20TH-CENTURY COMPOSERS

Jean Sibelius

Jean Sibelius

by Guy Rickards

For Alison

Phaidon Press Limited
Regent's Wharf
All Saints Street
London N1 9PA

First published 1997
© 1997 Phaidon Press Limited

ISBN 0 7148 3581 1

A CIP catalogue record for this book is
available from the British Library

Printed in Singapore

Frontispiece, Jean Sibelius,
cigar in hand, at his home in
February 1939. Later that
year this photograph was
circulated with the headline
'Sibelius Feared War
Victim'.

Contents

Preface

No one who listens to and enjoys the music of Sibelius, let alone endeavours to write about either the man or his music, can do so without owing an immense debt of gratitude to the late Dr Erik T. Tawaststjerna (1912–93), who was given unrestricted access by the composer's family to Sibelius's papers. Dr Tawaststjerna's huge and authoritative multi-volume study forms the bedrock of Sibelius scholarship and proved an indispensable source for the present book, particularly as many documents – the composer's diaries not least – have now been locked away until 2017. Dr Tawaststjerna did not always overburden his readers with details of his sources, some of which remain shrouded in mystery. It is also clear that he trod a careful path through Sibelius's life, largely one suspects out of delicacy to the composer's family. Until these papers enter the public domain, any biographer hoping to achieve a rounded picture must perforce chart the terrain with Tawaststjerna in both hands for much of the time, especially since he has shown that earlier studies – such as those of Erik Furuhjelm, Cecil Gray and Karl Ekman – must be treated with a certain amount of caution. That said, I take entire responsibility for the views of the music as well as interpretations for Sibelius's actions expressed here. Faber and Faber I must thank for permission to quote liberally from all three volumes of the English edition of Tawaststjerna's study. I owe a more personal debt to Robert Layton, a valued friend and colleague and a noted Sibelius expert in his own right, who gave me sight of the then unpublished final instalment of his elegant translation of Dr Tawaststjerna's study, and much advice besides.

The state of Sibelius scholarship at the time of writing is one of ferment, as was shown by the papers read during the Second International Sibelius Conference, held in Helsinki from 26 to 29 November 1995. Glenda Dawn Goss I must thank especially for sharing her remarkable discoveries concerning the composer's earliest

7

years, including the exact form of his full name; Dr Kari Kilpeläinen
for his painstaking research into Sibelius's manuscripts and the dating
of his earliest works, expanding on Fabian Dahlström's pioneering
work; plus Peter Revers, Tina K. Ramnarine, Veijo Murtomäki, the
composer Erkki Salmenhaara, and Anna Krohn, secretary to the
organizing committee. After the Conference, Markku Hartikainen,
who acted as guide at Ainola and was a childhood friend of many of
the composer's grandchildren (recalling how they adapted the two
phrases of the second subject of the Violin Concerto's finale as a
musical challenge and password), freely shared knowledge from his
twenty-year study of the composer's letters. (Mr Hartikainen is also
one of the few people to have been able to inspect the diary kept from
1904 until the 1950s by Sibelius's longstanding nanny and housekeeper
Aino Kari and has waged a long campaign to prevent it from being
destroyed.)

Sickan Park, Cultural Attaché at the Finnish Embassy to the Court
of St James, her predecessor Frank Hellstén (now working at the
Department for Press and Culture at the Ministry for Foreign Affairs
in Helsinki) and his colleague Christian Lindholm all provided
considerable assistance whilst I was in Finland, and with material
subsequently. The experience of watching, from the upper storey of
Halosenniemi (the log-cabin-cum-museum of the artist Pekka
Halonen, who first brought Sibelius to Järvenpää), the sun set over the
frozen Lake Tuusula is something that I will never forget. (A line of
trees now blocks the view of the lake from Sibelius's house, Ainola.)
Others whom I must thank in Finland include Kaarlo Paloheimo and
Petri Blomstedt of the Collegiate body, 'The Legal Successors of Jean
Sibelius', Anne Alakallaanvaara of Helsinki University Library, the
composers Einojuhani Rautavaara and Paavo Heininen, Ms Kitty von
Wright of the Sibelius Museum in Turku (part of the Musicology
Department at Åbo Academy), Ms Ritva Eskola at the Sibelius
Birthplace Museum in Hämeenlinna, and Jaana Manner in
Hämeenlinna church registration office. In Britain, I am indebted to
Grainne Devine (Conifer), Alexandra Spicer (Select), Richard
Dinnage (RCA), Paul Westcott (Chandos), Karen Pitchford (Koch
International), Harriet Capaldi (Warner Classics) and Peter Horton of
the Royal College of Music in providing recordings and information.

I should also record my appreciation to Ingalo Thomson, Roger Sears and Deirdre O'Day at Phaidon Press, and Hans Dieter Reichert at hdr design.

Finally, I am very grateful to the composer John Pickard for reading through a draft of this book, and for his many helpful comments, and to my wife Alison, whose intuitive love of the music of Sibelius was a constant inspiration.

Guy Rickards
Horsham, 1997

A Note on Naming Conventions

Finland is a nation with two distinct languages, Finnish and Swedish. I have followed modern practice for place-names in using the Finnish name, although in the nineteenth and early twentieth centuries the Swedish versions were more prevalent. Where appropriate, as with Hämeenlinna for example, I give the Swedish equivalent (Tavastehus) in parenthesis on first reference. With Sibelius's own works, some are titled in Finnish, such as *Kullervo*, *Oma maa* and *Maan virsi*, others – such as the majority of the solo songs – in Swedish. The situation is complicated further by many pieces, especially for orchestra, being known outside Finland in the local language, as with *Öinen ratsastus ja auringonnousu* and *Aallottaret*, in English respectively *Night Ride and Sunrise* and *The Oceanides*, in German *Nächtlichter Ritt und Sonnenaufgang* and *Die Okeaniden*. I have in general referred to Sibelius's compositions by the most familiar names to English readers, with appropriate cross-references where necessary.

Introduction

More than any other single factor, the music of Jean Sibelius (1865–1957) is quintessentially the product of the natural landscapes (physical, ethnic, historical and political) of his native country. Finland is a country of extremes and opposites, a young nation in an ancient land. Situated in the remote north-east of Europe, abutting the vast expanse of the Russian Empire that sweeps unbroken to the Bering Straits and the northern reaches of the Pacific, Finland is none the less a distinct geographical unit. The geological strata are of great age yet the surface topography is relatively recent, a complex latticework of forests and over 100,000 lakes formed by the grinding process of the ice sheets' last recessional some 15,000 years ago. The extreme latitude (from 60° north through ten degrees almost to the Arctic Ocean) and not-quite-landlocked Baltic Sea have together determined the climate of short, hot summers and long, cold winters, managing to avoid the permafrost prevalent due east in Siberia.

The first migrations of people into the Finnish shield occurred around 10,000 years ago, and continuous settlement has obtained ever since. At some point in remote antiquity peoples of the Finno-Ugrian ethnic group moved west of the Ural Mountains, dispersing not just in present-day Finland, Karelia and Estonia but south and west towards the Hungarian plain. (Migrations ever westward undoubtedly continued, the last traceable remnant probably being the trans-Pyrenean Basques of France and Spain; the modern Finnish, Hungarian and Basque languages are related to each other – however dimly – rather than to any of the prevailing Indo-Aryan tongues of the rest of Europe.) In the early centuries of the Christian era, migrants from eastern Europe moved northwards to rejoin their sundered relatives (perhaps to escape the ever-increasing barbarian incursions that would eventually bring down the Roman Empire of the West). Yet as recent analysis of blood groups has revealed, modern Finns possess a rather more varied racial background than might be expected from their isolated position; for while their language has retained its eastern, Asiatic roots, the current population is of western, predominantly Germanic, ethnic origin. This can only partly be explained by the waves of crusade, conquest and settlement from Sweden, Frisia and Germany from at least the eleventh century onwards; clearly the recorded movements of peoples in this area are only one chapter of the story. Nor was it a one-way traffic, since over the centuries a smaller but steady number of Finns emigrated west to Sweden.

Finland is unusual amongst the developed European nations in being a political creation of the twentieth century without any tradition of independence or self-determination. Norway, whose current nation-statehood dates only from 1905, Germany and Italy all have traditions stretching back more than a millennium; even short-lived artificial constructs like Czechoslovakia or Yugoslavia were formed around the memory of ancient states. Finland has no such history. The first glimmerings of the country as a coherent political unit, rather than as a collection of provinces to be squabbled over by the Swedes and Russians, date only from the formation of the Duchy of Finland in 1556 by the Swedish king, Gustavus I Vasa. The Grand Duchy's perpetuation after annexation by Russia in 1808, completing a process begun a century earlier, secured for the Tsar a loyalty from the Finns that forestalled for a time the onset of nationalist sentiment endemic in other parts of Europe in the mid nineteenth century, such as in Austria-Hungary. The liberal policies of the Tsarist administration also unfettered the native Finnish tongue from its centuries-old overshadowing by Swedish, and it became an official language of government in 1863. Finnish literature existed only fitfully prior to this period, starting with Mikael Agricola's translations of the New Testament and the Prayer Book in the 1540s, although a Finnish-language edition of the Bible did not appear for another hundred years. But with the publication in 1835 of the *Kalevala*, a collation of legends and folklore by Elias Lonnrot (and revised in expanded form in 1849), a uniquely Finnish written tradition was born overnight. No matter that the subject was mythological, that Lonnrot could only find the majority of the stories from Karelian villagers and had compressed and telescoped characters and tales into composites blurring regional variations. Its impact was immense, both for the nation as a whole in focusing a latent sense of national identity that was independent of the domineering cultures of neighbouring Sweden and Russia, and for Sibelius in providing a rich source for a whole series of musical works, large and small.

Sibelius's own background was just as mixed as his country's. His remoter forebears on the paternal side were largely, though not exclusively, of peasant Finnish stock that had farmed the land for hundreds of years, eventually intermarrying with incoming Swedish settlers and being assimilated into their more organized European culture. This may be reflected in the appellation by which Sibelius's great-great-grandfather, Matts Mårtensson, is known, though the name Sibelius itself was of more recent provenance. In the early eighteenth century Mårtensson's son took the name of Sibbe from his wife's family and the estate which they farmed. His son in turn, Johan Sibbe (1785–1844, the composer's grandfather), latinized his name after the bourgeois Swedish fashion to Sibelius. He married Katarina Frederika Åkerberg, some fifteen years his junior and the daughter of the local doctor, Matthias, who was a noted amateur violinist and cellist. Of their five children only one, Christian Gustaf (1822–68, the composer's father), had any progeny, he too marrying into a Swedish family of more elevated social standing, and also possessed of some musical talents, with his union on 7 March 1862 with Maria Charlotta Borg (1839–97).

Sibelius might then have inherited his musical disposition from the Swedish side of his ancestry, although it may be just as likely that the music-making in his mother's and paternal grandmother's families was merely of a more developed nature, and therefore more likely to be recorded in a country with precious little musical infrastructure. Music was a pastime of the home, or of small social gatherings arranged on an *ad hoc* basis. No orchestras, opera houses or concert circuit existed; indeed the capital, Helsinki, would only acquire a permanent professional orchestra in 1882. Finnish composition, like its literature, was still in its infancy when Sibelius was born. There had been a few notable figures who had flourished under Swedish or Russian patronage, such as Bernhard Crusell (1775–1838) or Axel Ingelius (1822–68), drawn from the Swedish-speaking minority. Even then, most of Crusell's career was spent abroad, in Sweden, Germany and elsewhere; Ingelius's *Kalevala*-inspired symphony of 1847 was a landmark work, but ultimately of purely local interest. So was the

Aino Symphony (1885; properly titled a symphonic poem, 'Aino – the Mystery') by Sibelius's future friend and champion, the conductor Robert Kajanus (1856–1933). But the dominant composer in the country up to the late 1880s, composer of the first Finnish opera (set in Swedish) and of the tune that would become the national anthem, was the German-born Fredrik Pacius (1809–91), who had settled in Finland in 1834.

It is not surprising then that Sibelius's music should bear signs of the dichotomies investing almost every strand of the nature and history of his homeland. Throughout his life he oscillated between such extremes: composer-laureate of the pro-Finnish patriots despite his Swedish upbringing; abstract symphonist of imposing classical severity yet perpetrator of light music pot-boilers of embarrassing vacuity; highly successful nature tone-poet ('When we see these granite rocks,' he once remarked to pupil and fellow-composer, Bengt de Törne, of the rocky approaches to the southern coast, 'we know why we are able to treat the orchestra as we do.') but failed violin virtuoso. Contradictions in his attitude to his own music abounded throughout his life. His fierce self-criticism could lead to either the suppression of works, such as the epic, nationalistic *Kullervo* symphony, two of the colourful *Lemminkäinen* tone-poems and the Eighth Symphony, or to their wholesale recomposition: for example, *En saga*, the Violin Concerto and the Fifth Symphony (twice over in the case of the last work) on the one hand, yet he appears to have been untroubled by the quality of such pieces as the vapid *Suite champêtre* and *Suite caractéristique* (the last-named his one hundredth published opus). In his personal life, matters were often little different: a devoted husband and father, his family life was nearly wrecked by alcohol; a man who, for instance, demanded absolute quiet from everyone around him – even his young children – so that he might pursue his muse, yet whose own self-control was utterly emasculated by his addiction. In his final years disparities in his lifestyle continued to make themselves apparent, on the one hand as a living national monument whose very physical appearance seemed an archetype of Finnish legend, on the other as the elegant Swedish gentleman with a weakness for fine living and especially cigars. Most bizarre of all, perhaps, was his role as cultural ambassador for his country, for he barely ever set foot outside his front door.

In the last analysis, such considerations may help to define the character of the man and his music, but not to gauge its worth or explain its appeal. Why, for instance, did Sibelius find such a ready and enduringly faithful audience in the Anglo-Saxon cultures of Britain and North America, while signally failing to make an impact in Latin countries like Italy and, until very recently, France? What raises Sibelius above the level of a curiosity with a particular accent, the largest fish in a remote backwater, is the sheer quality of his finest music which ranks as high as anything produced in the last hundred years. And as the tides of fashion have ebbed and flowed towards the end of the second millennium, Sibelius's most important works have come to be seen, if not as revolutionary as some of Stravinsky's or Schoenberg's, then certainly as prophetic of the compositional trends that seem likely to dominate the opening of the third.

I

The surgery of Dr Christian
Sibelius, the composer's
father, in Hämeenlinna,
now the site of the Sibelius
Birthplace Museum

*While I was a child and youth, life and people
in Hämeenlinna formed an environment that
had a stimulating effect on the mind of an
impressionable young boy. Hämeenlinna was,
above all, a very civilized town.*

Jean Sibelius to Karl Ekman

Youth in Hämeenlinna 1865-85

Jean Sibelius was born on 8 December 1865 in the thriving town of Hämeenlinna (Tavastehus in Swedish), an old settlement by Finnish standards, a castle having been founded there by the Swedes as early as 1240. Its position at the south-western reaches of Finland's lake system was of obvious strategic importance; in 1862, just three years before Sibelius's birth, the first Finnish railway linked Hämeenlinna with the still relatively new capital at Helsinki, thirty or so miles to the south. The townsfolk were predominantly Finnish speakers, the surrounding rural population almost exclusively so but, as elsewhere, the professional and educated classes spoke Swedish (the main language of administration since the early 1600s). This was the tongue used in the Sibelius household.

His parents named the boy Johan, after a seafaring uncle who had died the previous year en route from Havana, Christian, after his father, Julius, after his maternal grandmother, Katarina Juliana Borg, although the family almost always called him by the diminutive Janne. The budding composer reversed the order of his second and third names in adolescence, adopting the now familiar French form of Jean only in his late teens, as an affectation following the example of his namesake uncle; Sibelius even reused some of Uncle Jean's old printed cards. Janne was the second child in the family, his sister Linda Maria preceding him by two years, his brother Christian following over three years after. His father, Christian Gustaf, was the town doctor, though his professional position did not bring with it an overly comfortable living. The precariousness of the family's finances was made worse by his irresponsible way with money, the good doctor preferring to live well and buy books and musical instruments rather than pay the rent or the house servants. His wife, Maria Charlotta, was a preacher's daughter of a more restrained, even austere, disposition.

As Janne had been named for his recently deceased uncle, so little Christian was likewise for his father. The doctor had died of typhus on 31 July 1868, several months before his second son's birth. The previous year, 1867, had seen the onset of a catastrophic famine, the result of consecutive crop failures over several years, bringing epidemics in its wake. The disaster claimed the lives of over 100,000 people across the country, some seven per cent of the total population. Christian Gustaf was placed in charge of an isolation hospital; years of indulgence had lowered his resistance and he succumbed rapidly once infected, aged only forty-six. Sibelius retained almost no recollection of him, beyond dim sensations of his physical presence. It may be that Sibelius's lifelong love of cigars derived from the odour of tobacco that permeated every fibre of his father's clothes and every nook and cranny of the house. Precious little of that home stayed with the still-pregnant widow and her young family: the estate was declared bankrupt, the effects sold to cover debts of over 4,500 marks (more

The composer's parents, Christian and Maria Charlotta Sibelius, shortly after their marriage in 1862

than two years' salary). Maria did manage to retain some clothing, linen and bedding, and removed to her mother's house across town.

The stigma of insolvency never left Maria, casting a gloom over the family, and this may account for an emotional distance between her and the children. Much as he professed throughout his life to have loved his mother, Sibelius and she were not really close. As a student in Berlin and Vienna around 1890–1 his letters to her are usually short

The infant Janne, aged about eighteen months, on his mother's knee

and somewhat stiff, whereas those to friends, and particularly to his
fiancée Aino Järnefelt, positively overflowed by comparison. His
mother's physically undemonstrative manner deprived him of tactile,
sensory contact, compounding his sense of isolation. As a boy, Sibelius
was of a dreamy, intermittently remote nature; his sense of fantasy and
separateness was remarked on by many and found expression in some
of his drawings. One is of a family outing to the country with Janne
depicted flying overhead in a hot-air balloon. On another occasion,
one winter evening six-year-old Janne came in late from play claiming
to have seen a house ablaze, which he described in graphic detail,
explaining how he helped local people carry water to extinguish it, as a
result of which he had become drenched. On removing the child's
clothing his mother found him to be quite dry, and after repeated
questioning elicited the admission that the boy had merely seen a
house and imagined what would happen if it caught fire.

These instances may even be suggestive of his having suffered from
a mild form of what is now known as 'Attention Deficit Disorder'
(ADD). This condition is caused by a chemical imbalance in the brain
and often translates in children into self-obsession, a difficulty in
concentrating (most usually at school) or behavioural problems; the
young Winston Churchill amongst many others is thought to have
been afflicted by this ailment. As an adult Sibelius not infrequently
craved to be 'caressed' (as he put it in a letter to Aino in 1891), a need
his future wife was prepared to indulge him in, whereas his mother
would not. This mutual attentiveness of son and daughter-in-law may
partly explain why Maria, in her final years, felt jealous of Aino.

Sibelius, his brother and sister grew up surrounded by women. In
addition to their mother and sister, there was the formidable presence
of his maternal grandmother with her two unmarried daughters:
Tekla, an invalid, and Julia. As Maria Sibelius's children grew older,
conditions became increasingly crowded. The family moved house in
Hämeenlinna three times in as many years before finally settling at
number 15 Läntinen Linnankatu (later renamed Sibeliuksenkatu) in
May 1874. During the summer months the three children would
stay at the paternal family home in the coastal town of Loviisa. There
Sibelius's paternal grandmother, also called Katarina, lived with
her daughter, his much-loved aunt Evelina. The only male family
influence in the children's lives was provided intermittently by

Christian Gustaf's sole surviving brother, Pehr, who lived and worked
in Turku, the old 'Swedish' capital (known as Åbo) on the south-
western coast.

Evidence of Janne's musicality emerged only gradually through his
childhood. His gift of perfect pitch, the ability to recognize and
distinguish notes precisely by ear alone, even with birdsong, may have
been masked by the out-of-tune piano at his grandmother's house in
Hämeenlinna. As a young child Janne would crawl underneath it
when it was being played and may have related certain keys to
particular colours. He started to sit at the keyboard and experiment
about the age of five, often in the key of G major because – according
to a much later recollection – both it and the instrument were brown!
It was not until Sibelius was seven that his aunt Julia began to give
him some rudimentary tuition, usually culminating in raps across the
knuckles when he started to extemporize instead of playing his
exercises. Not surprisingly, the future composer never grew to like the
piano, nor did he write any successful major pieces for it (although
there are many minor ones and arrangements), believing that the
instrument could not 'sing'. Nor did he endear himself to his aunt by
his undiplomatic criticisms of some of her other pupils, even telling
one: 'Don't bother coming any more. You'll never be a pianist
anyway.' Sibelius's musical capabilities developed apace, demonstrated
impressively in October 1875 when, not yet ten, he played from
memory at the piano extracts from a concert given by the Swedish
harp virtuoso, Adolf Sjödén.

Sibelius had started school in 1872, and coming from a culturally
Swedish (though racially equally mixed) background, he was sent first
to a Swedish school. He was not a good student. Music was already
beginning to take its hold of his imagination, and he neglected his
schoolwork to scribble down musical phrases, bringing him inevitably
into conflict with his teachers. His first attempts at composition – at
least those which still exist – are traditionally dated from around his
tenth year. These included *Water Drops*, a tiny duo for violin and cello
played pizzicato – plucking the strings rather than using the bow –
from which no hint of the mature symphonist of thirty to forty years
later may be discerned, and the more ambitious *Aunt Evelina's Life
in Music*. (*Water Drops* survives only in a much later copy by the
composer's first biographer, Erik Furuhjelm, and may have been

written rather closer to 1880.) With other school friends, Sibelius put on short improvised plays and formed a toy orchestra, conducting the latter from the piano. At this time, he also made a first acquaintance with the folklore collection *Kalevala*, albeit in a Swedish translation, but it failed to make a lasting impression. However, the establishment of the first ever Finnish grammar school in Hämeenlinna meant that Sibelius was eligible to be enrolled there, which he duly was in 1876 after a year in a local Finnish preparatory school.

The education system in Finland at the time, as in almost every other country, was hardly conducive to the discovery and development of an innate musical talent such as Sibelius's. As elsewhere in the Grand Duchy, policy was dominated by the growing linguistic struggle between the majority Finnish- and minority Swedish-speakers, the former wanting full equality in the use of both languages, the latter defending the dominance of Swedish. Despite being a province of the Tsarist Empire, the impact of Russian in Finland was negligible. In 1863 Tsar Alexander II had given the Fennoman (pro-Finnish) camp a huge boost on decreeing Finnish to be an official language of administration, requiring the routine translation of governmental documents. By 1869 the increasingly defensive Svecomen (pro-Swedish) lobby had become more vocal. They outraged the Fennomen with the ominous declaration in the Swedish-language newspaper, *Hufvudstadbladet*, that Swedish-speakers were ethnically superior because the largely peasant Finnish population were of an 'essentially primitive nature', a nature reflected by their alien-sounding language.

At the Finnish school, Sibelius's academic prowess did not improve, and he continued to dream his way through class. Just as the rigour of regular tuition and practice at the piano bored him, so in the main did schoolwork. 'I look back for the bright spots in vain,' he remarked late in life. Some subjects did hold his attention though (not the *Kalevala*, even in the original), and in these – mathematics, history and especially natural science – he generally performed very well: his collection of wild flowers and fauna was recognized as being the best in his year. A friend from the toy orchestra who attended the Finnish grammar school and with whom the composer maintained a lifelong friendship, Walter von Konow, recalled how as a youth Sibelius would entertain him during walks around the Konows' estate at Lahis, peopling the surrounding woods with all manner 'of trolls, witches, goblins and the like'. But Sibelius's poor academic record created difficulties for him at home as well. However much his mother, whose family had a longstanding amateur tradition of music-making, was prepared to encourage his interest in music, it could not be at the expense of studies. His grandmother took a dim view, labelling the boy 'Slapdash Janne'. Eventually though, something had to give and at the end of his fifth year he suffered the indignity of being kept back while all his friends moved on.

In 1880, it was felt that Sibelius's musicality required more expert guidance and he was sent to the local bandmaster, Gustaf Levander, to learn the violin. The instrument immediately captivated the boy, whose sights were set firmly on a virtuoso career despite several compelling obstacles. Not the least of these were his having taken up the instrument too late for such an exalted ambition, and the breaking of his right arm near the shoulder a year or two before, which inhibited for a time his bowing action (a weakness in the limb would persist into adult life, to impair his conducting from time to time). Sibelius bombarded his uncle Pehr, an amateur composer who had an impressive collection of instruments, with requests for a violin, replacement strings and musical scores. Sibelius progressed quickly, and some element of discipline from within at last manifested itself, as he devoted much time to the practice needed to fulfil his dream. Yet even here he turned to improvisation to improve his dexterity, offering 'meandering concertos to the birds' in the open air, sometimes aboard boats picking their way through the islands off the coast at Loviisa. One attempt to form an accompanying farmyard orchestra of chickens, cows and pigs ended with the apprentice virtuoso beating a hasty retreat because of the animals' unbearable stench.

Pehr Sibelius, the composer's paternal uncle, in the 1880s

More solid instruction was gained from the local composer Emil Genetz and the study of textbooks in the school library. Recalling this period at the time of his fiftieth birthday in 1915, Sibelius singled out Adolph Marx's *Die Lehre von der musikalischen Komposition* (published in Leipzig in four volumes, 1837–47), yet his letters to Uncle Pehr mention rather Johann Lobe's *Lehrbuch der musikalischen Composition* (Leipzig, 1850–67) – used by Tchaikovsky as a student in Russia – as well as an anonymous *Compositionslehre* (Lobe published a manual of that name in 1884). Practical knowledge followed when he formed a

The Sibelius family trio at Loviisa, 1888; left to right: Janne (violin), Linda (piano), Christian (cello)

trio with his sister at the piano and brother on the cello. Having worked their way for a year through a large swathe of the output of Haydn, Mozart and Beethoven, they began to investigate the Romantic repertoire, ranging from Schubert and Mendelssohn to Tchaikovsky and Grieg, the last two very much contemporary figures who both made a firm impact on the young composer. But a disturbing trait now appeared during some of Janne's solo turns: stage fright. On one occasion he became so nervous he had to turn his back on his audience in order to perform.

None the less, Sibelius became a much sought-after chamber player in Hämeenlinna's musical circles, primarily Swedish-based but including some of the Russian garrison officers. (Sibelius incidentally never learnt to speak Russian.) In the Finland of the early 1880s, concerts by touring performers were rarities, so the vast bulk of activity – especially at provincial level – was amateur in origin. In 1882 the capital, Helsinki, finally acquired a permanent orchestra, founded by the young composer-conductor, Robert Kajanus, while the country's first Music Institute (doubling as Helsinki University's music faculty) was established only in that same year, by Martin Wegelius. Yet even these advances were limited in scope. Kajanus's orchestra was a chamber band by the standards of the day, while the Institute could not run to putting its house string quartet on a professional footing, let alone develop a student orchestra, both *de rigueur* on the continent. Kajanus and Wegelius would come to dominate Sibelius's development in the late 1880s, but their rivalry, exacerbated by the former's foundation of an orchestra school in 1885, undermined some of the gains of their enterprise.

Another practical upshot of Sibelius's experience of performance was an expansion in scale of his compositions. In the main these were for himself and his siblings to play, and included a trio for two violins and piano in 1883, a violin sonata the next year, plus a whole range of pieces for violin and cello with piano. Most of these were undated at the time, and as an old man Sibelius attempted to assign approximate years of composition. One such work is the five-movement Sonata in E major for violin and piano – later the title was altered to Suite – which Sibelius hazarded in the 1940s to have been composed in 1883. A suite there may have been, but internal evidence suggests the work dates from about five years later during Sibelius's formal studies at Wegelius's Institute. That the violin formed the centre of his musical universe can be heard in the Piano Quartet in D minor of 1884. Instead of being a true ensemble piece where the four players are equals, the piano quartet sounds in places like a sonata for violin accompanied by a piano trio. As with all of his output of these years, the quartet and suite are derivative, and bear no hint of the recognizable Sibelian voice. Instead they betray the influences of other composers such as Grieg, Sinding and Sarasate whose pieces Sibelius played as a violinist. Yet there can also be no doubting the lively imagination that had created them.

One work which can be pinpointed in time with certainty is the sunny, Haydnesque String Quartet in E flat. This, his most ambitious piece yet, was completed in June 1885, following his final school examinations. The quartet does evince a sound knowledge of Classical style, blending well with a cleanness of texture quite Nordic in tone. The whole, for all its awkwardnesses in parts, is a remarkably assured piece for a student yet to receive any advanced formal training, especially in the large first movement, as long as the other three put together. Despite unimpressive grades (he was placed nineteenth out of a class of twenty-eight) occasioning further opprobrium at home,

Sibelius was able to enrol that autumn at the University in Helsinki. After toying with the idea of medicine, he opted for law and music. Law was a sop to placate his family (his maternal grandmother in particular), for he never really intended to pursue any career other than the latter. Such was his growing self-confidence that during the summer break he contemplated writing an opera on a subject suggested by Walter von Konow. Prophetically for his career as a theatrical composer, nothing came of it.

2

Sibelius, the dapper student,
in Berlin, 1889

*He was a real natural genius, thoroughly
individual, without the slightest relationship
to others.*
                    Adolf Paul, *A Book about a Man*, 1891

Helsinki, Berlin, Vienna 1885–92

By the standards of the major European nations, Helsinki in 1885 was
more a thriving provincial town than a capital city. Busy as it was, it
could not even compete with its approximate contemporary in status
Budapest in Hungary, which was probably the fastest-expanding
economic unit in the whole of Europe as well as joint capital of the
Hapsburg Empire. Helsinki's role as the seat of the administration
dated only from 1812, when the Tsar had removed it from the older
Swedish foundation of Åbo (modern-day Turku), initiating a
rebuilding of Helsinki on a lavish scale that would not be complete for
another half-century. The new foundation lacked many of the
facilities taken for granted in even mediocre centres on the continent,
such as an opera house, and those that did exist were, as was painfully
obvious, still in their infancy.

Even before Sibelius had enrolled at the University, his family had
taken the decision to remove from Hämeenlinna to the capital.
Modest accommodation was secured and Aunt Evelina joined the
household, augmenting the meagre income by taking in needlework
and dressmaking. Sibelius threw himself into his musical studies with
as much relish as he ignored law. The tutor for his principal subject,
the violin, was Mitrofan Vasiliev; instruction in music theory came
from the Institute's director, Martin Wegelius. Sibelius made an
immediate and favourable impression, Vasiliev declaring him excitedly
to be a 'genius'. Wegelius was more circumspect but nonetheless
confident even at this early stage that Sibelius 'would become a
great musician'.

Yet the director was responsible for placing an obstacle in the way
of that forecast being fulfilled. His antagonism to Kajanus had
increased when the latter formed his orchestra school, pointing up
the Institute's deficiency in this respect. Wegelius saw Kajanus as a
dangerous rival and declared the conductor's concerts off-limits to
the Institute's students. Kajanus's advocacy of Russian music was
anathema to Wegelius, who had strong Central European sympathies,

Wagner and Liszt being particular enthusiasms. The interdict severely restricted the development of Sibelius's orchestral imagination; only later, as a student in Berlin and Vienna, did he finally make contact with even the basic orchestral repertoire such as the symphonies and concertos of Mozart, Beethoven and Brahms. It would be another five years before he seriously attempted to write for the medium with which ultimately he came to be associated above all else.

Sibelius endeavoured, largely successfully, to keep out of this and most other faculty quarrels. He integrated himself only gradually into the social fabric of University life, avoiding the autumn freshmen's party, though such caution did not last long. In the 1930s Sibelius recalled of these times (through heavily rose-tinted glasses) that 'no political clouds darkened the horizon, economic problems did not assume the proportions that they came to do in later years … There were riotous parties that could go on for two or three days at a time.'

Mitrofan Vasiliev (centre) photographed with his violin students c. 1886; Sibelius is standing at the rear and to the left.

True, there were as yet no difficulties with the Russian government, but this decade saw an upsurge in radicalism across the whole range of the Fennoman movement, from the staging of Minna Canth's caustic and graphically realistic plays *A Worker's Wife* in 1885 and *The Ill-fated* three years later, to the political split of the Fennoman party into Old and Young camps. The Young Fennomen took an increasingly aggressive line with respect to the language question. In the context of the University this centred on the vexed question of the use of Finnish in all the courses. As a natural Swedish-speaker, Sibelius was careful to avoid being embroiled in the argument. His brother Christian, on attending the University three years later, was not so reticent, aligning clearly with the Finnish-speakers.

Sibelius had more pressing concerns during his first term, finding Vasiliev's requirement that he practise the violin four hours daily a trial. His solo début at an Institute concert, in a movement from a Viotti concerto, had to be postponed in November due to ill health. When he finally appeared on 14 December, the press had all gone to hear Tchaikovsky's then still novel First Piano Concerto. Progress during the next two terms was more assured, the influential critic Karl Flodin being particularly impressed with a performance of Ferdinand David's E minor Concerto in May. Sibelius joined Richard Faltin's University orchestra (run externally to the Institute) in the spring of 1886, becoming concertmaster later in the year.

Another question now resolved itself, that of music versus law. His uncle, Otto Borg, had noted during a visit that a law textbook left strategically open on a desk had remained untouched for so long that the pages had become discoloured. Sibelius closed the book – and any pretence of study – there and then. His good marks in music at the end of the first academic year mollified his family's doubts, although Grandmother Borg's view of him as 'Slapdash Janne' was hard to dislodge. Only his piano-playing let him down.

Sibelius's progress in his second year continued to be good. At the start of the spring term in 1887 he joined the Institute's Quartet as second violin and began composition studies with Wegelius. At the end of the term, he was awarded the University's music scholarship, for which he had been repeatedly nominated by Faltin, although his limitations as a soloist had now become clear. A performance of the second and third movements of Mendelssohn's E minor Concerto – a

Martin Wegelius, founder-director of Helsinki's Music Institute and Sibelius's tutor in music theory and composition, 1885-9

step up in difficulty from his previous repertoire – was marred by 'thin tone and wayward intonation'. Stage fright, occasioned perhaps by a dawning realization that he really could not cope at this level, had got the better of him. To his credit, Sibelius stuck at his task, even making a little progress the next year under a new teacher, Herman Csillag. But this level was one he could not pass beyond, and whether through temperament, recurrent (perhaps psychosomatic) ill health or both, he did not complete the solo violin course.

Some minor pieces aside, Sibelius composed little in his early period at the Institute. On entering the composition class, however, he began to work on his own music aside from the exercises Wegelius required of him. As with his violin studies, the young composer found these classes hard going. 'Often I wanted to throw in the sponge,' he later recalled, adding – perhaps echoing his maternal grandmother's expressed opinion of him – 'and live the life of an idiot for which I have always felt myself well qualified. But it was my fate to want to compose.' Holidays were the most profitable times for composition, and the summer of 1887 saw the creation of a host of chamber and instrumental pieces, most with a practical or local connection. The largest is a Quartet in G minor for piano, harmonium, violin and cello, made to measure for Janne to play with the Sucksdorffs, family friends in Loviisa.

However discouraged Sibelius might have been – and during the winter months throughout his life he would often slide into a decline, symptomatic of Seasonal Affective Disorder (SAD), an affliction well known to modern-day Finns – his teacher Wegelius knew exceptional talent when he saw it. In the spring term of 1888, Sibelius earned top marks in composition and was permitted to collaborate with the director in writing incidental music to Gunnar Wennerberg's fairy-tale drama, *Näcken* ('The Watersprite'). Faltin was deeply impressed by the potential Sibelius the composer displayed, and praised the Theme and Variations for string quartet performed at an Institute concert at the close of the summer term. Wegelius invited his protégé to stay at his summerhouse at Granholmen in the Helsinki archipelago shortly afterwards. The two men played violin and piano duets for a month, concentrating on the Classical sonata repertoire. Wegelius allowed his pupil to choose some pieces, probably against his better judgement: Tchaikovsky's *Sérénade mélancolique* was dismissed as 'violinistic drivel'.

Following page, Granholmen, Wegelius's summerhouse, where Sibelius was invited to stay during summer vacations from 1888

The academic year 1887–8 was a crucial one socially for Sibelius, not just in his relationship with Wegelius. Towards the start of the year he had made the acquaintance of Armas Järnefelt, a student of piano and theory. Armas came from the highest echelon of society, being the third son of General August Aleksander Järnefelt, a Fenno-Swede aristocrat and one of the provincial governors in the Grand Duchy who was strongly Fennoman in outlook. General Järnefelt's German-born wife Elisabeth, who refused point-blank to speak Swedish, 'collected' musicians and artists, so it is no surprise that she warmed to the charming, good-looking Sibelius, then twenty-two years old. Her husband's transfer as governor of Vaasa on the west coast led Elisabeth to rent an apartment in Helsinki, the better to mix in with city and artistic life. Armas and his two sisters Elli and Aino came with her.

Christian Sibelius had enrolled in the Medical Faculty this same year. With Richard Faltin's medical student son – also named Richard – and Ernst Lindelöf, the Sibelius brothers formed an impromptu string quartet which duly played its way through much of the Classical repertoire from Haydn to Beethoven. Another piano student who came within Sibelius's circle was Adolf Paul, a budding playwright and apostle of the Swedish writer August Strindberg. Paul clung to Sibelius like a limpet and vainly hoped to create 'an art of the future' in collaboration with him. But of considerably more moment was the arrival at the Institute of the international virtuoso and

The virtuoso pianist and
composer Ferruccio Busoni
(1866–1924), photographed
during his period teaching
in Helsinki in the late 1880s

The artist Eero Järnefelt,
Armas's brother and
a member of Busoni's
'Leskovites'

composer, Ferruccio Busoni, as piano tutor. The half-German, half-Italian Busoni was five months younger than Sibelius, a fact not lost on the Finn. Busoni was aghast at the Institute's restricted syllabus compared with mainstream European colleges – with no student orchestra, courses for wind instruments, or professional quartet – and rapidly came to understand how much of a provincial backwater Helsinki was. He resolved to move on as quickly as possible, but in the meantime consoled himself by cultivating a circle of friends amongst the student body. This group came to be known as the 'Leskovites' – after Busoni's dog, Lesko. Armas's brother Eero, a painter, joined the group on his return from St Petersburg and became a lifelong friend of Sibelius, with an ability to puncture the young composer's wilder flights of fancy. The movements of Busoni's *Geharnischte Suite* of 1889–90 (subsequently rewritten in 1894–5 and again in 1903) were dedicated respectively to Sibelius, the Järnefelt brothers Armas and Eero, and Adolf Paul.

　　Sibelius's friendship with Busoni lasted until the latter's death in 1924. The two men were of completely contrary, yet complementary, creative characters: the Finn nervous and instinctive, the Italian intellectual and philosophical. Busoni was of inestimable benefit in expanding Sibelius's horizons, both musically and personally, beyond Finland's parochial confines. The meetings of the Leskovites revolved primarily around impromptu recitals by Busoni of his favourite pieces – many of them quite unknown to his young audience – as well as improvisations by the students, something at which Sibelius shone. Busoni soon realized that however much his own technique as a performer exceeded that of his less experienced friend, as creative artists the gap between them was not so wide. He was the first figure of international standing to appreciate the young Finn's outstanding compositional talent. Sibelius for his part was dazzled by Busoni's pianistic prowess, but seems never to have thought highly of the latter's music. They are known to have performed together in public on only one occasion: at an Institute concert on 14 February 1889, in Schumann's Piano Quintet in E flat.

　　Towards the end of the previous year, Sibelius had achieved his first work in print – the song *Serenad*. Setting words by the national poet Runeberg (whom the composer, as a boy, had once met; half a century earlier Runeberg had taught Sibelius's father), *Serenad* appeared in a

collection of Finnish songs. Around this time, Sibelius composed
several pieces for violin and piano, including the Suites in D minor
and E plus a Romance and *Perpetuum mobile*, the last two known
today in revisions from 1912. In 1889 he tried his hand with limited
success at larger projects, notably the piano suite *Florestan*, inspired by
Busoni's interpretation of Schumann's *Kreisleriana*, plus a Violin
Sonata in F. However, a Suite in A minor for string trio, given its
première in April, made a real impression. 'Far more than a student
work,' Busoni called it – he had earlier amazed the composer by
playing it at sight on the piano ('and how he played it,' Sibelius
recalled in old age) – while Csillag, incensed at Flodin's remark that
the suite had 'a total absence of melodic invention', hailed his pupil as
'a richly endowed melodist'. At the end of May, the première of a new
string quartet, again in A minor, led Kajanus to remark that there
seemed little point in anyone other than Sibelius bothering to write
any more. Wegelius was peeved by this acclamation, declaring the first
movement to be 'far from good'. But the A minor Quartet, for all that
it is an apprentice piece anonymous in style, is a much more assured
composition than its predecessor of 1885.

One side-effect of Sibelius's increasing celebrity in the capital's
musical circles was the frequency of his visits, usually with Christian,
to the Järnefelts' Helsinki flat. There they would often improvise with
Armas. On one such occasion, accompanying a pantomime in which
the ladies of the house partook, Janne first set eyes on Armas's sister
Aino. So intense was his gaze – he later told her father that he had
fallen in love with her there and then – that she was quite transfixed
and unable to go through with her part. Armas and Eero were
immediately aware of the budding relationship and became very
protective of their sister. Sibelius was, after all, not of equal social
standing and Aino, 'the prettiest girl in Finland' as Wegelius called
her, was a considerable catch. The Järnefelts' reserve and his own
insecurity led Sibelius to court instead for a time the vivacious Betsy
Lerché, also from an aristocratic-diplomatic background. Sometime
that year he even penned for her a short piano waltz. Aino was hurt
by his avoidance of her, all the more as Eero repeatedly implored his
friend to visit during the summer.

Sibelius graduated from the Institute with flying colours, despite
having withdrawn from the violin course. Busoni suggested that the

'The prettiest girl in Finland': Aino Järnefelt, aged about eighteen, c. 1890

24-year-old should study with Rimsky-Korsakov but Wegelius would not hear of it, believing Berlin to be a more wholesome environment for his star pupil. While his fate was being decided for him, Sibelius continued to compose, including a Fantasia for cello and piano and the beginning of another string quartet – his third – this time in the key of B flat. Christian declared the Fantasia 'one of the most beautiful cello pieces I have ever heard', which may have prompted its composer to designate it for a time as his Opus 1; only the cello part now survives. Wegelius was also complimentary about the new quartet's first movement. Armed with a scholarship of 2,000 Finnish marks (enough to last a year) and letters of introduction from Wegelius to the German pedagogue Albert Becker, Sibelius in early September 1889 set sail for Berlin. He did not travel alone; Eero Järnefelt and the writer Juhani Aho were on board en route to Paris. The director and his wife came to the dock to see him off. Hanna Wegelius wept to see him go, as did Aino for a rather different reason. The Järnefelt family were on hand mainly to bid Eero goodbye, but Sibelius – whether wary at the thought of engendering any commitment, or to avoid a confrontation with Eero – affected not to see the girl, who was utterly mortified.

On Sibelius's first night in Berlin the historian Werner Söderhjelm, whom Wegelius had requested keep a watchful eye on the budding composer, took his young charge to see Mozart's *Don Giovanni* at the Kroll Opera. Artistically, the whole city operated at the level of excellence – if not quite the virtuosity – that Sibelius had only previously encountered in Busoni. The sheer cosmopolitanism of the German capital overwhelmed the Finn for a while and he felt quite unable to write a note. The adjustment from being perceived as a figure of national consequence to being just another foreign student proved extremely tough to make. A sense of inadequacy developed such that even the whistling of street-boys seemed of more moment than anything he could produce, something his new teacher Becker inadvertently exacerbated. The German pedant, a favourite composer of Kaiser Wilhelm I but 'a stuffed shirt from head to toe' according to his new pupil, was unimpressed by Sibelius's technical ability and started him on a thorough and strict grounding. Sibelius found the regime gruelling and complained by letter to Wegelius, who was unsympathetic despite Becker's implied criticism of his teaching methods. However, Becker wrote to Wegelius that he thought Sibelius 'exceptionally gifted'. When Wegelius paid a visit to Berlin shortly afterwards he was pleased with the progress made, unlike Busoni who called in to see his friend a little later. But Sibelius's morale was further dented by a performance of Richard Strauss's orchestral tone-poem *Don Juan*. Strauss was only a year older than the Finn, yet was writing sensational music of astonishing maturity – well in advance even of Busoni's. Sibelius by contrast was still in the process of discovering large swathes of the fundamental repertoire – such as Mozart, Beethoven and Brahms – that Finland had not been equipped to acquaint him with.

He found solace for his distress in the cultivation of a bohemian lifestyle that involved spending large amounts of money on eating out, the best seats at the opera, cigars, subsidizing the constantly penurious Adolf Paul (who visited frequently from Weimar) and drinking large quantities of alcohol. He fell in with a number of other hard-drinking students who orbited around the Norwegian composer Christian Sinding. Many were string players – such as the Dane Fini Henriques

Adolf Paul, writer and
fellow Leskovite, who hoped
to establish an artistic
partnership with Sibelius

– and students of the pre-eminent virtuoso (and colleague of Brahms), Joseph Joachim. Sibelius had resumed his own violin studies with Fritz Struss, a friend of Becker's and himself once a pupil of Joachim, but this was more to show potential scholarship assessors how diligent he had been than a serious revival of his soloist dream. With Adolf Paul he accompanied Busoni to Leipzig where the latter performed Sinding's Piano Quintet in E minor with the Brodsky Quartet. For this occasion Sibelius extravagantly bought a new top hat which was ruined by being worn constantly in the rain; on returning to Berlin, he donated it to the cab driver who drove him home.

By November, with winter approaching, he had already run short of money and succumbed to an attack of 'nerves', requiring a brief hospitalization during which the respite from the bottle was the most beneficial treatment. Sibelius petitioned his family and Wegelius for more funds at regular intervals from this time. His family raised another 2,000 marks over a period of six months through loans and selling off personal items, even clothing. On one occasion, Sibelius's plea had been in such a panic that he neglected to forward his latest address. His brother Christian vainly implored him to be more prudent but money just ran through his fingers like sand. Having been brought up in financially straitened circumstances with no resources of his own, Sibelius possessed little understanding of how to manage his affairs – a failing he would never really overcome.

He continued to make first acquaintance with the bedrock of European music, particularly orchestral and operatic works, that had been denied him in Helsinki. Wagner's *Tannhäuser* and *Die Meistersinger* aroused in him feelings of 'surprise, disappointment, joy' as he reported to Wegelius, but the crucial, formative musical experience from this year in Berlin was Beethoven. He saw Hans von Bülow, the champion and friend of Liszt and Wagner, conduct the 'Eroica', Fifth and Ninth Symphonies and play the last five great piano sonatas. In February 1890, Kajanus conducted the Berlin Philharmonic in his own *Aino Symphony*. The musical potential of the *Kalevala* – from which Kajanus had drawn his subject – rather than the music itself, impressed Sibelius greatly.

The combined effects of a strange city, acute homesickness (in one letter to his mother he begged her not to forget him), burgeoning alcoholism and an increasingly nervous disposition played havoc with his health, though the string of minor ailments do not seem to have interfered with his capacity to drink. The death of his Uncle Pehr, who had been so supportive of his musical ambitions, in January 1890 came as a shock, yet as winter gave way to spring, inspiration began to flow. Christian suggested that Sibelius attempt a big new work, an idea Wegelius welcomed, no doubt thinking of the unfinished B flat String Quartet. What resulted was the Piano Quintet in G minor, suggested by Sinding's example, by some way the largest in scale of Sibelius's early chamber compositions, with more character than anything he had achieved thus far. He completed the work in April and sent it off to Wegelius but doubted how well it would be received at home, writing to Werner Søderhjelm that it was 'absolute rubbish'. His fears proved only partially ill-founded; while Busoni thought the impassioned first of its five movements 'wonderful', he did not care for the folk-like and gentle second, nor did Wegelius like the fourth at a run-through. The finale seems to have remained untouched so only the first and third movements – the most original – were given a première by Busoni and the Institute Quartet (led by the young Norwegian composer Johan Halvorsen) on 5 May, with some success. Hanna Wegelius wondered at possible autobiographical associations in the turbulence of the first movement; her husband tartly responded to Sibelius that 'a composer ought to keep his gropings to himself' in a long, rather sour critique. A performance then took place in Turku in October with Adolf Paul as pianist, but omitted the finale. Not until 1982 was the quintet played as a whole in public.

By the end of the academic year, Sibelius had established very cordial relations with Becker, who wrote a long testimonial for his student's application for a continued State scholarship, noting his 'original talent' of which he had 'high expectations'. The application was successful and another 2,000 Finnish marks was awarded. In June, Sibelius was ill again and delayed his return from Berlin. Most likely nervous exhaustion was the cause, convalescence in his home environment the only necessary curative. His gaunt appearance came as a shock to his family and friends in Finland; Aino happened to meet him in the street and was rather taken aback.

After a brief spell resting at Aunt Evelina's house in Loviisa, Sibelius went to stay with Wegelius and his wife at Granholmen. In August he moved on to Ätsäri to join the Järnefelts and go with them to Vaasa where the General was provincial governor. Delayed by storms, Sibelius arrived at the railway station there only to see Aino and the others leave from another platform. Matters were a little tense between Aino and Sibelius after his treatment of her the previous summer, but over the ensuing weeks an understanding between them developed. Armas in particular was protective of his sister and hoped she would forget his friend, but a month after they had all returned to the capital Sibelius proposed to her, and she accepted. By an odd twist of fate, the very next day Aino read a short story by her friend Juhani Aho, *Yksin* ('Alone'), in which the author also declared his love for her. Sibelius quickly heard about his rival's interest and when she returned to Vaasa had her train compartment filled with flowers. He then returned to Loviisa to finish the B flat Quartet. This lyrical work was well received at its première in Helsinki in October and is the most expertly written, if not the most original, of his early chamber works. The B flat Quartet marks the apogee of his student chamber output, the model of Classical balance that the Piano Quintet had failed to be. With it, he bid the discipline of chamber composition all but farewell, and it is one of the few early pieces he did not disown in later life, numbering it Opus 4. He tried in vain to interest the Leipzig publisher Kistner in the piece. Even at this early stage, he realized that Germany, not Russia, was the stage on which a budding composer needed to establish himself.

With his engagement still largely a secret, Sibelius left Helsinki that same month for further study, this time in Vienna. His travelling third class in order to economize impressed those who came to see him off, but if it augured well the new-found responsibility of attitude did not last. He passed through the German capital and renewed acquaintance with his old circle, as well as new arrivals Armas Järnefelt and the Dane Carl Nielsen, who in the fullness of time became his country's leading composer. Sibelius wrote to Aino telling her that Berlin was no longer a place where he could work. Vienna in its late Hapsburg glow, however, was a very different proposition: 'a place after my own heart'. The bars and restaurants of another great European city rapidly proved too great a temptation. His taste for the good life earned him the nickname 'le comte' (the count) and he quickly ran short of money. He took up the violin again, mainly as a possible fallback for earning some cash. He joined the Conservatoire orchestra, and had

soon established a drinking circle amongst the student players.
However, he did at least reap some practical benefit from this group
by having them demonstrate their instruments' potentials to him.

In contrast to his year in Berlin, Sibelius arrived in the Austrian
capital with no arrangements made for his studies. Busoni had written
a letter of introduction to Brahms, who was no longer interested in
teaching. Nor was Bruckner. Wegelius suggested Karl Goldmark, one
of the most successful Viennese composers of the day by virtue of his
opera *The Queen of Sheba* (1874) and enduringly popular *Rustic
Wedding* Symphony of 1876. It was not until the middle of November
that Sibelius managed to see him. In a rather informal morning
meeting Goldmark, who was only half-dressed, agreed to take him as a
pupil, but would not look at the B flat Quartet that Sibelius had
brought to show him. Sibelius was delighted to find that he attained
considerable kudos by being one of Goldmark's rare pupils; he soon
came to realize why his teacher did not instruct others on a regular
basis. Goldmark's tuition on orchestration was extremely valuable, as
was the advice to study the scores of Mozart and the Classical
composers and to work over ideas again and again, but he could not
provide the detailed technical instruction Sibelius desperately
required. He therefore followed the suggestion of the conductor Hans
Richter and enrolled at the Conservatoire in the composition classes
of another noted composer, Robert Fuchs. Several composers who
went on to achieve great fame later on had been or would be pupils of
Fuchs, such as Hugo Wolf, Gustav Mahler, Franz Schmidt and
Franz Schreker.

Just as in Berlin, where he had been astounded by the music he saw
and heard, so in Vienna the pattern repeated itself. As early as 21
November his high spirits at getting down to constructive work with
Goldmark were rudely shattered when he attended a performance of
Wagner's *Tristan und Isolde* 'staged … in so brilliant a fashion I could
not have believed it possible.' A month later he experienced Bruckner's
revised Third Symphony conducted by Richter. He wrote home
calling Bruckner 'the greatest of all living composers', even though he
was aware of the symphony's shortcomings. Outside the concert hall
he was involved in a scuffle with partisan supporters of Brahms, who
detested Bruckner's music as heartily as they did Wagner's, and hurt
his foot. Later in the season he encountered Wagner's *Siegfried*, the

The distinguished operatic
and orchestral composer
Karl Goldmark, one of
Sibelius's tutors during his
year in Vienna, 1891–2

'Waltz-King' Johann Strauss conducting his own works (Sibelius retained a love of Strauss's music all his life), and still more Beethoven.

Just before Christmas Sibelius wrote to Aino, echoing Goldmark's exhortations that a composer's most valued attribute was self-criticism. He recounted how he had written at least three orchestral overtures, all of which he had destroyed. Yet the passage into the New Year was one of mounting insecurity. On Christmas Eve, Sibelius read Juhani Aho's *Yksin*, immediately recognizing the depiction of Aino and his rival's (or 'the author's') declaration of love for her. His first reaction was to challenge Aho to a duel (echoing one of the characters in the book), but he soon thought better of it. In the first week of January 1891, he set to music Runeberg's poem 'The Dream'; although the text was in Swedish, Sibelius felt it was 'new and also Finnish' (by which he probably realized that it was more personal in style and tone) but was unsure how effective a setting it was. Two days later his self-esteem suffered a more severe blow when an attack of nerves wrecked his audition for a post in the violin ranks of the Vienna Philharmonic Orchestra. So upset was he by this failure that he returned to his room and wept. To add insult to injury, Goldmark had become more aloof. Ostensibly this was because the older man wanted time for his own compositions; however, it might have had rather more to do with his niece. She had taken a fancy to the handsome young Finn and endeavoured to be present whenever Sibelius called on his teacher. Sibelius exploited his attractiveness to women; Adolf Paul later described him at this time in a thinly disguised portrait (in the autobiographical novel *En bok om en människa* – 'A Book about a Man') as the 'worst skirt-chaser of us all'. Goldmark became aware of their mutual interest and made sure the two did not meet again.

A further distraction was provided by the return of the nobility from their seasonal retreats. Sibelius had begun to move amongst the culture-loving aristocracy and *cognoscenti* prior to Christmas and up to a point pursued their acquaintance even though it proved highly damaging to his pocket. At times, he was careful to keep some distance, often despite earnest entreaties to become more involved (not least from the famous operatic diva, Pauline Lucca). His attitude to his social superiors was ambivalent: he wrote to Aino that the aristocratic of temperament were the ones with whom he most felt at home, yet in replying to a form sent by his mother – desperate to find

'The worst skirt-chaser of us all': the student Sibelius in Vienna, 1890

out what he was doing – he noted sourly that he usually dined 'with the lower orders'.

At the time Sibelius was seeing little of Goldmark, he was also at odds with Fuchs over an orchestral piece which Fuchs had found 'crude' and 'barbaric'. Stung into action by his recent string of disappointments, he ruthlessly revised the work, possibly an early version of the Overture in E major. Fuchs was much more impressed with the newer version, so much so that he wrote a glowing testimonial for Sibelius which secured a second Nylands Nation scholarship. Sibelius then showed the piece to Goldmark, who reinforced in his pupil the importance of constantly honing his musical material: 'Beethoven recast his some fifty times.' Sibelius had grand schemes in mind, namely a symphony 'permeated by the … intensity of spring'. The Overture was to be the first movement, followed by 'an idealized Ball scene', a short interlude and a set of variations to finish. The first two movements were completed by April, but Sibelius realized that his handling of symphonic form was not sure enough. The Overture, for all its bustle and infectious vitality, does not really go anywhere during its ten minutes and is constructed a little crudely. The more complex 'Ballet Scene', as the 'Ball Scene' was titled, is more deftly scored but still expressively elusive, with disparate elements from the Nordic to the Mediterranean pressed uneasily together. Nonetheless, he dispatched the Overture and 'Ballet Scene' to Kajanus. He was plagued by self-doubt on account of these two pieces; during their composition he had written to the conductor asking him to play them, suggesting he was not going to live much longer (a recurrent motif in his correspondence when depressed). Two days after he had posted them, he telegraphed to Kajanus begging for them not to be performed. Kajanus played them anyway at one of his regular Helsinki concerts. Critics and public alike were puzzled, particularly when both movements were played together, and did not know what to make of either work.

After producing some small chamber pieces, the largest of which was a rather slight piano quartet, Sibelius started to sketch ideas for another symphony. The spur was, most likely, a performance of Beethoven's Ninth Symphony by Richter. It is no accident that the work that resulted, *Kullervo*, would prove to be a symphony on the largest scale, employing vocal soloists and a chorus in two of its five movements. But more important was the subject; Sibelius had been re-reading the *Kalevala* in Finnish since the autumn of the previous year and the tragic tale of Kullervo, orphaned as a boy and who as a man unwittingly seduces the sister he believed was long dead, seemed ripe for a full-blooded choral-and-orchestral telling. Fuchs lauded the opening section of the first span so much he made the young man blush.

Robert Fuchs (1847–1927), composer of the highly popular *Serenade*, and Sibelius's other principal tutor in Vienna

Work was interrupted when Sibelius was suddenly admitted into hospital in May. He concealed the nature of his ailment for some time, causing disquiet at home, until treatment was proved to be progressing satisfactorily. He wrote to Aino telling her that he had had an operation to remove a kidney stone, but in a letter to Kajanus on 14 March revealed that he was in fact suffering from a venereal disease. Sibelius had in earlier letters to his fiancée admitted some infidelities, but infection was really beyond the pale. As if that were not bad enough, the clinic would not discharge him until the bill was settled. Christian was only able to send the requisite funds in June, and on the eighth of that month Sibelius left Vienna for Berlin. There he met up again with his old cronies and drank so much he had to sell most of his clothes in order to pay for his passage home, finally arriving in Helsinki in evening dress.

His return to Finland involved coming to terms with some unpleasant realities, including a growing band of creditors who were anxious to be repaid. Sibelius eventually (in October) took some violin students in Loviisa – the first time he had earned his own living – but still needed to borrow funds. A few older debts were reduced with what was left after he had kept himself supplied with cigars. Composition had become difficult, with only a solitary song produced all summer. And the idyllic atmosphere at home now seemed parochial and stultifying compared with Vienna. The publication of Adolf Paul's book, in which Sibelius was depicted as the skirt-chasing boy-genius Sillén, embarrassed him publicly; privately, Aino was highly displeased. *Kullervo* beckoned him on, and in November he travelled to Porvoo to hear the Karelian runic singer Larin Paraske. She had perhaps the largest repertoire of Finnish folk-songs of anyone alive at the time, had even composed songs of her own, and was a vital source that Sibelius needed to tap in order to get close to the spirit of Finnish legend. In later years, Sibelius maintained that he had not met Paraske until 1892, after *Kullervo* had been finished, but there were several witnesses – such as Yrjö Hirn – whose accounts confirm that they met in late 1891. Sibelius recorded his progress in letters to Aino, who remained in Helsinki.

In January 1892 Sibelius moved back permanently to the capital where he cemented his relationship with Kajanus, usually over dinner in restaurants. With Wegelius, matters became gradually more tense, not only by virtue of Sibelius's fraternization with his arch-rival, but also his increasing involvement with the Finnish-speaking camp. Wegelius upheld the Svecoman position, and when Sibelius told him that he was setting lines in Finnish from the *Kalevala*, responded 'Ugh!' Through February and March, Sibelius worked in an increasing fever of inspiration, detailed in almost daily reports to Aino. The huge score, lasting seventy minutes overall and the largest composition he is known to have written, was completed in the first few days of April. The première was fixed for the twenty-eighth of that month, so on completion of the music Sibelius plunged immediately into an equally frenetic round of editing, copying, checking and rehearsing – for he was to conduct the work also.

Programme listing for
the première of the *Kullervo*
Symphony; it incorrectly
marks the fourth movement,
Kullervo Goes to War,
as having a sung text.

Konsert den 28 April 1892.

Program.

Kullervo, symfonisk dikt för orkester, soli och kör . . . . *Jean Sibelius.*

I.

Inledning.

II.

Kullervos ungdom.

III.

Kullervo och hans syster.*)

IV.

Kullervo tågar ut till strid.*)

V.

Kullervos död.*)

Orkesterföreningens orkester, fru E. Achté, herr A.
Ojanperä och manskör (musikvänner) under ledning
af undertecknad.

Konserten börjar kl. 8 e. m.

Jean Sibelius.

*) Se texten.

Helsingfors, Tidnings- & Tryckeri-aktiebolagets tryckeri, 1892.

Sibelius had made his début on the podium in the previous November conducting the Overture and 'Ballet Scene', but was still untested as a conductor. He encountered incomprehension and derision at first from the orchestra, many of whom were German. By force of personality Sibelius imposed his will on the players, his ability to speak the three languages of his performers – the choirs were a mix of Swedes and Finns – helping to overcome their resistance. *Kullervo* played to a packed house, the Fennoman nationalists having come out in force, and was an unqualified triumph, even if the performance itself and Sibelius's conducting of it were less than ideal. Even Flodin had to concede that the composer had created 'his own music in our own music'.

The sheer power of the writing and *Kullervo*'s epic scale were quite unprecedented in Finland; indeed in Europe only Berlioz, Bruckner and Mahler had achieved a like monumentality. The symphony represented an enormous leap forward in Sibelius's development. Here for the first time his own voice was heard unequivocally, unlike in the Overture and 'Ballet Scene' where it had been glimpsed only fitfully. Nothing in his earlier output prepared anyone for the work's size or quality, nor its nationalist ardour. Acclaimed by the irredentists, the music's Finnish elements, such as the runic patterns (derived from Karelian folk-ballads) of the choral declamations, were stressed by many commentators at the expense of the whole's internal coherence, over which Sibelius had laboured long and hard. Perhaps aware that in some measure the work had run out of control, he referred publicly to *Kullervo* as a symphonic poem, though in his letters and in later life he retained the title 'symphony'. And while *Kullervo* is programmatic (in that it relates a story – or programme) rather than abstract, it possesses an inner cohesion that fully justifies such an epithet.

3

The two-headed Russian eagle tears a statute-book from a helpless Finnish maiden in Eero Isto's allegory of Tsarist oppression, *The Attack* (1899).

... Then Janne stopped, glanced at his watch, got up suddenly from the chair, bowed and left the house. We knew that he was hurrying to catch the train, and none of us was surprised that he did not say goodbye. We went on crying after he had left, for we knew that this son of Hämeenlinna, Janne Sibelius, would no longer belong to us; we already knew that he belonged to the whole of Finland.

reminiscence (unattributed) of Sibelius
at his grandmother's funeral in 1893

The Nationalist Poet 1892–9

Kullervo's success changed Sibelius's life. First of all, it enabled him to marry Aino. Neither his mother nor the Järnefelts had believed that the young composer, with no regular employment or prospects as a violinist, could support a wife and family from composition alone, but *Kullervo* showed that the potential was there. The wedding took place at the Järnefelt home in Tottesund in early June but Maria Sibelius was prevented from attending due to the sudden onset of a nervous disorder. The newlyweds travelled to the south-eastern province of Karelia for their honeymoon, financed by a grant of 400 Finnish marks for Sibelius to research folk-songs. It was typical of the composer that he set out with no route planned, or accommodation booked. Fortunately a base was established at Monola, where three more songs were composed to texts by Runeberg: *Under strandens granar, Kyssens hopp* and *Till Frigga* ('Beneath the Fir Trees', 'Kiss's Hope' and 'To Frigga', Op. 13, Nos. 1, 2 and 6), the most ambitious in scope that he had yet attempted, marking a considerable advance on his earlier efforts. Realizing that travel in the remoter regions of Karelia was perhaps too much of a hardship for Aino, he rather unromantically proceeded alone to Karpiselkä and rejoined her at Kuopio at the end of July. There they visited the playwright Minna Canth, whose other house guests included the poet Karl August Tavaststjerna, some of whose verses Sibelius had already set, and ironically Juhani Aho.

But *Kullervo* had wider implications for Sibelius since it propelled him to national prominence as a spokesman for Finnish culture at a time of uncertainty. Finnish-Swedish antagonism in the capital had been fanned again in the spring of 1892 by the hounding of the pro-Fennoman Tavaststjerna by the Swedish press. More ominously, unease was beginning to appear in the hitherto unproblematic relationship with Russia. For seventy years after Finland's absorption into the Tsarist Empire, the administration in St Petersburg had been of a liberal disposition and gloried in the cultural and ethnic diversity of its many subject peoples. In the last two decades of the nineteenth century, however, increasingly aggressive pro-Slavic elements in the government emerged who wanted to promulgate a more integrated political union by imposing greater uniformity from the centre. In autonomous Finland, 'Russification' began insidiously in 1890 with the incorporation of the Finnish postal service within the Russian system, followed by Tsar Alexander III's annulment of criminal law reforms previously assented to. Pressure began to be applied for the use of Russian as the language of government. Sibelius's music began to assume the role of totem for the Finns' growing cultural awareness, an awareness increasingly at odds with the designs of their overlords across the Gulf of Finland.

On their return from Karelia, Janne and Aino set up house in a rented Helsinki flat with Christian as a lodger. Sibelius had warned his

An oil painting of
Sibelius, around the time
of his wedding in 1892,
by Eero Järnefelt

wife of the ground rules for married life with a composer prior to
their wedding:

> *The last thing he must become is the kindly, drowsy, pipe-smoking*
> *head of the house. He must be free to continue his imaginative life*
> *undisturbed ... that is absolutely essential! The sort of marriage centring*
> *solely on rearing children is anathema to me – there are other things to*
> *think about if you are an artist.*

Believing absolutely in his genius, to which she would effectively
sacrifice the rest of her life, Aino accepted her role with little or no
demur. In the short term, Sibelius needed to earn a regular living so he
applied for – and secured – teaching posts in theory and violin at both
the Institute and the orchestra school. However much Wegelius and
Kajanus despised each other, both wanted the new force in Finnish
music in their camp. So Sibelius resumed his position as second fiddle
of the Institute's Quartet and composed a new, purely orchestral work
for Kajanus, the tone-poem *En saga* ('A Tale'). Unlike *Kullervo, En
saga* was cast in a single, atmospheric movement evoking the spirit of
Nordic myth rather than any particular legend. The lack of explicit
programme surprised critics such as Flodin and Oskar Merikanto at
the première the following February, which Sibelius directed.
Merikanto, who would become a distinguished song composer in his
own right, had already found the three Runeberg songs composed
during Sibelius's honeymoon 'bizarre and tiring ... to the unitiated
ear', and thought *En saga* needed to be cut. However, the new piece
was programmed no less than five times in 1893, and by the end of the
year had largely won round its audiences.

Gratifying as the success of *Kullervo* and *En saga* was, Sibelius was
not entirely satisfied with either. He began now to evolve a process
affecting his major pieces which would be repeated throughout the
rest of his career of composition, performance (usually with himself
wielding the baton) and revision prior to publication. Sibelius
eventually followed Merikanto's advice on overhauling the overlong
and somewhat diffuse tone-poem ten years later, in time for him to
conduct the work in Berlin at Busoni's instigation; the revised score
was printed in 1903. *Kullervo*, though, was another matter. Revived
three times during 1893, Sibelius became aware of the work's

unevennesses, and uneasy at its overtly folkloristic aspects. Even at this early stage in his creative life, he was concerned to foster an idealized conception of himself as a unique, Classically oriented composer, uninfluenced by Romantic trends whether Nordic, Russian or Central European. The motivation for this, at least within the Finnish context, may have been so that he could be experienced as a truly national but factionally neutral figure, standing above the squabbles of Finns and Swedes. *Kullervo* was withdrawn, ostensibly for revision, but no attempt was made to alter the work. The huge score remained suppressed until 1935, when the third movement was played in celebration of the centenary of the *Kalevala*'s publication. The symphony was not heard again in its entirety until 1958, a year after Sibelius's death.

   The spring of 1893 saw the first strains emerge in Sibelius's marriage. On 14 March, Aino had given birth to their first child, Eva. Towards the end of May, in order to save money, the couple moved out of their flat in Helsinki and rented a cottage on the outskirts of town, only securing a new apartment in the autumn, a pattern

Aino Sibelius with her first child, Eva, in 1893

followed each summer for several years. But at this same time, the painter Axel Gallén – who had not yet adopted the more familiar form of his name, Gallen-Kallela – returned from Paris and around him an intellectual drinking circle quickly formed known grandly as the 'Symposium'. Sibelius began to spend less time at home, preferring to squander his money on drinking, smoking and playing the gentleman about town. Aino, feeling deserted if not actually maltreated, returned home – not for the last time – with her child to Vaasa. However, the delicate state of her parents' own marriage made her sojourns there of temporary duration.

The regular members of the 'Symposium' with Sibelius were Gallén, Kajanus, Armas Järnefelt and Paul; occasional guests included Oskar Merikanto (whose wife had also given birth in 1893 to Aarre, who would become one of Finland's most advanced composers between the two world wars), as well as the violinist Willy Burmester

The Problem (1894) by Axel Gallén (1865–1931), depicting a typically alcoholic meeting of the 'Symposium'; left to right: Gallén himself (standing), Oskar Merikanto, Robert Kajanus, Sibelius

– leader of Kajanus's orchestra – and the pianist and former Liszt pupil Alfred Reisenauer. Meetings generally took the form of involved philosophical debates, usually initiated by Paul, or musical marathons. Once, Burmester and Reisenauer performed all ten of Beethoven's violin sonatas – and one or two of Grieg's – in a single night. The common factors of all the events were alcohol and cigars, both consumed in prodigious quantities. That New Year's Eve they drunkenly telegraphed Paul's mentor, the playwright August Strindberg, in Brno to inform him they were drinking Pommery. 'Life must be very boring in Finland,' he is said to have commented. When Gallen-Kallela later exhibited a painting of the group, *The Problem*, with Sibelius, Kajanus and Merikanto all looking very much worse the wear for drink, Finnish society was scandalized, Aino not least. The 'Symposium' broke up not long afterwards.

Having made his mark as an orchestral composer, Sibelius turned his attention to the potentially more lucrative areas of piano music and opera. During the summer he produced one of his most charming sets of piano pieces, the Six Impromptus, Op. 5, the first ideas for which dated from 1890, and a Sonata in F major. The Impromptus were given premières piecemeal throughout November 1893 by Karl Ekman, Merikanto and Armas Järnefelt. The larger-scale Sonata – at which Sibelius tinkered for a further two years – is hampered by unidiomatic keyboard writing and, despite the winning sweep of its opening ideas, one of his least successful works for the instrument. At this same time he worked out the skeleton scenario for an opera, *The Building of the Boat*, inspired by an episode in the *Kalevala*. The story concerned the hero Väinämöinen's attempts to win the love of Kuutar, daughter of the moon, by trying – in vain – to construct by the power of song alone a boat made out of splinters. Although he later strenuously disavowed any influence from Wagner, Sibelius's attitude to the operatic genre at this time contains many resonances of the German master's:

Music alone, that is to say absolute music, is not enough … Music is like a woman, it is only through a man that she can conceive and that man is poetry. Music attains its fullest power only when it is motivated by poetic impulse … when words and music blend.

He reckoned it would take him two years to complete the project and intended to enter the opera for a competition to be judged in 1896. Promisingly, the overture was drafted during the summer, but as autumn drew on progress on the opera itself became erratic.

Aside from over-indulgence at meetings of the 'Symposium', distractions from his task came mainly from commissions. One such was for incidental music to accompany a series of historical tableaux on Karelian subjects, for which Sibelius wrote some dozen songs and short orchestral pieces. The music, crowned by Pacius's anthem 'Maamme', prompted considerable acclaim at the Helsinki première on 13 November, although the composer believed this was due more to burgeoning national sentiment than musical appreciation. Nevertheless, six days afterwards he followed up this success by conducting a concert suite of eight numbers (including two of the songs), and in the following year finalized the definitive extract for concert performance of the *Karelia Overture*, published as Op. 10, and the *Karelia Suite*, Op. 11. The latter, in three movements, established itself rapidly as one of the composer's most popular works. Sibelius may have entertained similar hopes for success in his next completed item, *Rakastava* ('The Lover'), a suite of four songs for male chorus drawn from the collection of folk-songs, the *Kanteletar*. This was entered into a choral competition in Helsinki but, to the surprise of several observers, was beaten into second place by a song by Emil Genetz, Sibelius's former teacher in Hämeenlinna. (In 1911–12, Sibelius recomposed *Rakastava* as a three-movement suite for strings and percussion, in which form it is best known.)

Sibelius's financial difficulties worsened through the winter of 1893–4. In January, he visited his aunt Evelina in Loviisa (for the last time as she would die later in the year), using her house as a base to successfully secure yet another loan of 3,000 marks. But he now entered an unsettling compositional fallow period. Work on *The Building of the Boat* proceeded slowly, interruptions including a short spell lecturing at the University and further commissions. The biggest of these were a rather feeble cantata to celebrate the University's graduation ceremony at the end of May and an orchestral Improvisation, better known in its revised form with the title *Spring Song* (Vårsång), first played outdoors at the Vaasa Festival three weeks later. A short lyrical tone-poem with a gently Nordic atmosphere,

Spring Song was well enough received but Sibelius felt overshadowed by the success of Armas Järnefelt's *Korsholm*. The presence of his father-in-law in the audience only added to Sibelius's discomfiture.

In July, having decided that he needed to get away and concentrate on his opera, he left Aino for a trip to Europe's high temple of Wagnerian music theatre, Bayreuth. On the day of his arrival he went straight to hear *Parsifal*: 'Nothing in the world has ever made so overwhelming an impression on me,' he wrote to Aino, 'all my innermost heartstrings throbbed.' The performance encouraged him greatly in his hopes for *The Building of the Boat* by demonstrating what might be achieved on the stage: 'We must each commend our children to the holy spirit's protection. I can even feel my child gradually coming to life. I felt it only today.' Nothing else he heard at Bayreuth measured up to *Parsifal*, and after a few days despondency set in. Sibelius moved on to Munich to work on his 'child', and there renewed his acquaintance with *Tristan und Isolde*, which he had first seen in Vienna and which now left him thoroughly dispirited. He gave vent to his frustration in a letter home on 10 August: 'I want to settle down somewhere and get an ordinary manual job [in a factory!] … nothing, not even *Parsifal*, made so overwhelming an impression. It leaves one feeling that everything else is pale and feeble by comparison.' Twelve days later, the dominance of Wagner purged away despite his having been 'completely bowled over' by *Die Meistersinger* twenty-four hours earlier, Sibelius declared: 'I must be led by my inner voices.' *The Building of the Boat* expired in the Bavarian heat; from its ashes came a new idea for a sequence of purely orchestral tone-poems, though as yet he had not decided upon the subject.

On 23 August Sibelius quit Germany for a brief visit to Venice. He slowly picked his way back home via Innsbruck and Berlin – where he had a reunion with Busoni and Paul – and spent time visiting art galleries with Armas. He returned to Helsinki in mid September, in time for the new academic year, and a new flat in Brunnsparken. He immediately obtained a leave of absence from some of his teaching duties, but if this was intended to allow him to devote time for composition he had little to show for it by the time of the birth of his second daughter Ruth, on 23 November. The highlights of the first half of 1895 were an all-Sibelius concert in Helsinki in mid April, at which the Piano Sonata (championed by Merikanto), a new tone-poem *The Wood Nymph* ('Skogsrået') and the revised *Spring Song* were all given their premières, and the visit the next month of Busoni to give three concerts. Busoni persuaded Sibelius to offer some scores to the Russian publisher Belaiev; the virtuoso had some hopes of publication, having enlisted the composer Alexander Glazunov to Sibelius's cause. Nothing came of it, however, and Sibelius already knew that Germany was the vital arena for his music to appear in.

The summer months were spent in the idyllic surroundings of the lakes of Vaania, with little composition achieved. But on his return to Helsinki, Sibelius began to develop his idea of a cycle of tone-poems, taking the epic adventures of Lemminkäinen from the *Kalevala* as inspiration, something Flodin had urged on him three years before. For *Lemminkäinen and the Maidens of the Islands, Lemminkäinen in Tuonela, The Swan of Tuonela* and *Lemminkäinen's Return* Sibelius cannibalized material from the aborted opera – the overture was recast as the bleak and haunting third piece, depicting the baleful black swan which swam on the waters of Tuonela, land of the dead. In contrast to the gloom-laden atmosphere of the central pieces, the first and last are more extrovert and powerful, the set closely resembling a traditional symphonic scheme. The cycle was completed early in 1896 and given its première, conducted by the composer, in Helsinki on 13 April. The day after, Aino's father died. Using her share of the estate, she and Janne headed off to Berlin in late spring to visit Busoni, returning for the summer to Vaania.

The *Four Legends* or *Lemminkäinen Suite* as they are commonly known (the full title given by the composer is 'Symphonic Poems on Motifs from the Lemminkäinen Myth') achieved a more marked success even than *Kullervo* had enjoyed. Critical argument centred on whether the cycle was more or less Finnish in national character than the earlier symphony. As yet, no clear definition existed as to what constituted 'Finnish music' in a wider sense, though it was becoming clear that its kernel was formed from Sibelius's works, and most were agreed the tone-poems were his finest to date. Indeed, *The Swan of Tuonela* should really be considered as his first incontestable masterpiece. Nevertheless, he revised all four tone-poems in 1897, having revisited the subject in the short cantata *A Song for*

Lemminkäinen's Mother, painted in 1897 by Axel Gallén, from one of the episodes in the *Kalevala* that inspired Sibelius's so-called *Four Legends,* Op. 22

Lemminkäinen. The new version of the cycle was received as rapturously as the original, except ironically by Flodin, who found the music 'purely pathological'. Flodin's comments indicate how strongly he believed Sibelius should move away from the illustrative type of composition that he had mastered in the *Lemminkäinen* cycle to a more abstract concept. The Beethovenian format of a symphony by the twenty-year-old Ernst Mielck, given its première a few days before *Lemminkäinen* and acclaimed by audiences and critics alike, provided the goad with which Flodin urged Sibelius towards the Classical ideal of the symphony. In the event, only the third and fourth *Legends* were released (all four had been designed to be played separately as well as part of a set), after further revision in 1900, and both went on to establish a firm place in the orchestral repertoire. The other two were again held back until 1935 (partly because Kajanus did not rate them highly). However, in his old age Sibelius permitted all four to be published and performed, but with the order of *Lemminkäinen in Tuonela* and *The Swan of Tuonela* reversed.

Lemminkäinen put an end to the compositional impasse that had crippled his operatic ambitions, and is his major achievement of the middle of the decade. Yet ironically, amongst a host of songs and salon pieces (and a feeble cantata to celebrate the coronation of the new Tsar, Nicholas II) composed between its two versions, Sibelius did manage to compose an opera, the single-act *The Maiden in the Tower*. Created not through any inner compulsion but for a lottery raising funds for the Philharmonic Orchestra, Sibelius suffered acute self-doubt bordering on depression while composing it. Lasting little over half an hour, *The Maiden in the Tower* is bedevilled by a dire libretto. The naïve plot concerns the abduction of the maiden of the title by a lustful bailiff and her rescue by her lover, who alone believes her still unsullied. Applauded at the première in November, the general view was that Sibelius's music had been wasted on the subject. The composer quietly buried the score, despite requests for revivals. Although he considered writing another opera at various times in the future, *The Maiden in the Tower* is the only one he completed.

While completing the opera, Sibelius was busy preparing to take on a new academic role. At the end of the summer term, Richard Faltin had retired from his university professorship and Sibelius was considered the foremost contender. The post carried with it a reasonable salary – his financial situation was still precarious despite concert successes and the award of two scholarships (one shared with Kajanus) in the preceding two years – but was not uncontested; two other composers, Ilmari Krohn and Kajanus also applied. To support his candidature, Sibelius delivered a lecture on folk music and its influence on 'composed' art music. While the originality of his ideas made an impression, his paper's haphazard, improvisatory nature did not make for a good demonstration of his academic attainment. Worse still, the première of the Coronation Cantata for Tsar Nicholas II was a fiasco; Sibelius later placed the blame on a drunken tuba-player. Under pressure now, however much self-imposed, the composer became noticeably irritable and ill-humoured.

The decision of who would fill Faltin's chair rested not with the academic authorities but with the minister of Finnish Affairs in St

Petersburg, who happened also to be the University Chancellor. A committee was set up in the late spring of 1897, with Faltin as chairman, to make a recommendation to the minister and by an overwhelming majority Sibelius was chosen. Kajanus appealed on the grounds that Sibelius should be left free to create, and was anyway unsuited for the task. He even cited his friend's recent unsatisfactory showings as composer, conductor and lecturer. Kajanus seems to have been peeved by Sibelius having been the automatic choice. The latter felt terribly betrayed but made no response, other than with his new cantata for the University's graduation ceremonies, which was received rather better than any of his efforts for similar occasions in previous years. Yet although public sympathy was with Sibelius, at a deeper level there was a realization that Kajanus – for all that he did not need the post or the money – was the right man for the job. That was also the minister's view, and Kajanus was duly appointed. The affair opened a chasm between the two former cronies that would never be entirely closed, and right until Kajanus's death in 1933, Sibelius – who was in Italy with Walter von Konow when the decision was announced – remained distrustful of Kajanus's motives when programming his works.

On his return he went with Aino and the children to her mother's house in Lojo, but after a month he came back alone to Helsinki to compose the large and bracing orchestral song *The Rapids-Rider's Brides*. The rest of his family moved on to von Konow's estate where Aino could be near her mother-in-law, whose health was failing. Maria Sibelius had moved to Tampere, where Linda was a teacher, some years before, possibly to put some distance between herself and Aino, whose attentiveness to her son she resented. Christian made visits and prescribed medicines but Janne stayed away. Maria died before the year was out without having seen her elder son again.

Sibelius's next major première – on 24 February 1898 – was of four numbers (*Elegy, Musette, Minuet* and *The Fool's Song of the Spider*) for the first production of Adolf Paul's historical drama, *King Christian II*. It scored a modest but satisfactory success with two dozen performances at the Swedish Theatre in Helsinki. Credit was due to Sibelius for producing music of charm and dramatic effect, and for a revival in the summer he added three more pieces (*Nocturne, Serenade* and *Ballade*). At the end of February, Sibelius and Aino visited Berlin,

The conductor and composer Robert Kajanus, the first and most faithful of Sibelius's champions

where he composed the cantata *Sandels*, inspired by a famous general in Finnish history. Styled an 'Improvisation for male chorus and orchestra', this jaunty, rather unwarlike evocation of militarism won a competition run that same year by the MM ('Muntra Musikanter') Choral Society in Helsinki, but had to wait until March 1900 for its première. Sibelius revised the score in 1915. Aino returned alone in early April, but crossed with Christian who arrived to study pathology in the Wilhelmine capital. In between carousing with Busoni and Adolf Paul, and visiting the opera with his brother, Sibelius finally made his breakthrough with a German publishing house, placing the suite from *King Christian II* with the Leipzig firm of Breitkopf und Härtel. It was largely due to Paul that the young composer secured a reasonable deal:

Everything made a solemn and awe-inspiring impression. Paul seemed to feel very much at home in these surroundings – it looked as if his hopes grew the nearer the decisive moment arrived. Our progress through the huge rooms had just the opposite effect on me. My confidence decreased at every step I took, and when we came at last into the holy of holies, the manager's room, where the head of the firm, O von Haase, sat enthroned at a monumental desk under Beethoven's autograph portrait, I was almost ready to sell my compositions for nothing.

Successful as the incidental music had proved, Sibelius's thoughts were now fixed on the idea of the symphony, though as yet he was still undecided whether to follow the illustrative road of *Lemminkäinen*, so execrated by Flodin and Wegelius, or an abstract work. He began to sketch the latter at the end of April, but the convivial atmosphere of Berlin, now that Aino had left for home, deflected his attention away from composition at this crucial stage, especially when Gallén arrived and resurrected the 'Symposium'. Even a head injury obtained during a drunken brawl with some Polish workers failed to bring him to his senses.

The country he returned home to in June was caught in a growing state of unease. Tsar Nicholas had acceded to the demands of the pan-Slavic elements in his administration, and the autonomous Grand Duchy of Finland was a prime target for 'Russification'. The appointment as Governor of General Nikolay Bobrikov was widely interpreted as a stepping-up of the pressure to make Finland 'outwardly … recognizable as Russian'. Up until now, for all his use of Finnish elements in his music and the wider interpretations the politically minded placed on them, Sibelius's brand of nationalism had been purely cultural, with no political edge. He had taken care not to become bound up in radical causes even when they involved those he knew well and respected, such as Tavaststjerna, and did not share the anti-Russian sentiments of Wegelius. Indeed, the First Symphony on which he was at this time hard at work bears prominent echoes of Tchaikovsky and Borodin. As 1898 wore on he became more and more involved with its composition, so much so that he declined to attend Busoni's Helsinki concerts at the end of September. He excused his absence by citing Aino's pregnancy but like as not the symphony was the real reason. As the political screw began to tighten he

General Nikolay Bobrikov,
Imperial Governor of the
Grand Duchy and
enthusiastic implementer of
'Russification'

concentrated on the composition, aided by the final awarding of a
3,000 mark per annum pension in part recompense for being rejected
for Faltin's professorship. He endeavoured to keep distractions to a
minimum – the birth of his third daughter, Kirsti Marjatta, on 14
November was one he could not evade – by removing himself and the
family to the suburb of Kerava to keep away from the Helsinki bars
(his attendance there being so familiar that the *Musette* from *King
Christian II* had been turned into a drinking song by a local wag).

Events finally forced Sibelius to make a public demonstration of his
sympathies on 15 February 1899, when Bobrikov issued the infamous
'February Manifesto', designed to force Finland into a closer union
with the Empire. The Finns were incensed at this betrayal of their
rights but divisions opened up over how best to react. The older
Fennomen believed 'Russification' to be a temporary phenomenon;
their caution drove the previously antagonistic younger Fennomen
and Swedish liberals together in an unholy anti-Russian alliance which

advocated passive resistance as the best policy. Half a million people, a third of the population, signed a petition in protest at the Manifesto, which was delivered in person by 500 representatives to Nicholas II, who refused to see them. International opinion was mobilized across Europe, with over a thousand public figures adding their support, including Émile Zola, Anatole France, Florence Nightingale and even the author of *War and Peace*, Count Nikolay Tolstoy, but all to no avail. Sibelius's practical response was the choral-and-orchestral *Song of the Athenians*, evoking the defiance of the third-century Greeks under Dexippos resisting the invasion of the Heruli. Song and symphony were given their premières in April; whilst every movement of the symphony was applauded, the thunderous reception of the *Song of the Athenians* caused it to be instantly encored.

It is curious that at the very point when Sibelius for the first time openly took a political stance in his music, he should also have produced his first abstract symphony. In *Kullervo* and the *Lemminkäinen* cycle, the Finnish colours of the music had been the most immediately striking feature for all the hints of Wagner or Liszt in their construction. Yet amidst the turmoil of the winter and spring of 1898–9, Sibelius appropriated the Russian symphonic model, with its evocative and colourful orchestration and tendency towards illustrative or programmatic subjects, and made it his own. There is no evidence to suggest that this was anything but a musical decision, but its timing was extraordinary. In other circumstances, the Symphony No. 1 in E minor might even have suggested an artistic rapprochement with the Russians; yet in context it sounded more like a Finn beating them at their own game. A turbulent opening movement is followed by a passionate slow second, vibrant, dancing scherzo and dramatic finale. Much of the musical material is derived from a long melody of brooding and distinctive character prefacing the first movement which returns in the last, along with the slow movement's principal theme. In recognition of his achievement, and one suspects not only musical, Sibelius was awarded a Finnish State grant of 2,500 marks. In the following year the symphony was withdrawn (the original full score has not survived), revised and given a new première, to equal acclaim.

4

A care-worn Aino, in a
1907 portrait in oils by her
brother Eero

'*Romanticism is the innermost essence of music,*'
he once said as we were engaged in a discussion
of modernism.
    '*What is Romantic is imperishable. It always
has been, and always will be, as long as people
inhabit the earth.*'

Santeri Levas, *Sibelius : A Personal
Portrait*, 1972

The Way of the Future 1899-1907

One of the earliest casualties of the February Manifesto was the freedom of the press. Newspapers were summarily closed down for periods running to months if they offended the censor. Two such were *Aftenposten*, the paper Karl Flodin wrote for (his views on the première of the First Symphony therefore went unrecorded), and the Young Fennoman organ *Paivälehti*. To alleviate the financial strains put on disadvantaged newspaper staff an elaborate, three-day festival was mounted in Helsinki in early November 1899 to raise funds for the Press Pension Fund. That it might also boost the Finns' morale was an added bonus, something not lost on the ever-astute Bobrikov, who wryly auctioned seats in the Imperial box 'to assist such a good cause'. Sibelius contributed the music for the climactic series of seven tableaux illustrating episodes in Finland's past, culminating – as had the *Karelia* pageant seven years before – in a stirring, patriotic finale. However, the music made its deepest impact a month later when Kajanus reprised four of the numbers in concert: the opening *All'overtura*, *Scena* – depicting the Finns' involvement in the Thirty Years War (1618–48) – *Quasi bolero* and the finale, *Finland Awakes*. This last, with its dramatic demeanour and anthem-like central section, quickly came to be in demand as a separate concert work, and the composer revised it the following year as a self-sufficient item with the title – acting on a suggestion in a letter from an anonymous fan – *Finlandia*.

Born out of political struggle, *Finlandia* itself became over the years a constantly evolving symbol of the country's predicaments, whether it were the emergent nation seeking self-determination before 1917 or the fledgling state resisting Soviet aggression in 1939. And while Finland remained a Russian possession, performances within the empire had to take place under the covert title of 'Impromptu'. Whatever it was called, *Finlandia* achieved and sustained a position with an international audience much of which was only dimly aware of Finland's geographical situation; it only knew it loved the music.

Although none of the other Pension Fund pieces rivalled *Finlandia* in this respect, the three remaining movements from the concert extract enjoyed continuing popularity in their own right under the title *Scènes historiques*. (In 1911–12, Sibelius revised the set, renaming *Quasi bolero* as *Festivo*, and wrote a second, newly composed triptych.)

The poor receptions accorded to the cantatas *Sandels* in March 1900 and *Snöfrid* the following October were uncomfortable proof that a rousing, nationalistic tone was not in itself a guarantee of success. And though Sibelius was seen to have allied himself firmly

Photographic portrait of the composer as a public figure; Sibelius in the early 1900s

with the dissenting lobby through such works, in no sense was he a political animal. He believed in the right to existence of the Finnish language and culture and resisted any attempt, whether from bigoted Fenno-Swedes or imperialist Russians, to suppress or supplant them. If he never took an active part in the resistance to the Tsarist regime, he made the acquaintance of many who did, such as the civil rights campaigner R. A. Wrede and the writer Maxim Gorky. But he was a native Swedish-speaker first and last, and saw no conflict between his position as the musical voice of Finnish nationalism and a song-composer with a gift for setting Swedish poetry – particularly Runeberg's. His even-handedness in this respect was prophetic of the moral stance of present-day Finland, where although the Swedish-speaking element has dwindled to just six per cent of the population it is treated as a cultural equal. In the first decade of the twentieth century, however, his fellow countrymen were not all of so accommodating a cast of mind. One such was Heikki Klemetti, the dominant choral conductor in the country, who gave the first performances of many of Sibelius's Finnish part-songs. Klemetti fuelled the Finn–Swede divide by constant carping at the prevailing tendency amongst Finnish composers of the time, many of whom like Sibelius were of Swedish or mixed background, to prefer Swedish texts. Sibelius maintained a scrupulous detachment from this quarrel, producing as far as was possible vocal works using texts from both languages, though it may be no accident that his solo songs with piano are predominantly in Swedish, while his choral works with or without orchestra use Finnish texts more often.

In the wake of the First Symphony and Press Pension Fund music, Sibelius turned to writing songs in Swedish, and the three sets eventually published as Opp. 36, 37 and 38 (some sixteen in all, dating from 1898–1904) constitute one of the high-points of his early career. Indeed, it can be argued that they form the richest seam in his output of some hundred solo songs. The best of them, such as *Svarta rosor* ('Black Roses', Op. 36, No. 1), *Säv, säv, susa* ('Sigh, Sedges, Sigh', Op. 36, No. 4) and *Höstkväll* ('Autumn Night', Op. 38, No. 1), have remained among his best-loved and most-performed pieces, standards of the repertoires of a legion of the world's finest singers. As with his piano pieces, Sibelius collected the songs into fairly arbitrary groupings throughout his life, even where they shared common features, as with the two sets of Runeberg settings, Opp. 13 (1890–2) and 90 (1917). He never composed a true song-cycle in the tradition of Schubert or Schumann, and it is as individual works that his songs are best appreciated.

February 1900 saw the outbreak of a severe typhus epidemic in southern Finland. Amongst its victims were the young child of Arvid Järnefelt and Sibelius's youngest daughter, the 'radiant' fifteen-month-old Kirsti. Aino was inconsolable, having nursed both children unsuccessfully, and blamed herself for their deaths; Sibelius was equally devastated but withdrew into a shell. So great was his grief that it is said he could never again bring himself to speak of her, even after three more children had been born and grown to adulthood. He attempted to sublimate his feelings in the large-scale fantasia for cello and piano *Malinconia* ('Melancholy'), in which an atmosphere of despair manages to emerge despite some unidiomatic writing for the instruments.

The conductor and pianist Georg Schnéevoigt, who with his wife Sigrid gave the first performance of Sibelius's *Malinconia* in 1900

The first performance of *Malinconia* was given in Helsinki a month after Kirsti's death by Georg and Sigrid Schnéevoigt as part of a fund-raising concert for the Helsinki Philharmonic's proposed European tour, the Finnish Senate having at first refused to grant support to the enterprise. The intention was for Kajanus to take the orchestra across Scandinavia and Northern Europe during the summer, culminating with a concert in Paris as part of the Finnish contribution to the 1900 World Fair. The desirability of asserting Finnish cultural independence took on an added urgency with the proclamation in June of an Imperial decree gradually introducing Russian as the official language of the Grand Duchy. Sibelius's music was to be featured most prominently of all, with the revised versions of the First Symphony and *Finlandia*, as well as *The Swan of Tuonela*, *Lemminkäinen's Return* and *King Christian II*. Kajanus and Armas Järnefelt were represented by two works apiece. Sibelius was even drafted on to the tour as unpaid assistant conductor – though in the event Kajanus jealously guarded his position on the podium and Sibelius had to rest content in the wings. The tour got off to an inauspicious start in Stockholm, as the Olympia Hall they booked to play in turned out to be a large circus tent, with problematic acoustics and the overpowering reek of animals. Further engagements in Sweden proved even more farcical; they arrived in Malmö to discover that no one had booked the hall! Despite these difficulties, which left the composer somewhat dispirited, Sibelius's music was in general well received. Parallels were even drawn with the national role Chopin had assumed earlier in the century for Poland where, ironically, Finnish levies had assisted the Russians in suppressing the national uprising in 1830.

Sibelius's morale rose when they reached northern Germany, where performances of the *King Christian II* pieces had made his name familiar. Tension between composer and conductor, stemming back to the conflict over Faltin's professorship, began to ease as Sibelius came to understand the terrible strain the tour was placing on Kajanus. Writing home to Aino, who was still depressed over Kirsti's death, he reported: 'I try to help him as much as I can by at least always appearing cheerful … Sometimes I get into a silly frame of mind which seems to do Kajanus and the members of the orchestra good.' The better-prepared concerts in Lübeck and Hamburg were

The Finnish Pavilion, designed by Gesellius, Lindgren and Saarinen (with frescoes by Gallén), at the Paris World Fair in 1900

enthusiastically received, and the orchestra moved on to Berlin for the crucial test. The critics in the German capital regarded themselves as the arbiters and guardians of the Classical tradition. As such, they were unresponsive to the idiom of the First Symphony, with its to them parochial Finnish accent, though many gave credit to its 'fine craftsmanship and seriousness of tone'. The shorter items, not only Sibelius's, elicited much more favourable comments, and the party felt overall quite satisfied as they moved on through Holland and Belgium. Sibelius, despite this, began to feel homesick: 'I long for Finland which I love more than ever. I intend never to leave it. If it is necessary I'll be chained to it: I can die for it.'

In the event, the orchestra's concerts in the French capital were an anti-climax. The holiday season and a heatwave had driven most of the Parisians out of town. Those that remained who did attend (and the tourists attracted by the Fair) reacted more positively than the Berliners to all of Sibelius's pieces, particularly to the symphony, *The Swan of Tuonela* ('a remarkable poetic vision' one critic thought it) and, inevitably, *Finlandia* (under the title *La Patrie* – 'The Fatherland'). Sibelius was in general unimpressed by the French capital – especially its cigars, which he declared 'beneath criticism' – though at least one observer commented that both he and Kajanus were 'too young and immature as personalities' who 'could not resist the temptations of Paris'.

After his return to Finland in August, Sibelius came into contact with Axel Carpelan, the formerly anonymous fan who had suggested the idea of a piece called *Finlandia*. Carpelan was full of good ideas and suggestions: Sibelius should write a violin concerto, another symphony, music to Shakespeare; Sibelius should visit Italy for inspiration. It is a measure of what Carpelan came to mean to Sibelius that all of these suggestions, and many others, would in the fullness of time be acted on. Indeed, over the next nineteen years until his death Carpelan became as indispensable to the composer as he was indefatigable in his support, particularly in the crucial role of unpaid and self-appointed fund-raiser. Carpelan himself had no wealth, but his connections in moneyed circles enabled him to secure enough financial support for Sibelius to start devoting himself to composition.

The first fruit was a sum of 5,000 marks so that Sibelius with his family could winter in the aesthetically congenial setting of Italy. After

securing deputies to take over his teaching duties, Sibelius, Aino and
the children set off at the end of October for Berlin, where the
composer wanted to build on his successes earlier in the year. To this
end he stayed on until January 1901, by which time he had little more
than a few promises of performances to show for his efforts, and he
began to run low of funds, partly as a consequence of drowning his
sorrows in alcohol. He wrote to Carpelan asking for more money: the
latter retorted that Sibelius should fulfil the objective of the trip and
move on to Italy. Sibelius finally acceded at the end of the month,
thereby missing Ida Ekman's rendition of his song *The Tryst* (Op. 37,
No. 5) at the home of Otto Lessman, a German businessman whom
she successfully cultivated to Sibelius's cause.

In the first week in February the Sibelius family arrived in Rapallo
on the Ligurian coast in north-west Italy. Janne rented a study in a
local villa and immediately began to sketch ideas for a cycle of tone-
poems, similar in design to the *Lemminkäinen* set but on a topic more
familiar to a continental European audience: Don Juan (the Don
Giovanni of Mozart's opera). After a month, however, the idyllic
setting soon turned sour: inspiration had dried up, news from home
of increasing attempts at Russification proved a constant distraction
and then six-year-old Ruth contracted typhus. This time Aino
successfully nursed her child back to health, but for Janne the
memory of Kirsti's death barely a year before was a horror not to be
contemplated. The combination of composer's block, financial
uncertainty and Ruth's illness proved too much of a strain and
without warning he abandoned his family and took off for Rome.
Aino was left to fend for herself with a few hundred lire while her
husband wandered in and out of Roman art galleries and heard
Palestrina masses in church. His letters to her are eloquent testimony
to the blind egocentricity of the artist:

> *I realize what a hell both Rapallo and Berlin were for me. I am*
> *working very hard here and – I hope – writing well. And there are so*
> *many artistic diversions when my imagination runs dry. I seem to need*
> *this stimulus and it also seems that I need total solitude when I am*
> *working … I have now fallen fatally in love with my orchestral fantasy. I*
> *can't tear myself away from it.*

Sibelius with his second daughter Ruth in Rapallo, Italy, in 1901. When she contracted typhus, he abandoned his family and fled to Rome for a fortnight.

Ruth's condition improved but it dawned on Sibelius that his marriage was reaching breaking-point. He conceded that his selfishness was intolerable, but believed he was not wholly at fault: 'You must also love me,' he wrote to Aino, 'otherwise our relationship will perish.' That it did not was due in large part to his wife's unswerving belief in his genius and importance as a composer to their country, for which great cause she was prepared to endure much.

Sibelius slunk back to Rapallo after a fortnight and the reunited family edged homeward, stopping off in Florence, Vienna – where he received an invitation to conduct *The Swan of Tuonela* and *Lemminkäinen's Return* at Richard Strauss's Heidelberg Festival in June – and Prague, where he met the two leading Czech composers of the day, Antonín Dvořák and his son-in-law Josef Suk. The Sibeliuses arrived back in Finland in early May and Aino and the children went to stay at the Järnefelt estate at Lojo. Sibelius returned to Berlin a few weeks later to prepare for the Heidelberg concert. This went very well despite a touch of stage fright and difficulties at rehearsal. Strauss's officiating at the festival ensured the presence of many leading Berlin critics who hailed the two tone-poems as 'highly sensitively wrought' and 'brilliantly accomplished'. Both were taken up by orchestras in several German cities, Berlin included, in the ensuing concert season.

Back in Lojo for the summer, Sibelius took stock of his situation. Devoting time to his compositions as well as wife and family was a priority after the upheavals in Italy, but his duties as a teacher, even though he had found deputies to relieve himself of many of them, were a burden he wanted to be rid of. It was a combination of Russian oppression and Axel Carpelan that provided the way out of the impasse. In the summer, the Tsarist regime made the first of several misguided attempts to forcibly conscript Finns directly into Russian-speaking regiments, rather than within the purely Finnish battalions hitherto. A wave of protest swept the country, prompting a new petition, which Sibelius was one of the first to sign, and the formation of the secret Kangal group who organized a successful campaign of passive resistance. With Sibelius's status as national icon bolstered by such events, Carpelan was able to secure for the composer a regular though hardly lavish quarterly allowance of 500 marks from a group of patriots that beneficiary and sponsors both firmly believed it was their duty to provide. Sibelius duly resigned his teaching posts, though it might be more accurate to say that he formalized his state of absence. If he thought the new arrangement would provide financial security for the future, he was much mistaken: within a few years the loss of his regular teaching income would leave bankruptcy a real danger.

The new-found freedom allowed Sibelius to progress with the 'orchestral fantasy' that he had been working on in Italy. But if Don

Axel Carpelan, Sibelius's indefatigable counsellor and impoverished organizer of financial support

Juan had proved to be the wrong subject, so too was Dante's *Divine Comedy* which he considered at Lojo. What finally emerged was indeed a cycle of four orchestral pieces, but now in the form of his Second Symphony, the profile of which was very different from its predecessor. The movements describe a clearly interrelated mood-progression of pastoral calm, conflict, an urgent call to arms and concluding defiance and triumph. The resonances of Finland's situation are clearly audible, but more personal events also found expression in the music, not least a brief mournful episode in the finale occasioned by the suicide of Aino's sister, Elli. The symphony took shape steadily through autumn, but by November Sibelius had decided to subject the still incomplete score to a thorough revision and postponed the January première until March. The delay also gave time for him to write two smaller supporting items for the March concert, the merry Overture in A minor and a rather bland Impromptu for female voices and orchestra (Op. 19).

The Second Symphony was presented four times between 8 and 16 March. It was an immediate success, the combative tone and blazingly affirmative conclusion according with the spirit of the times, as was much remarked on – by Kajanus for instance – although it was not designed as an overtly political work. Accordingly, the Second has occupied a special place in Finland and has remained the most popular and often-played of his symphonies. Most commentators cared not to look past the extra-musical significance. Those that did, such as Cecil Gray, noted that 'the Second strikes out a new path altogether' and that the 'internal organization of the movements reveals many important innovations, amounting at times, and particularly in the first movement, to a veritable revolution', though the nature of that revolution has been hotly debated ever since. Many who had been lukewarm towards the First Symphony were won over by Symphony No. 2 – including the composer Wilhelm Peterson-Berger in Stockholm who had found its predecessor 'moribund, shoddy' and full of 'bogus philosophical poses'. The Second was not to be subjected to revision.

A month later the new Finnish National Theatre was inaugurated, for which occasion Kajanus conducted *Snöfrid*, with an alternative text provided by Volter Kilpi, and a new cantata for baritone, chorus and orchestra, *The Origin of Fire*, derived appropriately from the *Kalevala*. A near-masterpiece – at least in its final version from eight years later – *The Origin of Fire* is let down only by its final chorus, but after the overwhelming impact of the symphony neither the composer nor the audience seemed able to work up much enthusiasm for it. Sibelius rapidly entered an emotional trough and slunk off to Berlin to see Christian. He excused himself to Aino (who remained in Helsinki) by saying he was following 'the bidding of his genius'. Whilst in Berlin he made the usual round of conductors, but the only concrete offer came from the ever-stalwart Busoni: that Sibelius conduct *En saga* with the Berlin Philharmonic in November. He accepted with alacrity. That summer he rented a summer house alone; Aino and the children went as usual to Lojo, in the coastal resort of Tvärminne where his sister Linda – whose mental health was causing the family some concern – was also staying. In August he went off to visit Wegelius at Pojo, and then returned to Helsinki to flat-hunt. With Aino still away, he could not decide which flat to choose and had to rely on his brother-in-law Eero for help.

In mid September, Sibelius worked on two projects: a thoroughgoing overhaul for the Berlin concert of *En saga*, whose première was conducted by Kajanus in Helsinki, and a concerto for his old instrument, the violin. Busoni had given Sibelius the option of substituting the Second Symphony in Berlin but the latter stuck to his original task. *En saga* was well received, its composer's pleasure increased by the critical savaging given to the other works on the programme, by Delius, Mihalovich and Théophyle Ysäye. After the concert, Busoni gave a lavish reception at which he and Sinding toasted the Finn's success at prodigious length. His esteem in Germany was bolstered further in December by the publication by Breitkopf und Härtel of the First Symphony, which led to further favourable comment, albeit outside Berlin.

On his return to Finland, Sibelius became involved with a new cultural club, the Euterpists, centred around Flodin's arts periodical, *Euterpe*. Although made up largely of the Swedish-speaking élite, the group had wide-ranging aesthetic and political sympathies, and Sibelius was the only regular composer-member. One common propensity all the attendees shared was the ability to drink heavily. This inevitably put still more strain on his marriage, all the more so since Aino was in the final stages of her fourth pregnancy, and indeed Katarina Elisabet, usually called 'Nipsu', was born on 12 January 1903. Throughout the new year, Sibelius was too often to be found in Helsinki bars instead of being at home writing the concerto. He might disappear for days at a time. Aino occasionally tried to locate him herself, though if she did manage to track him down as like as not he would refuse to see her. His drinking also worried his brother, Christian, who had seen it at first hand in Berlin and who had been dissecting the brains of alcoholics as part of the pathology course he was pursuing. Christian exhorted Janne in the strongest terms to turn teetotal, but the latter had a repertoire of excuses to counter these suggestions:

There is much in my make-up that is weak ... When I am standing in front of a grand orchestra and have drunk a half-bottle of champagne, then I conduct like a young god. Otherwise I am nervous and tremble, feel unsure of myself, and then everything is lost. The same is true of my visits to the bank manager ... The worst thing is when I go to concerts given by rivals and imagine that everyone is looking at me to see whether I'm suffering from envy. I get then an expression round the mouth that has

done me much harm in the eyes of other people. If I have a few glasses of
wine, that's all gone … You can see from this that my drinking has
genuine roots that are both dangerous and go deep. I promise you to try
and cope with it with all my strength.

All his strength was insufficient for the task, so Aino and Carpelan
joined forces to extricate him from the centre of temptation, Helsinki
itself. Arvid Järnefelt, the artist Pekka Halonen and Sibelius's one-time
rival for Aino's affections Juhani Aho had established a small artists'
colony in the village of Järvenpää, twenty miles north of the capital,
near Lake Tuusula. There in 1903, with borrowed funds, Sibelius
bought a plot of land with a fine prospect of the lake and arranged for
a house to be built to a design – supplied free of charge – by the
eminent architect Lars Sonck. The house, which Sibelius named
Ainola, was completed in the following year.

    In parallel with the construction of the house, the Violin Concerto
slowly took shape, in between binges. Sibelius had originally arranged
with the former leader of Kajanus's orchestra and 'Symposium'
member, Willy Burmester – at the time one of the leading solo
violinists in Europe – to give the première of the work in Berlin in
March 1904. Pressure of money worries made the necessity of
presenting the concerto before then and in Helsinki of paramount
importance, so he entrusted it to the local professor of violin, Viktor
Nováček. Burmester was furious but bided his time: the composer
had pleaded poverty, and on receiving copies of the first two movements Burmester knew he was looking at a masterpiece. 'Wonderful!
Masterly!' he wrote back. As the deadline for the completion of the
concerto drew ever nearer, Aino enlisted Kajanus's help in dragging
the distracted composer out of bars to finish the finale. The première,
originally set for the autumn, was postponed until February (just
one month before Burmester would have tackled it). Even then,
Sibelius took time out to compose incidental music for Arvid
Järnefelt's play *Kuolema* ('Death'). His music accounted in large part
for the play's successful first production, and orchestral versions of
two of the numbers, the *Valse triste* and *Scene with Cranes*, went
on to achieve great popularity in the concert hall. The *Valse triste* in
particular became a hit all round the world. Arrangements
proliferated for all manner of instrumental combinations but in

Winter at Ainola, Sibelius's villa in Järvenpää in which he lived from September 1904 until his death fifty-one years later

perhaps the greatest irony of his life the composer received nothing from its success. Under the terms of the publishing contract, Sibelius was paid royalties only on his own versions – but the publishers, Fazer and their German agents Breitkopf, were free to make others with no obligation to pay the composer a penny. Time and again for the rest of his life he encountered his simple, wistful little tune, in concerts, restaurants, cafés, almost always in arrangements other than his, earning his publishers the small fortune the near-penurious composer had missed out on; though how much of it he would have drunk away can only be wondered at.

The Violin Concerto's first performance did not go well. Nováček staggered as best he could through the score, one of the most demanding ever written, into which Sibelius had poured all the

Opposite, 'polonaise for polar bears': sketch in Sibelius's hand for the opening of the finale of the Violin Concerto

virtuosity he had once dreamed of displaying himself. In several places soloist and orchestra came unstuck, so that a clear view of the piece was hard to obtain. Flodin was one of the most outspoken: 'boring' was his judgement. Burmester could afford to be smug over the notices and offered to play the concerto three times that October. But Sibelius declined his offer and withdrew the work for revision, yet he barely even looked at it for a year. Built on a Beethovenian scale, the concerto in its original form is perhaps too self-consciously a vehicle for display. The large first movement was episodic in construction, with two large cadenzas for the soloist, unlike the two symphonies which were more integrated in design. That failing Sibelius rectified in his complete rewrite of the concerto (excising around ten per cent of its original length including that second cadenza), as well as lightening the orchestral textures to achieve a brighter sound. The final version was launched by Karl Halir in Berlin under Richard Strauss's direction in October 1905, much to Burmester's justifiable disgust. Sibelius had decided again that he could not wait for Burmester to fit it into his busy schedule; the virtuoso had threatened never to play the work if he did not give the première himself and was true to his word. The great Joachim, present in the audience for the revision's first performance, echoed Flodin's opinion of the original: 'terrible and boring'. The concerto, with its 'jolly, tearing finale' (to quote Ralph Wood), the main theme of which was described by Sir Donald Tovey as 'evidently a polonaise for polar bears', only set public enthusiasm alight in the 1930s through the sustained advocacy of the leading virtuoso of the day, Jascha Heifetz. Thanks to his commitment, and a brilliant recording made in 1935, the work went on to become one of the standards of the modern violin repertoire. With the establishment of the quinquennial International Jean Sibelius Violin Competition in Helsinki in 1965, the concerto became the principal test-piece, one of the ultimate challenges any aspiring violinist must face but one its composer could never have met himself.

Between the two versions of the concerto Sibelius entered a brief fallow period. He concluded the set of solo songs eventually published as opus 38 and composed a series of minor orchestral pieces, including a Dance Intermezzo based on Heine's poem 'A fir-tree ... dreams of a palm' and an Andante for strings that has become better known under the title Romance in C. In the meantime, the Second Symphony was

The Italian maestro Arturo
Toscanini c. 1904, in which
year he first conducted a
Sibelius score, *The Swan
of Tuonela*

enjoying rather mixed reviews outside Finland. The best reception was
accorded in Hamburg, where Sibelius's music had been known for
several years, but critics in Boston, USA, and St Petersburg were not
impressed. To offset these negative developments, Arturo Toscanini
scored notable successes in Italy with *The Swan of Tuonela* and *En saga*.
In the summer, Sibelius turned his thoughts to another symphony, but
quietly shelved this project in the following year. He did manage to
complete his first big piano composition since the Sonata of ten years
before, the three 'lyric pieces' *Kyllikki*, named after a character in the
Kalevala (though not, according to the composer, inspired by her). But
in *Kyllikki* as with his other keyboard compositions, the piano did not
draw out the best in Sibelius and, despite some fine moments, it
cannot be counted amongst his best works.

Politically, the early months of 1904 became increasingly tense.
Russia suffered a calamitous defeat in Manchuria in February at the
hands of the Japanese. The Pacific Fleet was destroyed and Tsarist land
forces driven into retreat following invasion. The Baltic Fleet was duly
dispatched to retrieve the situation but was sunk as well. Bobrikov's
popularity was at its lowest ebb following further attempts at
conscription and he was assassinated in April by Eugen Schauman,
who then shot himself on the spot. (The doctor who treated the dying
Governor was Richard Faltin, Sibelius's one-time quartet partner. Five
years later, Sibelius incorporated a theme inspired by Schauman's
death into his tone-poem *In memoriam*.) Two months later the
Interior Minister Plehwe was murdered in St Petersburg. With the war
lost, the administration needed to quell provincial discord. In Finland,
this was translated into the conciliatory appointment as Governor of
Prince Obolensky.

The move of the Sibelius family into their new home of Ainola was
delayed by Janne's hospitalization (for an ear complaint) until late
September. The Järnefelts and Ahos welcomed them in but Sibelius
himself needed time to settle. His uneasiness found expression in
continuing ill-health and protracted drinking sessions. The doctors in
Helsinki suggested diabetes, or at least a susceptibility to diabetic
symptoms, but incipient alcoholism was the real cause. On his thirty-
ninth birthday, Sibelius went to conduct a concert in Uleåborg but on
his way there received a furious missive from Aino about his drinking;

his letters home show how severely his handwriting had deteriorated, evincing signs of tremor, a symptom of alcoholism. In January 1905 Sibelius travelled with Aino's blessing to Berlin, ostensibly to conduct the Second Symphony at one of Busoni's modern music concerts and to keep abreast of musical developments. Both the music and his conducting drew praise, and in February he was able to take advantage of his increasing fame to negotiate a deal with a new publisher, Robert Lienau of Schlesinger. While in Berlin Sibelius consulted a diabetes specialist, Dr Klemperer, who found him to be in perfect health but a hypochondriac. Klemperer lectured the composer on the perils of wine and then dismissed him.

Sibelius had hoped that by changing publisher he would maximize his income from future compositions, the royalties from *Valse triste* being irretrievably lost. Any possibility of an accommodation with Fazer, who had printed much of his output thus far in conjunction with Breitkopf und Härtel, evaporated in July with the sale of all of their rights in Sibelius's music to their German partners. Lienau investigated whether their rivals might sell these in turn, but Breitkopf were content to stick with what they had. Sibelius was contracted by Lienau for four years to provide four major works per year for a minimum sum of 8,000 Reichsmarks. The first work covered was the revised Violin Concerto and it was Lienau who arranged the prestigious première that October. The second work was a concert suite of nine of the ten numbers Sibelius had composed as incidental music to a production at Helsinki's Swedish Theatre of Maurice Maeterlinck's play *Pelléas and Mélisande*. The play was popular with composers at the time: Debussy had already composed his only opera on it in 1902, Arnold Schoenberg had given the subject the full Expressionist treatment in his huge forty-minute-long symphonic poem the following year, while Gabriel Fauré had composed incidental music (orchestrated by Charles Koechlin) as far back as 1898. For this highly symbolic story of a love triangle set in the semi-mythical Merovingian France of the sixth or seventh century AD Sibelius produced with minimal means music of remarkable evocative power and range, from the stirring prelude *At the Castle Gate* to the delicate albeit tragic poetry of *The Death of Mélisande*. The suite was taken up rapidly in Germany.

SVENSKA TEATERN.

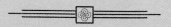

Fredagen den 17:de Mars 1905 kl. 7,30 e. m.

(Gästuppträdande af fru Gabrielle Tavaststjerna).

För första gången

Pelléas och Mélisande

Skådespel i fem akter afdelade i 13 tablåer af **Maurice Maeterlinck.** Öfversättning af **Bertel Gripenberg.** Musiken af **Jean Sibelius** under medvärkan af Filharmoniska sällskapets orkester. Dekorationerna af **P. Knudsen.**

Personerna:

Arkel, konung af Allemonde	Herr Malmström.
Geneviève, Pelléas och Golauds moder	Fru Brander.
Pelléas ⎫ Arkels söner	Herr Wingård.
Golaud ⎭	Herr Tallroth.
Mélisande	Fru Tavaststjerna.
Lille Yniold, Golauds son (i ett tidigare gifte)	Athenaïs Stavenow.
En läkare	Herr Ahlbom.
Portväktaren	Herr Lindh.

Tjänarinnor, m. fl.

Akt I { Vid slottsporten. / I skogen. / Ett gemak i slottet. / Utanför slottet (Vid hafvet).

Akt II { En källa i parken. / Ett gemak i slottet. / En sal i slottet.

Paus.

Akt III { Ett torn i slottet. / Slottets underjordiska grottor. / Ett torn i slottet.

Paus.

Akt IV { En sal i slottet. / En källa i parken.

Akt V { En sal i slottet.

Börjas kl. 7,30 och slutas omkring kl. 10,30 e. m

Hvita biljetter.

Opposite, poster for the
first night in Helsinki of
Maeterlinck's play *Pelléas
and Mélisande*, for which
Sibelius provided one of his
most popular scores

Sibelius's music had by this time spread to Great Britain, where in
general it had been received enthusiastically, especially *Finlandia* and
the two symphonies. Symphony No. 1 had been acclaimed as 'full of
character as in the best Russian music'; the composer had pulled out
of an engagement to conduct it in Liverpool in order to complete and
give the première of the *Pelléas* music in March, prompting
speculation in the English press that the Russians would not let him
out of the country. However, in November he finally arrived in Dover
to fulfil the request belatedly but he immediately ran into trouble with
Customs for carrying with him an illegal quantity of cigars and was
fined on the spot.

Sibelius stayed in Britain for just five days as a guest of Sir
Granville Bantock, one of the leading conductors and composers in
Britain before World War II. Bantock proved to be a stalwart
champion of Sibelius's music over the years – he had taken over the
performance of the First Symphony Sibelius had cancelled – and
introduced the composer to many influential contacts who would
carry his banner over the next forty years, such as Sir Henry Wood
(the first person to conduct a Sibelius score in Britain, the *King
Christian II* suite in 1901), the critic Ernest Newman (who had already
acclaimed the Second Symphony) and Rosa Newmarch, who

The eminent English
conductor and composer
Granville Bantock, who first
enticed Sibelius to Britain
in 1905, and who became
the dedicatee of the
Finn's Third Symphony two
years later

maintained a correspondence and friendship with Sibelius until her
death in 1940. He also met up with Busoni, who was giving concerts
in England. Sibelius approved of the stiff manners and social code of
the English upper echelons (about which Carpelan had briefed him
thoroughly), and ensured that he behaved and was attired impeccably
at all times. After his successful British début, again in Liverpool,
Sibelius headed off to Paris. In the French capital, however, he was an
unknown figure, the World Fair being long forgotten, and he did not
stay long.

During his absence from Finland much had happened politically.
The fall-out from the Russians' ignominious defeat by Japan had led
to increased calls for a democratically elected parliament, culminating
in a five-day general strike in late October. If there were fears that the
strike might share the fate of the abortive protest-cum-uprising in St
Petersburg which had been bloodily suppressed on 9 January, that did
not stop its spread, even to Finland, where the Finns rescinded all the
Imperial political appointments of officials since 1900. At the end of

the month, the Tsar gave way and permitted the Duma, the Russian
parliament, to be constituted. On 4 November, Tsar Nicholas
retracted many of Bobrikov's decrees in Finland and Leo Mechelin
was invited to submit a bill for the universal suffrage of Finnish men
and women over the age of twenty-four – the first modern state in
Europe to enfranchise women. This led in May 1906 to the creation of
a single-chamber Finnish parliament of 200 elected members, the
Eduskunta, reported to by an executive Senate. This was ratified by
the Tsar in July. But in the wake of these successes an ominous
factionalization occurred in Finland. An armed volunteer vigilante
force which had formed to maintain public order after the Russian
police in Finland had been disarmed had almost immediately split
into 'Red' (socialist) and 'White' (conservative) groups. Before the end
of 1906, these groups clashed in Helsinki, as a result of the mutiny by
sailors of the Russian Baltic Fleet in Viapori (or Suomenlinna;
Sveaborg in Swedish), the military fortress guarding Helsinki. A Red-
sympathizing commander of the volunteer force had armed his men
to secure the streets; the Senate duly mobilized the pro-White
'Protection Force' to oust the Reds and a pitched battle ensued in
Hakaniemi Square. Order was restored only by the arrival of the
Russian garrison.

Along with the majority of his compatriots, Sibelius deplored the
factional split and the violence. He had become increasingly aware of
the tendency to more direct action during the year through Axel
Gallén's contacts with Russian dissidents like Gorky, who found refuge
in Finland's more liberal administration. And as with all such
arguments, Sibelius kept away from the extremists and confined his
efforts to music, exemplified at this moment with the cantata *The
Captive Queen*, which marked the centenary of the nineteenth-century
economic reformer, J. V. Snellman. The obvious symbolism of the
title alone was too much for the censor, and the work had to be
performed using the first line of Paavo Cajander's text, 'There sings
the Queen', instead.

Sibelius's principal work of 1906, however, was a large-scale
orchestral tone-poem which again looked to the *Kalevala* for
inspiration. He had become very taken with the idea of a work based
on the ancient creation myth, concerning the daughter of the heavens
and mother of the waters, Luonnotar. But with what he had termed a

'symphonic fantasia' substantively complete, Sibelius changed the programmatic inspiration to that behind his abandoned opera of ten years before, *The Building of the Boat*, and amended his proposed title to *Väinämöinen*. As such he submitted it to Lienau, who thought the title would not appeal to a Central European audience unversed in Finnish mythology. Sibelius then suggested the more neutral *A Hero's Life*, but Lienau – perhaps not wanting too direct a comparison with Richard Strauss's epic symphonic poem of the same name – opted for *Pohjola's Daughter*, which title has stuck ever since. *Pohjola's Daughter* is one of Sibelius's most accomplished orchestral works, a marvel of internal construction (the late composer and musicologist Harold Truscott regarded it as a 'genuine one-movement symphony') decked out in the most brilliant orchestral garb he had yet devised. The work was received with rapture almost universally at its first performances, whether in Finland, Germany or Russia, so effectively had he captured the spirit of Finnish legend. In Sweden, the usually hostile Peterson-Berger wrote of its 'radiant and new beauty'. For no readily accountable reason, *Pohjola's Daughter* has tended to be overshadowed by earlier works, such as *En saga* and *The Swan of Tuonela*, or later ones like *The Oceanides* and *Tapiola*.

Behind the creation of *Pohjola's Daughter*, and sundry minor pieces to satisfy Lienau, such as a set of six songs to German poems (published as Op. 50) and another, smaller tone-poem, *Pan and Echo*, lay the Third Symphony. The initial ideas for the symphony had been sketched in 1904, but the work had been set aside. One reason was that Sibelius wanted to compose more overtly dramatic and illustrative works, such as the tone-poems; another may have been the subconscious awareness that this next symphony would be radically different from its predecessors and that he needed time to work the music out fully. There were plenty of distractions along the way, not least the composition of yet more incidental music to a feeble play by his friend Hjalmar Procopé, *Belshazzar's Feast*. So good was Sibelius becoming at theatre music that his Oriental-sounding numbers quite outshone the text and converted very happily into a four-movement concert suite. The Third Symphony was scheduled to be given its première in London in the spring of 1907 but this had to be cancelled as the finale was not ready. Lienau was extremely unhappy but arranged for a run-through with a provincial German orchestra in

June; this, too, was cancelled. Under increasing pressure, Sibelius turned, as usual, to the bottle, though now he began to realize that his drinking as well as financial mismanagement were out of control. In a letter to Gallén's brother-in-law, Sibelius admitted:

> *In my case something has to be done. I am now in my prime and on the threshhold of big things, but the years could easily melt away with nothing to show for them … This drinking – not that I don't enjoy it – has gone too far … There need be no real fear of 'bankruptcy' since my income is rather better now; it's rather my ability to manage money. Aino is quite at the end of her tether. I really must have it out with her … it's not just the boozer Sibb who is at stake but the composer in whose music I believe, and which can still develop into something much bigger … All this is not easy for me to admit to myself, as I am spoilt, superior and weak-willed.*

Opposite, 'On the threshold of big things': Sibelius at Ainola, c. 1906

In August, Sibelius travelled to Germany but what he did there is shrouded in mystery; a scribbled note on a postcard to Gallén aside, there are no letters – not even to Aino – to trace his movements.

The Third Symphony, dedicated to Bantock, was completed on his return and given its première in Helsinki before September was out, alongside *Pohjola's Daughter* and the suite from *Belshazzar's Feast*. The last two were received more enthusiastically by the audience than the austere, pared-down textures of the symphony, with its oddly elusive atmosphere, restrained mid-nineteenth-century orchestration and telescoped scherzo-and-finale. Flodin, though, was delighted, calling the composer 'a Classical master' and the music 'revolutionary, new and truly Sibelian'. Flodin was right – the Third Symphony was indeed a quietly radical work, where all the most extraordinary activity occurred below the surface, unlike in the Second with its grander, romantic mien. Harold Truscott believed it to be the first Sibelius symphony to evince 'complete mastery' and was 'the key to all that followed it', while others like Julian Herbage have commented on its innovative key-scheme, harmonic side-slips and the individuality of the finale. In many ways Symphony No. 3 accorded with Busoni's ideal of 'Young Classicality', a return to the musical spirit of the past and not to be confused with the mannered neo-classicism that became the rage amongst composers of the post-World War I years. As such, the Third – the first of the truly great Sibelius symphonies – has been generally misunderstood and did not succeed with audiences or the bulk of critics to anything like the degree of the First or Second. So complete was the incomprehension that greeted the work that its lack of success was at least partly attributed by many to the composer's use of Finnish folk elements, whereas in fact this was intentionally the most cosmopolitan and international score Sibelius had yet attempted to compose.

5

Sibelius with his youngest
daughters Margareta (left)
and Heidi (right)

'One could have said of Beethoven – if one
absolutely insists – that he wrote programmatic
music. For his point of departure was always a
specific idea, whereas I ...'
    The sentence broke off. Sibelius noticed that
he had trodden on dangerous ground and
changed the subject.'

Santeri Levas, *Sibelius: A Personal
Portrait,* 1972

Miraculous Logic 1907–14

The true nature of the Tsarist government's intentions towards
Finland became apparent during 1907 and 1908. The new Prime
Minister, Pyotr Stolypin (appointed the previous year), took measures
to curb the legislative authority of the Eduskunta and begin drawing
the Grand Duchy back under more direct control. Russification was
again propounded to the Pan-Slav rallying cry of 'Finis Finlandiae'. To
further these objectives, by 1910 the Russian Prime Minister had
outflanked the new assembly by replacing a majority of the Senators
with his own stooges. Just how jejune the Finnish members were in
matters governmental can be gleaned from the recollections of one of
those inaugural members, the future Prime Minister, Oskari Tokoi.
He recalled of his fellow Social Democrats, who had won eighty seats
through their championing of the rights of the population at large to
become the leading party: 'Almost all its members came from the
labouring classes; and as farmers, chiefly from tenant families. Only
one man among them was a Doctor of Philosophy, another was a
Master of Arts. Six had studied a term or two at the University; and
there were seven grammar-school teachers.' Another member – from
the Old Fennoman party – elected was the former Paymaster-General,
and future President, Juho Kusti Paasikivi, who had studied at the
Finnish grammar school in Hämeenlinna that Sibelius had attended.

   In October 1907 Gustav Mahler paid a visit to Helsinki to conduct
the Helsinki orchestra. There he renewed his acquaintance with Axel
Gallén, whom he had known in Vienna. The 47-year-old Mahler was
one of the leading international conductors of his day. At this time he
had just resigned his directorship of the Imperial court opera in
Vienna and was due to take up the post of principal conductor of the
Metropolitan Opera in New York. Mahler was also one of Europe's
most controversial composers, especially with regard to his then eight
symphonies, all enormous in dimensions, scope and resources. The
Eighth, later christened the 'Symphony of a Thousand' by his agent,
he had only completed a few months before, requiring a vast array of

Gustav Mahler, one of the leading international conductors and composers of the day, in 1907, the year he visited Finland and discussed the nature of the symphony with Sibelius

orchestral musicians, vocal soloists and choirs. Gallén took his guest to see Kajanus conduct the orchestra; included on the programme were Sibelius's *Vårsång* and, as an encore, *Valse triste*. Although Sibelius's music had received considerable exposure in Germany, very little had found its way to Austria and these were the first pieces that Mahler had heard. He was not much impressed, as he noted in a letter to his wife, Alma:

At the concert I also heard some pieces by Sibelius, the Finnish national composer who they make a great fuss about, not only here but elsewhere in the musical world. One of the pieces was just ordinary 'Kitsch', spiced with certain 'Nordic' orchestral touches like a kind of a national sauce.

They are the same everywhere, these national geniuses. You find them in Russia and Sweden – and in Italy the country is overrun by these whores and their ponces. Axel is made of altogether different stuff with his twelve schnapps before the soup, and one feels that there is something genuine and robust about him and his kind.

He modified his view of Sibelius a little when the latter paid him a visit at his hotel: 'He, too, like all Finns, seems a particularly sympathetic person.' The two composers met several times over the next few days, often taking walks together, during one of which occurred a famous exchange over the formal qualities of the symphony. Sibelius recalled:

I said that I admired its style and severity of form, and the profound logic that created an inner connection between all the motives ... Mahler's opinion was just the opposite. 'No!' he said, 'the symphony must be like the world. It must be all-embracing.'

Nowhere is their fundamental difference of approach encapsulated more dramatically than in the two symphonies that they had completed that very year: Sibelius's half-hour-long Third, a model of Classicist restraint, Mahler's Eighth a vast and unwieldy excrescence of late Romanticism three times as long, requiring eight or nine times the number of performers. Mahler never conducted any of Sibelius's music: the Violin Concerto would be scheduled in his 1911 season with the New York Philharmonic Orchestra, but ill-health prevented his directing it (he was replaced by Theodore Spiering and died in May that same year).

Mahler moved on to St Petersburg in the first week of November to fulfil an engagement there. Sibelius followed a few days later, to conduct his own Third Symphony at one of the new music concerts organized by Alexander Siloti, which functioned in a similar way to Busoni's series in Berlin. The performance went well, but the reception was lukewarm. Aino, who attended this performance and unlike her husband spoke Russian, recounted to Erik Tawaststjerna towards the end of her life how a member of the audience had delivered a stream of invective about the work at Siloti's wife without realizing who Aino was. The young Sergey Prokofiev, then a composition student of Rimsky-Korsakov (with whom Busoni had suggested Sibelius study many years before), was also in the audience and was much taken with the symphony. His teacher was not: 'God in Heaven! Sibelius! Why listen to Sibelius?' Critical reaction was little better, one commentator asking 'Is it really possible that he has already written himself out?' The only favourable notice he received was due as much to antipathy to Mahler (an Austrian Jew), very probably anti-Semite in origin. Sibelius presented the Third again in Moscow in December, along with a mixed bag of other pieces hastily assembled because the soloist engaged to perform the Violin Concerto could not cope. These included *Pohjola's Daughter*, which made a strong impression with critics and audience alike.

Whilst in the Russian capital, Sibelius suffered from a severe sore throat. This had occurred before, and the composer had a set treatment for it, but the ailment persisted into February, when a bout of influenza (still very much in these years a killer) led him to cancel several conducting engagements abroad. He occupied his time by writing incidental music to August Strindberg's play *Swanwhite*, an allegorical fairy-story of good versus evil, with a sleeping prince awoken by the princess's kiss, and a wicked stepmother transmuted into good. Sibelius responded enthusiastically to the play's magical atmosphere and in April turned down a request from Lienau to travel to Berlin to conduct the Third Symphony, although six weeks earlier he had interrupted composition to go on a short trip to London to direct the very same piece, incidentally renewing acquaintance with Rosa Newmarch, Bantock and Henry Wood. The reasons for Sibelius's refusal to his publisher are complex: his throat was still worrying him – and the London smog did it no good whatsoever – and he was preoccupied with *Swanwhite*. There was also his chafing under the terms of Lienau's contract. Sibelius wanted to reduce the number of works required per year from four to two – in order to prevent submitting 'hasty and shabby work' he told Aino – but for the same price, which Lienau just would not agree to.

The score for *Swanwhite* originated in the enthusiasm of the actress Harriet Bosse, a long-time lover of the playwright's, for Sibelius's music. Sibelius in turn had been a lifelong devotee of Strindberg and harboured a wish for a protracted collaboration much along the lines that Adolf Paul, himself a disciple of the writer and a future biographer, had wanted with Sibelius. In this he was to be disappointed; Strindberg remained polite but never heard Sibelius's music and his relationship with Harriet Bosse finished at around the time of the première. Of the fourteen evocative items for the stage production, the composer extracted seven to form a delightful concert suite, the popularity of which has been unfairly eclipsed by *Pelléas and Mélisande.*

Through April into May Sibelius's sore throat worsened, his voice rendered increasingly hoarse. Finally seeking medical attention in Helsinki, on 12 May a biopsy was performed on what was thought to be an 'incipient tumour'. From this, the doctors diagnosed that the tumour was not malignant but recommended Sibelius consult as soon as possible a specialist in Berlin, one Dr Fränkel. Sibelius simply could not afford to go; he was a year behind in his contractual deliveries to Lienau, and had already borrowed heavily against the security of his annual state pension (still 3,000 Finnish marks per annum and worth somewhat less after ten years than when first given). Even Carpelan could not help at such short notice; news of the composer's illness had spread widely and it was rumoured he was dying – accordingly several sponsors literally gave him up for dead and refused appeals for funds. Towards the end of the month Sibelius and Aino spent a dispiriting day visiting the banks and financial houses of Helsinki to try and raise the money; only the very last, an insurance company, yielded success: the director promptly donated to the composer the entire day's takings!

Sibelius visited Dr Fränkel at the end of May (Christian took the precaution of consulting a second specialist, Rosenbach). The doctor declared from the specimen Sibelius brought from Helsinki that it was not cancer, though it might later develop that way, and immediately forbade the composer to drink any alcohol or smoke cigars what-soever. During the month of June, Fränkel attempted thirteen times to remove the growth, eventually succeeding with the assistance of a younger colleague. Sibelius returned home barely able to speak and fearing a relapse at any time. Sibelius stuck to Fränkel's regimen of abstention for seven years, until his dread had abated sufficiently. That dread overcame the symptoms of nicotine and alcohol withdrawal, and his letters and the diary that he started keeping in 1909 record how desperately he missed them at times, especially on social occasions. Almost the first musical expression of his state of mind can be heard in the fevered atmosphere of the song *Teodora* (Op. 35, No. 2). Set against the other-worldly air of *Swanwhite*, the song's ambiguity of key is electric by comparison. *Teodora* signalled the start of a period of experiment that would take the composer to the very boundaries of tonality and place him briefly at the forefront of the pre-World War I international avant garde. It was not a role that Sibelius sought, or was well suited for temperamentally. Nor, in the end, did he create anything that he would not otherwise have done in the fullness of time, but the severity of his illness – the 'frightening warning from above' as he later referred to it – accelerated his musical evolution. The change had begun already and found first expression in the leaner textures and compound forms of the Third Symphony.

A less welcome legacy of Sibelius's illness was his increasingly parlous financial situation. Although his treatment had been successful, neither Sibelius nor his doctors knew whether or not the tumour would recur, or turn into a cancer. The uncertainty over his health was hardly conducive to fund-raising and the composer had to find other means of support. His debts had gradually been mounting for some years, especially following the establishment of Ainola and the retinue of several staff the Sibeliuses maintained. Aino tried to keep costs down as much as possible by acting as her daughters' teacher – and was able to educate three sufficiently well for them to enter university – as well as running a small kitchen garden. The birth on 10 September of his fifth daughter, Jeanne Margareta, hardly helped matters. Sibelius tried to make up part of his backlog in deliveries to Lienau – and drum up some quick cash – by offering the publisher earlier, unpublished works, *The Origin of Fire*, *Malinconia* and the Romance in C. Lienau were not interested. Sibelius began to take private composition pupils, such as Toivo Kuula, a former pupil of Armas Järnefelt, and Leevi Madetoja. Kuula's musical idiom was more folk-oriented than that of Sibelius and he only had a handful of lessons, but the older man thought highly enough of him to help secure Kuula a scholarship with Enrico Bossi in Bologna and

The sauna block at Ainola,
built after and separated
from the main house

recommend his near-hour-long Piano Trio to Siloti (who had it performed in St Petersburg). Madetoja studied with Sibelius over a period of two years; 'I am a poor teacher,' the composer told his pupil and Madetoja recalled later the lessons were 'not teaching in the normal sense', consisting of 'short, searching comments', such as 'No dead, unnecessary notes – everything must live.'

For the remainder of 1908 Sibelius worked on the orchestral tone-poem *Night Ride and Sunrise*. At different times he suggested that this work originated on first seeing the Colosseum in Rome (during his two-week desertion of Aino in 1901), or on seeing a marvellous sunrise during a trip by horse-drawn sleigh to Kervo. The basic premise of this piece, implicit in its title, is the fusion of two rather different types of music and motion into an indivisible whole. There is a clear transition midway through marking the beginning of the dawn. Here the initial galloping rhythms subside, and after it the music builds towards its blazing sunlit apotheosis. So artful is the composer's execution of his design that this episode becomes the fulcrum upon which the whole composition turns. How intentional this was is open to debate: in response to some penetrating observations that he had made about the piece, Sibelius wrote to Carpelan:

> *You mention interconnections between themes and other such matters, all of which are quite subconscious on my part. Only afterwards can one discern this or that relationship but for the most part one is merely the vessel. That miraculous logic (let us call it God) which governs a work of art, that is the important thing.*

Another feature taken over from the Third Symphony is the music's unwillingness to indulge in the obvious displays of orchestral brilliance that had made *Pohjola's Daughter* such a hit. This did mitigate against the new work's popularity, as in the first performance (of a badly cut version by Siloti) in St Petersburg but its cumulative power generally made a marked impression on critics and audiences alike.

Following the completion of *Night Ride and Sunrise*, Sibelius embarked on a string quartet. This was his first piece of chamber music for seventeen years since the Quartet for piano, two violins and cello written while a student in Vienna, although this seems barely credible given the fluency of the writing. Sibelius called his new

quartet, actually the fourth he had composed, *Voces intimae* –
'Intimate Voices' – and this title neatly describes the work's character.
There is in this work a far greater sense of self-communion than in
the more public symphonies and tone-poems, or even the earlier
quartets which followed a broadly sonata-based design, and formally
Voces intimae is a very different proposition. Its expressive weight falls
unusually on the large slow central movement (rather than on the
opening or closing spans as convention dictated), an intense Adagio
which has drawn comparison with the slow movements of
Beethoven's late quartets. Sibelius's is framed by two pairs of shorter,
quicker dance-like movements, the first of each being moderately
paced and succeeded by one that is much fleeter. Nominally in five
movements, *Voces intimae* functions as if in three, an impression
reinforced by the dovetailing of the opening two movements,
intentionally not attempted with the same degree of subtlety as in the
tone-poem or symphony that preceded it. The work was completed
in April 1909 and quickly despatched to Lienau. The composer set
great store by the work – 'Believe me,' he wrote later that year, 'with
the quartet I have left the training ship and gained my master's
certificate.' It was launched in Berlin in January 1910 by the Czech
Cecil Quartet; initial reviews were mixed, the most favourable
drawing comparisons with Beethoven and praise for the technical
skill of the writing; others, such as Otto Taubman, were less
convinced. The Ševčík Quartet in Germany from 1911 did much to
establish the work in the quartet repertoire.

Much of *Voces intimae* was composed during a foreign trip of some
three months Sibelius undertook between February and May 1909. He
rationalized the need for such trips in a letter to his wife: 'Have been
cut off for too long and came away from Finland in the nick of time.
It is absolutely vital for me to be abroad now. My artistic development
necessitates it.' It started with his third trip to Britain where he
conducted *En saga* and *Finlandia* with great success. Many notable
figures in the English musical establishment encountered Sibelius
again at an ill-conceived soirée in London of the Music Club. The
Club regularly focused on the chamber and instrumental output of
leading international composers (Debussy was the subject a couple
of weeks later). As the main thrust of his mature career had been
orchestral, the reliance on Sibelius's songs proved embarrassing. The

Sibelius at work in his study
at Ainola; a roundel of his
parents hangs on the wall

8

composer Arnold Bax was in the audience and years later opined in
his autobiography:

> *The promoters of the concert ... may be charged with carelessly taking a*
> *chance with a growing reputation in that they did not first find out*
> *whether there was any chamber music ... worth listening to. I believe that*
> *this lamentable affair was a serious setback to the acceptance in England*
> *of Sibelius's best work, and delayed the recognition of the grandeur of the*
> *later symphonies for several years.*

That Sibelius had a nearly finished chamber masterpiece in his
room was a strange if ironic mischance. Bax also noted for posterity
his Finnish colleague's appearance, how he 'gave one the notion that
he had never laughed in his life, and never could. That strong, taut
frame, those cold, steel-blue eyes and hard-lipped mouth, were those
of a Viking raider, insensible to scruple, tenderness or humour of any
sort.' Even Bax, who dedicated his Fifth Symphony (1933) to Sibelius,
wondered whether the latter's grim demeanour was the result of the
soirée; Debussy remarked that he would rather write a symphony than
repeat his experience!

The effect of the London air on his throat alarmed Sibelius and his
voice became hoarse, so following a brief stopover in Paris, he
anxiously consulted Dr Fränkel again in Berlin. Fränkel put his mind
at rest: 'Everything is in good order.' Relieved, he stayed on in the
German capital where he hoped to settle matters with Lienau. With
Night Ride and Sunrise, Voces intimae and other pieces previously sent,
Sibelius believed his contractual obligations had been fulfilled, a
notion Lienau quickly disabused him of. Actually there were two
outstanding works, but the publishers were pragmatic enough to settle
for just one – a set of six songs on Swedish poems by Ernst Josephson
which Sibelius composed then and there. Composer and publisher
parted company amicably enough, but neither side wanted to renew
an arrangement both realized had proved unworkable. Nonetheless,
Lienau left the door open to future, if *ad hoc*, collaborations, and in
June received a group of Ten Pieces for piano (Op. 58). However, the
composer's asking price of 5,000 Finnish marks was far too high. In
August, Breitkopf und Härtel, keen to enter into a contract with the
composer, took the Ten Pieces for just 3,000 marks.

Sibelius returned home at the end of May to a financial crisis. Aino had fought an increasingly desperate rearguard action with their creditors in his absence, making herself ill through nervous exhaustion. He had totalled up a large number of his debts whilst still in London and these came to well over 50,000 Finnish marks, approximately five years' average income. The sales from his German publishers helped in the short term but over the rest of the year his debts still increased. The composition of several smaller items, such as some rather characterless incidental music to Mikael Lybeck's play *The Lizard* (Ödlan), two songs ('Come Away, Death' and 'When that I was a little tiny boy') for a Swedish production of Shakespeare's *Twelfth Night*, and the tone-poem *In memoriam*, brought in a little, much-needed money. The last-named, a short and powerful funeral march with rather Mahlerian resonances, alone earned the composer the sum of 3,000 marks. But by December, matters had come to a head and he put out a desperate appeal to Carpelan who came to Ainola to work out Sibelius's exact position. To the horror of all concerned, the final total debt was closer to 100,000 marks, and Sibelius's expenses exceeded his income annually by 6,000 marks, which was twice the amount of his state pension. By the time Christmas arrived, help was at hand after Carpelan had successfully petitioned the wealthy Dahlström family in Turku for funds to alleviate (but by no means clear) his debts. Such was the measure of security this afforded the composer that Sibelius immediately declared to Carpelan that he would devote himself to the composition of a fourth symphony – which was all the thanks that his correspondent had hoped for.

Sibelius's first thoughts for his Fourth Symphony found expression in two tone-pictures, 'The Mountain' and 'Thoughts of a Wayfarer', and it seems fairly clear that the initial impetus for the work arose from a trip he had made with Eero Järnefelt the previous September to Koli, a remote spot in northern Karelia. Indeed, Sibelius eventually inscribed the score of the completed symphony to his brother-in-law and neighbour. The composition took him until March 1911, longer than any of his symphonies except the much-interrupted Third.

The trip to Koli may explain the almost graphic physical imagery of the Fourth Symphony's final form, which depicts an at times desolate landscape, half real, half of the mind, in the icy grip of

Opposite, Sibelius in the
grounds of Ainola, 1912

winter. The starkness of his vision was emphasized by the use in every
fabric of the work of the tritone, the most dissonant interval in
western music. This interval is described right at the outset in the
shape of the first three notes, C–D–F sharp, and in the final
movement underpins the grinding clash of tonalities (A major and E
flat) at the main climax. As befits a world blanketed by snow, the
orchestral textures are bleached of colour in a symphony that sounds
like the equivalent of an enormous line-drawing compared to the
richer oil canvases of the First and Second. In this respect the Fourth
is a synthesis of the nature-painting in *Night Ride and Sunrise* with the
imaginary world of the slow movement of *Voces intimae*, but the
music's picturesque qualities are only a means to an end. Central to
the conception is the power of suggestion; compared to the Fourth
Symphony, the much busier Third, which is only around five minutes
shorter in performance, feels like a much smaller work. The final –
literally so – unique aspect of the Fourth is its close. The conventional
ending inherited from Beethoven was loud and affirmatory; Bruckner,
Tchaikovsky and Mahler had departed in isolated cases to conclude
softly. In Symphony No. 4, Sibelius brought the work to a stop
midway between, *mezzo-forte*, neither loud nor quiet, in a state of
near-exhaustion.

The Fourth pushed the symphony as a genre, and the use within it
of tonality, to the most extreme point possible – one critic called the
work 'the most modern of the modern' – though without bursting
over into the atonality, the total absence of key, that was the basis of
the music of Arnold Schoenberg. The music's glacial tone
dumbfounded the first audiences in Finland and Scandinavia. One

The Swedish composer
Wilhelm Stenhammar at the
piano. As chief conductor of
the Gothenburg orchestra,
he steadfastly championed
Sibelius's music in Sweden.

early performance in Gothenburg, conducted by the composer
Wilhelm Stenhammar, was hissed by an ultra-conservative audience
(although a repeat performance was received better shortly afterwards). When Paul Weingartner tried to perform the symphony with
the Vienna Philharmonic in 1912, the musicians simply refused to play
it – and it has still not been performed there. Many questions were
asked as to why he had chosen to write that sort of music at that time.
Naturally, his recent illness was advanced as one possible cause, if only
that he had lost his grip – after the première 'people avoided our eyes,
shook their heads; their smiles were embarassed, ironic or furtive', as
Aino recalled much later. Others wondered if it arose from 'the
unconscious result of a concern over his country's difficulties with
Russia' or the increasingly bitter antagonism between Finns and their
Swedish countrymen. It may be that elements of such external events,
or his brush with death, are reflected in the music, particularly in the
bleak third movement. But the finale is lighter in tone, suggestive of
the thaw when the ice cracks. The uncertainty of the final bars is quite
deliberate, with an expressive rather than formally experimental
purpose. The composer himself disavowed any programme, and even
took the unusual step of writing to the Swedish-language newspaper
Hufvudstadsbladet to protest at a symbolic explanation they had
printed of his score.

As with its predecessor, Sibelius's progress with the Fourth was
subject to many distractions. Early in 1910 he had written a short
tone-poem *The Dryad*, and in March had completely overhauled *In
memoriam* after receiving proofs of the score from Breitkopf, who reset
the piece without demur. The spring had seen the first performances
(at least in Finland) of the music to *The Lizard*, the newly revised
Impromptu for female chorus and orchestra (Op. 19) originally
penned in 1902, and *Voces intimae*. In May, Rosa Newmarch visited
Finland and Sibelius dutifully took her to see the Imatra Falls in
Karelia (still one of the area's leading attractions). She later visited
Ainola and noted how the composer seemed in real danger of
neglecting wife – Aino's health was still not good – and family. His
need for solitude to work imposed a severe regime; the children often
had to creep about the house when 'Papa was working', and any
musical education would take place at the house of either Eero
Järnefelt or Pekka Halonen nearby. But with five children in a not

very large wooden house, peace was impossible to attain consistently, and several times Sibelius escaped, whether to Helsinki or the coastal resort of Järvo, to work undisturbed, rigorously maintaining his ban on alcohol and cigars. October found him first in Oslo giving the premières of both *The Dryad* and *In memoriam*, then in Berlin. There he met the workaholic composer Max Reger and laid the symphony aside to revise the cantata *The Origin of Fire* for publication. In November, he was so engrossed in the symphony that he ignored the visits to Helsinki of Alexander Glazunov and Gabriel Fauré, who directed performances of their own works. Aino's hospitalization for suspected rheumatoid arthritis was something he could not ignore (she was carrying their sixth and last child), but the domestic staff he employed, such as the nanny Aino Kari, carried most of the actual burden.

The new year brought little respite, with Sibelius wrestling ultimately in vain with a commission from the soprano Aino Ackté for an orchestral song, *The Raven*, intended for a much publicized tour of Germany early that year (1911; the musical material was taken into the symphony), as well as for two new pieces for a production of Arvid Järnefelt's *Kuolema* and a wedding march for the Viennese première of Adolf Paul's *The Language of the Birds*. After the symphony's première, Sibelius made some minor alterations to the score and sent it to Breitkopf on 20 May. For a while, he remained creatively exhausted, unsure of how to proceed from the position the symphony had reached. Domestic matters took much of his attention in spring and summer. Heidi was born in June, and shortly after came the visit of his sister Linda for a few weeks, on holiday from the mental home she had been being treated in for the past five years. Her presence had a depressive effect on the post-natal Aino, who went to stay with the family of Arvi Paloheimo, her eldest daughter Eva's fiancé, close by for a rest. In the early autumn Sibelius managed to scrape enough money together to have an extension built to the house so that he could have a work-room in the upper storey. Still kicking his heels artistically, he updated the worklist he had provided for Breitkopf in 1909 and took the opportunity to excise references to certain early pieces, such as most of the chamber works and the opera *The Maiden in the Tower*. He also looked out the three tone-poems of *Scènes historiques* and revised them, amending their catalogue listing to Op. 25, instead of

the original Op. 26, moving *Malinconia* from Op. 25 to Op. 20.
(*Finlandia*, at one time merely the seventh sub-item of Op. 26, was
now assigned the entire number for itself.)

One gem from this fallow period, which stretched long into early
the following year, was the rewritten version, for strings and
percussion only, of the 1894 choral suite *Rakastava* ('The Lover'). In its
instrumental guise it has proved to be a work of enduring appeal, yet
in the pre-World War I heyday of the massive orchestra, works for
string ensembles were thought to be risky commercially and Breitkopf
declined to publish it, as did Lienau. A Finnish company eventually
accepted it, though their scores were pressed by Breitkopf, which
caused awkwardness on both sides. On a larger scale, Sibelius's
inspection of past follies and successes led him to compose a second
set of *Scènes historiques*, which have no thematic links with the music
written for the Press Pension Fund in 1899. In the new triptych, *The
Hunt, Love Song* and *At the Drawbridge*, Sibelius successfully
recaptured his earlier romantic manner, although not its freshness and
in places the music sounds close to pastiche. Sibelius had quite
consciously evolved a different approach in his symphonies to his
tone-poems and incidental music from the days of Symphony No. 1
and *King Christian II*, but the disparity in styles between *Scènes
historiques* and the Fourth Symphony is alarmingly wide. This gap
would never close, giving Sibelius's overall output from this time on
an almost schizophrenic quality, as if two composers – one an
intellectual abstract thinker in pure sound, composing from inner
compulsion, the other a notesmith with few pretensions of gravity –
were inhabiting the same creative persona.

If posterity has tended to value the creations of the 'abstract
thinker' side of Sibelius rather more highly than the 'notesmith', the
latter aspect formed as vital a part of his make-up. It was the
'notesmith' side that was able to keep on producing saleable pieces
when the 'thinker', at the mercy of the caprices of inspiration, stayed
silent. And the more pragmatic side of the composer did from time to
time achieve works of substance, as with the Three Sonatinas for
piano (Op. 67). These were composed in the summer of 1912 and
collectively are the most consistently successful of his keyboard pieces,
more restrained than the uneven Ten Pieces (Op. 58) although
restricted in formal design. Two Serenades for violin and orchestra

followed during the autumn and winter, exquisite miniatures which recaptured effectively some of the atmosphere of the Violin Concerto. The oddest commission he received was for a peal of bells at the newly built church at Kallio (for which he also composed a short motet for the consecration ceremony).

Sibelius managed a short trip to Berlin and Paris at the end of 1911. In the French capital, where he was joined for a week by Rosa Newmarch, he was mightily impressed by a production of Richard Strauss's opera *Salome* (based on Oscar Wilde's drama). Back in Finland for his forty-sixth birthday, his reacquaintance with his financial plight and his dependence on charity to avoid insolvency thoroughly depressed him.

My domestic harmony and peace are at an end because I cannot earn sufficient income to supply all that is needed. A constant battle with tears and misery at home. A hell! I feel completely unworthy in my own home … Poor Aino! It can hardly be easy to manage the house on so little. It makes me more than aware of the truth in the old saying: do not marry if you cannot provide for your wife in the style to which she was accustomed before. The same food, clothes, servants – in a word the same income.

Yet 'the same food, clothes, servants' were not requirements that his wife demanded. Her espousal of Tolstoyan simplicity, which aimed at social levelling between the classes – with nobles even waiting on their domestic staff – and which was fashionable amongst aristocratic circles at this time, did not require so grand a lifestyle. In truth, it was the composer himself who desired it. An opportunity for betterment presented itself early in 1912 when he was invited to take over Robert Fuchs's chair of composition in Vienna. Despite knowing in his heart of hearts that he was not suited to academic life he was sorely tempted and only turned it down on 1 March. Sibelius had not been the first choice – Strauss and Reger both declined the post – and the appointment fell shortly afterwards to the Austrian Franz Schreker, who went on to become one of Europe's most influential pedagogues.

In September 1912 Sibelius arrived in Britain for his fourth visit, to conduct the first performance there of the Fourth Symphony. The work puzzled most of the audience, but their reactions were much more open-minded and positive than elsewhere. 'No ordinary music' was the reaction of the composer Frederick Delius; the critic from *The Times* thought the orchestral effects achieved 'astonishing', especially given the relatively small number of performers. In his next orchestral work, the tone-poem *The Bard*, completed in early 1913, Sibelius revisited for the last time elements of the sound-world of the Fourth Symphony. Again the resources of the orchestra were deployed with extreme restraint; almost the only colouristic effect coming through the use of the harp (as surrogate for a bardic lyre), and the heavy brass used for a single chord only. Breitkopf at first rejected *The Bard* as being the first movement of something larger. Sibelius considered including it as part of a three-movement suite but in 1914 revised the piece as a concentrated single span, in which form it was published.

On his return to Finland from Britain, Sibelius had at last begun to give consideration to large-scale projects. His diary records his wish 'for no more than to be able, untroubled by material anxieties, to devote myself completely to bigger works', though he felt this to be 'impossible', perhaps because these projects all centred on the theatre. The Danish publishers Wilhelm Hansen asked him to provide music for a proposed pantomime on the subject of *Scaramouche*. Believing that only a few numbers would be required, he accepted without troubling to give the matter much thought, partly because he was becoming preoccupied by ideas for an opera. Various subjects were suggested, the driving force behind which being Aino Ackté; she and Juhani Aho consulted with the composer about a work derived from Aho's recently published novel *Juha*. The realism of this proved unconducive to Sibelius, but not to Aarre Merikanto and Leevi Madetoja, who both created powerful operas which are now corner-stones of the modern Finnish repertoire. For much of 1913 he toyed with a libretto taken from Adolf Paul's play *Blauer Dunst* ('Blue Smoke') but despite much initial enthusiasm he does not seem to have been serious about its composition.

Two important events occurred in Sibelius's life in June 1913: on the tenth of the month, his and Aino's twenty-first wedding anniversary, their eldest daughter, Eva, married Arvi Paloheimo; and he set down to work, under considerable duress, on the music for the ballet-pantomime *Scaramouche* for Hansen. Months after signing the contract for the commission, he realized that far from just a few items, as he had provided for many stage-plays, what was actually required

was an hour's worth of through-composed music. Sibelius begged to
be released to no avail. He struggled with the score on and off for
seven months, finally completing it on 19 December. The rather
tawdry tale of jealousy, attempted abduction and murder centred on
the hunchback Scaramouche, Leilon and his wife Blondelaine drew
from Sibelius music of an at times ethereal, other-worldly character.
Hansen had hoped for a new *Valse triste* writ large; as far as popular
appeal was concerned he was to be disappointed, yet in a sense that is
precisely what Sibelius provided – music deliberately conceived for the
theatre, an integral not incidental element of the drama. Yet despite
this, *Scaramouche* was not staged until 1922. Sibelius remained
ambivalent about the piece, but was proud of the instrumental setting
he had created. When in later years the conductor Jussi Jalas, who
became his son-in-law, produced a concert reduction, he took great
pains at the composer's request to preserve the essence of the original
orchestration. Yet much of the larger work's substance and subtlety
was still lost.

Sibelius still harboured the desire to write a work for Aino Ackté,
not least after twice disappointing her over *The Raven* and *Juha*. He
had also wanted to compose a tone-poem on the *Kalevala* creation
myth, centred on the daughter of the air, Luonnotar (and in 1905
Pohjola's Daughter had originated in this way), and decided to
combine this with a commission from the Three Choirs Festival in
Britain for a choral work. In July 1913, alongside the early stages of
Scaramouche, he set to work and completed the score, for solo soprano
and orchestra with no choral parts, in late August. Ackté went over
the piece, a unique fusion of orchestral song and symphonic poem,
with the composer at Ainola before travelling to Gloucester to give the
première on 10 September. Although well received, Sibelius made
some minor adjustments to the score and sent it off to Breitkopf in
October. They were nervous about publishing what they viewed as a
song of such large (at nine minutes' duration) dimensions, and it only
appeared in a voice-and-piano edition; the orchestral score was not
published until 1981.

Luonnotar is music at the highest level of inspiration, fully worthy
of comparison with *Pohjola's Daughter* and *Night Ride and Sunrise*,
though as different from them as these two pieces are from each other.
For his next orchestral work, *The Oceanides*, Sibelius stayed with the

AINO ACKTÉ

═══ *KONSERTTI* ═══

Yliopiston juhlasalissa tiistaina huhtik. 21 p. klo 8 i.p.

AVUSTAJAT:

Kapellimestari G. Schnéevoigt
Helsingin Sinfoniaorkesteri
Rouva B. Funtek

Ohjelma

1. **ALKUSOITTO OOPP. ›NOITA-AMPUJA›** .... Weber
   Orkesteri,
   joht. kapellim. G. Schnéevoigt.

2. a. **AARIA oopp. ›ELINAN SURMA›** .... Merikanto
   (Orkesterisäestys.)

   b. **FRÅN ANDRA SIDAN STYX** Melartin
   (Orkesterisäestys.) Orkesterille
   sovittanut L. Funtek.

3. **LUONNOTAR** .... Sibelius
   (Orkesterisäestys.)

4. a. **KLEIN GRETLEIN, laulu VII** v. Fieliz

   b. **IN DER NACHT** .... Faltis

   c. **FRÜHLINGSFLUTEN** ...... Rachmaninow
   • • • •

5. **SALOMEN AARIA oopp. HERO-DIADE** .... Massenet
   (Orkesterisäestys.)

6. **CLAIR DE LUNE** .... d'Indy
   (Orkesterisäestys.)

7. a. **JAG SER EN STJÄRNA FALLA** v. Schantz

   b. **PAA DEN ANDEN STRAENG,**

tone-poem. He had been asked in 1913 by the composer and pedagogue Horatio Parker (who taught at Yale University; one of his students in the 1890s had been Charles Ives) to set three songs for voices with or without piano for an American Schools compendium. Sibelius complied by the end of June and in August, as *Luonnotar* was almost complete, Parker wrote informing of a $1,000 commission for a short orchestral work to last not more than fifteen minutes. The request had been made by Carl Stoeckel and his wife Ellen, who ran a music festival in Connecticut. Other work and the severe illness of his brother, who recuperated for a time at Ainola, kept Sibelius from making much headway for the rest of the year. With Christian on the mend, *Scaramouche* out of the way, and the revised *The Bard* given its première in Helsinki, in January 1914 Sibelius slipped away to Berlin to concentrate on the score undisturbed. He took in much of the new music being played there, but was distinctly unimpressed. 'The latest fad here,' he commented, 'is "Back to Mozart". Those who know least about Mozart shout the loudest.' He noted how several composers, such as Paul Juon, Julius Weismann and Heinrich Zöllner, showed traces of his influence – indeed he felt Weismann's Piano Concerto plagiarized him. There were compensations in the form of works by Korngold, Mahler and Schoenberg which 'made a deep impression', as well as some Debussy piano music and a recital by Busoni. Having recharged his creative batteries, he hurried back to Finland to write *The Oceanides*. In fact, he composed it twice, first as a three-movement suite, a copy of which was sent to Stoeckel and survives in part in Yale University Library, the second in its familiar single-span form. *The Oceanides* is an extraordinary score, the subtlest, most magnificent evocation of the sea ever penned. It builds inexorably like the deep-sea swell to culminate in a huge climax like a breaker on some unknown shore. After sailing across the Atlantic Ocean, Sibelius, in the light of his experience, made some modifications to the music prior to the première.

The Oceanides, for all that it reflects the variability in mood of the sea, is music suffused by light. This quality of luminosity is a logical continuation from *Night Ride and Sunrise*, the Fourth Symphony and *Luonnotar*. (In a letter to Carpelan, Sibelius averred that *The Oceanides* was 'in the same style' as the symphony.) The score radiates a tremendous harmony with the natural world, although it was written at a time of deepening strain in his marriage. The strain of the past twenty-one years, with their disappointments, frustrations and tragedies, and through them all the near-limitless self-obsession of her husband, had taken its toll on Aino. Sibelius's annual trips abroad, made despite the constant state of penury with which she had to deal from day to day, were another source of discord. The invitation for him to conduct the première of *The Oceanides* (and *Pohjola's Daughter* as well) in the USA – to where they could not afford her to go – was the last straw. Rows ensued with the slightest domestic problems as flashpoints, so it was probably with a mixture of relief as well as anticipation that he boarded the steamship *Kaiser Wilhelm II* on 19 May to make the ocean crossing.

Sibelius enjoyed his visit to the USA, and it would not be unfair to say that the USA, or that small part of it that encountered him, enjoyed Sibelius. He was received by the press as a celebrity: the Fourth Symphony, called 'cubist' by one critic the previous year, had been more warmly received and he was awarded an Honorary Doctorate by Yale. Stoeckel wined and dined him to the degree of

Above, Sigurd Wettenhovi-Aspa's portrait in oils (painted in 1921 from a photograph) of Sibelius in his Yale doctoral robes; *right,* the Doctorate of Music awarded to Sibelius by Yale University in 1914

luxury that he had always felt was truly right for him, though he effected less enthusiasm in his letters home to Aino. He was the guest of honour at numerous functions, meeting a host of American composers and other worthies – the most eminent being former President Taft. He saw the skyscrapers in New York and was dumbstruck by the falls of Niagara. The icing on the cake was the orchestra Stoeckel had assembled whose technical ability dazzled him. The première on 4 June was a huge success, and while it did not occur at a major musical venue – such as Carnegie Hall – many influential critics from New York, Boston and Philadelphia were present. Sibelius returned home in late June on the liner *President Grant* to a hero's reception. There were plans for him to return to North America the following year for a concert tour, and Sibelius believed that he might then be able to wipe out his debts at one fell swoop. But while he was at sea something happened in the Bosnian capital, Sarajevo, which dashed all his hopes and plans: Archduke Ferdinand, heir to the throne of the Austrian Empire, and his wife Sophie, were assassinated by Gavrilo Princip. Five weeks later, World War I began.

6

Finland crucified by foreign
oppression, revolt and civil
war as portrayed in Tyko
Sallinen's *The Fanatics* (1918)

*My symphonies were a terrible struggle. But
now they are as they must be.*

Jean Sibelius to Santeri Levas

The Forging of Thor's Hammer 1914-19

The outbreak of war accelerated the polarization of Finnish life into factions looking to Russia or Germany for leadership. On the whole, the officer and upper classes, the industrialists and commercial groups sided loyally with the Tsarist government; those amongst the working classes who were politically active followed increasingly the line of the Russian revolutionary groups, especially the Communists. Those of lower military rank inclined towards Germany, especially after December 1914 when that country undertook the clandestine training of Finnish volunteers (Sweden having withdrawn from so doing). The volunteers, some two thousand of them, were enlisted into a special Light Infantry, or *Jäger*, Division of the Imperial Prussian Army. Sibelius, who knew one of the initiators of this secret programme, Dr V. O. Sivén, would in 1917 write a marching song for the *Jäger* as it prepared to take an active part in securing Finnish independence.

In August 1914 the prospect of a free Finland seemed as remote as ever: many feared that Russification, which had already arrived at the teaching of Russian in schools, would intensify still further. After the campaigns of passive resistance in the previous decade, the government in St Petersburg were in no mood to set any store by the loyalty of the Tsar's Finnish subjects, and were fearful of a German attack on the capital being launched through the Grand Duchy. The Tsarists moved quickly to insulate Finland from any direct involvement in the fighting. One of the first casualties was the Eduskunta, which was indefinitely suspended with many of its members summarily imprisoned across the border in Russia. The most dissident figures – such as the Speaker and future President, Pehr Svinhufvud – found themselves exiled in Siberia. Russian garrisons were increased both to repel any invasion and keep control internally. While there was at this stage no question of Finns rising in revolt, the situation was undeniably tense, the dissident elements – particularly the *Jäger* – being encouraged by the news of the annihilation in the first full month of war of the Russian Second Army under Samsonov at Tannenberg. Rather more damaging to the wellbeing of the populace at large was the economic disruption; if some of the small metallurgical industries saw a modest boom, Finland as a whole was more dependent for her wealth on timber, and her best markets – Britain and western Europe – were suddenly cut off. By the end of 1915, half of the timber workers, around 17,000, had been laid off, with thirty per cent redundancies. The needs of the Russian market, however, staved off total collapse until the revolutions in 1917 threw both economies into chaos.

World War I was an unmitigated disaster for Sibelius, although it took some time for its full scale to make itself apparent, as he later told his biographer, Karl Ekman:

The outbreak of the war was a complete surprise to me. I had never seriously imagined that the largest nations in Europe would start a war with each other ... I had the conviction that the Franco–Prussian War [1870–1] was the last armed conflict between civilized nations in Europe.

It was generally thought at first, as I did, that the war would not last more than three months. It was therefore impossible at first to take it as tragically as the situation demanded – it would have been another matter if one could have imagined in advance what years of indescribable misery it was to cause.

Quite apart from the horror at the endless slaughter month on month, year by year, his own circumstances were changed irrevocably by the conflict. Finland, as a Russian province, was aligned against Germany, where the vast majority of Sibelius's mature compositions had been published and from where his royalties derived. Breitkopf continued to champion his music – *The Oceanides* and some instrumental miniatures were issued by them in 1915, some songs the next year – but pieces by an enemy national were not in great demand, particularly as his reputation in Germany was that of a nationalist. In Russia, where Finns were viewed with some suspicion as being less than loyal subjects of the Tsar, the fact that Sibelius's works had been printed by enemy publishing houses put them out-of-bounds. Similar sentiments obtained to a degree in Russia's ally, Britain, although Breitkopf's London office, run by neutral Swiss nationals, was able to keep more popular items such as the *Valse triste*

The German conductor Karl Muck, one of the earliest advocates of Sibelius's music in the United States. He was interred during World War I for not starting his concerts with the USA National Anthem.

and *Finlandia* in circulation. Even in the USA, anti-German sentiment eventually injured his cause when the eminent conductor Karl Muck, perhaps the most sympathetic of Sibelius's interpreters in North America, was interred in Georgia in 1917.

Cut off from the largest part of his income, his financial plight rapidly became extremely precarious. His expenditure, even without the outlay on cigars and alcohol, was still extravagant. The protracted German submarine campaign – designed to break the British naval blockade of German ports but the most infamous event of which was the sinking of the passenger liner *Lusitania* in May 1915 – meant that there was no question of a concert tour in North America or of his hopes of earning sufficient fees to clear his debts (which had edged back up towards 90,000 Finnish marks), or even those of his brother Christian, which were not nearly as large as Janne's. Except for those in Gothenburg arranged by Stenhammar, conducting engagements in the neutral Scandinavian nations were scarce compensation, when they occurred (one in Malmö was cancelled on his way back from the USA). Sibelius's diary for 31 July records his frustration, and the sudden shift of the limelight away from him: 'In Helsinki in waiting. War is in the air. Impossible for me to negotiate a loan. Rebuffs from all sides! Strange, it is almost as if I no longer mattered.'

A further complication was Russia's – and consequently Finland's – failure to sign up to the Berne Convention on Copyright which was designed to protect internationally the rights to remuneration of creative artists from exploitation of their work. During peacetime, Sibelius's German publishers ensured that due payments were made, but in war such niceties could not be observed, and the composer lost out considerably from performances in Europe from which he derived no income. Eventually, through the good offices of the Danish publisher Wilhelm Hansen (who had commissioned *Scaramouche* in 1913), some royalties did percolate through, though the fall-off in performances meant that these were never enough.

The war also had a disruptive effect on Sibelius's compositional plans. The exhilaration he had felt at his success in the USA had spurred him to plan a whole series of new large-scale works, and he was beset by commissions. These included a tone-poem for chorus and orchestra, *King Fjalar*, and a ballet to a scenario by Juhani Aho, and there was always the *Juha* project on which he still had an option

until the autumn of 1914. But in his heart of hearts the symphony still
held sway, and he had plans for up to three more. A notebook in
which he began to sketch ideas for the first of these, the Fifth, in
September 1914 would also come to contain the seeds of material used
eventually in the Sixth and Seventh, a sonata for violin and piano and
what became, a full twelve years later, the symphonic poem *Tapiola*.
But in order to generate some money, Sibelius perforce had to set
these major projects aside. On Carpelan's advice he rejected *King
Fjalar*, the ballet and *Juha* finally to produce groups of instrumental
pieces which he hawked to local Finnish publishers, such as Lindgren
and Westerlund, as well as Hansen. These include various sets for the
piano, *Pensées lyriques*, assigned as Op. 40 to give the false impression
that they had been composed earlier than in fact they were, the Five
Pieces, Op. 75, often referred to as 'The Trees' since they celebrate in
turn the rowan, pine, aspen, birch and spruce, and a further set
(Op. 76) which grew eventually in 1919 to thirteen brief items.
Contemporary with these were an equal number for violin and piano,
his first for a quarter of a century, eventually published as Opp. 77, 78
and 79, and collections of songs for voice and piano and part-songs
for male chorus. Sibelius did not view this necessary enterprise with
equanimity:

> *I cannot become a prolific writer. It would mean killing all my
> reputation and my art. I have made my name in the world by
> straightforward means. Perhaps I am too much of a hypochondriac. But to
> waste on a trifle a motif that would be excellently suited to symphonic
> composition!*

That his heart was not truly in it can be heard from the finished
products: charming as they are, the instrumental pieces, unlike the
song sets, are uneven in quality and generally lacking in substance.
Working on such a restricted scale began to become a little too
habitual; the work sketched first as a sonata for violin and piano
ultimately became the Sonatina in E major, Op. 80, rather smaller in
scope than first envisaged. Its composition provided a welcome if
nostalgic diversion from the note-spinning of the miniatures: 'Dreamt
I was twelve again and a virtuoso.' But always in the back of his mind
was the Fifth Symphony: 'In a deep mire again, but I already begin to

see dimly the mountain that I shall certainly ascend ... God opens His door for a moment and His orchestra plays the Fifth Symphony.'

Opposite, Sibelius's original conception for the close of his Fifth Symphony: not six lone hammer-blows, but five blasts of light over a dark, long-held chord

The notion for writing a fifth symphony had occurred as early as 1912, but the form it should take was a problem it would take him seven years to resolve. In the wake of the Fourth he had begun to debate with himself the true nature of the symphony, recording in his diary on 5 November 1911: 'A symphony is not just a composition in the ordinary sense of the word; it is more of an inner confession at a given stage of one's life.' The following year he reached the conclusion that the symphonies should 'decide their own form', but as he commenced notating musical ideas for the Fifth he began to doubt whether a symphony, as opposed to an orchestral fantasia (the form *Pohjola's Daughter* had taken), was the most appropriate vessel for them. 'I wonder,' he wrote in his diary on 18 October 1914, 'whether this name "symphony" has done more harm than good to my symphonies. I'm really planning to let my inner being – my fantasy – speak,' adding a week later, 'One needs to broaden the concept.' By December ideas were coming to him in sufficient volume for him to think of other orchestral pieces, to which he gave rough working names of *Fantasia I* and *Fantasia II*. These would grow in time into Symphonies No. 6 and 7, plus *Tapiola*, but the 'fantasia' tag survived until very late on in the creative process – indeed the Seventh Symphony would be given its première in 1924 with the title *Fantasia sinfonica*.

From the first, the music he had jotted down bore associations with the natural surroundings observable from Ainola: the retreat of winter, the onset of spring, the migrations of birds and even Aino herself. On 21 April the sight of sixteen swans in flight enraptured him:

One of my greatest experiences! Lord God, that beauty! ... Their call the same woodwind type as that of cranes, but without tremolo. The swan-call closer to the trumpet, although there is something of a sarrusophone sound. A low refrain reminiscent of a small child crying. Nature mysticism and life's Angst! The Fifth Symphony's finale-theme: Legato in the trumpets!!

The connection between swans and a theme in the finale persisted in the finished work; that movement's – indeed the symphony's –

The Sibelius family at
Ainola, 1915; left to right:
Aino, Margareta, Heidi,
Katarina (standing), Sibelius
(standing by fireplace)

most memorable idea is a magnificent swinging theme in the horns
over which another melody plays in the strings or woodwinds. The
horn theme seems to have represented to Sibelius the slow graceful
beating of the wings of the swans he had seen about his home, an
association he communicated to Axel Carpelan who, writing to the
composer late in 1916, called this passage 'your swan-hymn beyond
compare'. For the American critic Olin Downes, however, it was the
composer's 'native heath and … the mood to which those who
understand him know and love'. Most famous of all, perhaps, is the
remark, covering the whole opening section of the movement, by the
English composer and musicologist Sir Donald Tovey: 'The bustling
introduction provides a rushing wind, through which Thor can enjoy
swinging his hammer.' (Apt as this analogy of the Norse war-god may
have seemed over the years to many listeners, Tovey's contention –
made through acquaintance only with the symphony's final version –
that it ended 'with the finality of a work that knew from the outset
exactly when its last note was due' could not have been more
mistaken.)

The force of nature, rather than mythology, made itself felt with
still more immediacy in May with the birth to Eva and Arvi
Paloheimo of his first grandchild, Anna-Marjatta. By June the long
process of sifting through the welter of ideas and selecting those for
the new symphony was complete, a task which had fascinated him 'in
a mysterious way. It's as if God the Father had thrown down the tiles
of a mosaic from heaven's floor and asked me to determine what kind
of picture it was. Maybe [this is] a good definition of "composing".
Maybe not. How would I know?!'

In the meantime, his abstinence from alcohol and tobacco was
beginning to be compromised. He had taken to drinking coffee as a
stimulant, as usual to excess, and during 1915 increasingly leavened his
diet with cigars. The smoking led to a return of his hoarseness, giving
him cause for some agitation. He was more cautious at first with wine,
remembering his problems of old, but this passed, especially in the
company of his son-in-law, Arvi Paloheimo, when Aino was not
around. During the summer, with progress on the symphony
stuttering, he indulged more and more. He felt ignored and neglected
by the musical public, and envious of younger colleagues such as
Selim Palmgren and even Madetoja. The refusal by several publishers

of the latter's projected biography of him – in Finnish – fuelled his depression, although one in Swedish eventually appeared late in 1916 written by Erik Furuhjelm.

Despite a comment in his diary in July that 'All threads lead toward the Fifth', Sibelius delayed the detailed construction of the majority of the symphony in order to finalize a series of miniatures and to revise for publication his early patriotic cantata of 1898, *Sandels*. Only in September did he resume work consistently on his 'grand and resonant' symphony, which was to be given its première at a special birthday concert in Helsinki on 8 December, as part of a series of events celebrating his fiftieth birthday. The composer, who would even be honoured by the Tsar at the same time, soon began to worry that he was running short of time, and the first movement was not completed until 1 November. Working sometimes until five o'clock in the morning, he finally managed to complete the finale on 1 December, when rehearsals began. The first performance was well received, the programme completed by the premières of the two Serenades for violin and orchestra from 1912–13 and *The Oceanides*.

Although much of the music of the familiar, final version is present in its original incarnation, the structure of the Fifth Symphony as first conceived, as well as much of the orchestration, is radically different. The original is in four distinct movements (the fusion of the first two into a single whole having not been achieved at this time), the work dividing into two pairs. Both pairs consist of a deliberately inconclusive first span which acts as prelude to the next, while the first pair itself paves the way for the second. Sibelius also adopted an overtly 'cyclic' form, much used in the nineteenth century by composers such as Berlioz, Liszt, Franck and Tchaikovsky, where material from earlier movements had reappeared in the finale. This 'cyclic' element, or at least its explicit manifestations, was one of the major casualties of the series of revisions the Fifth underwent over the next three years. Rather than being a half-formed or unfocused stage in the composition of the final version as is often averred, the original Fifth is really a fundamentally different conception to the final version and should properly be seen as a separate, albeit not fully successful, work.

The gala occasion celebrating his fiftieth birthday had been rounded out by a eulogy given by his old friend Werner Söderhjelm,

Sibelius rehearsing the Helsinki orchestra for the première of the Fifth Symphony in its original version, December 1915

who voiced the esteem in which he was held by the vast majority
of Finns:

> *… the whole of his country feels the necessity of offering him its
> gratitude and assuring him of its admiration and love … How many of us
> really know what it is that makes Jean Sibelius stand so great, so unique
> and lonely in the annals of modern music, makes him a renovator of
> forms, makes him blend realism and romanticism like all great artists in
> reality, frank feelings and a strong sense of reality with the flight of the
> imagination and the mysticism of poetry? Yet, more than one of his works
> has grown into the national consciousness of us all and become national
> poetry, and for more than one of us laymen, who listened unreflectingly to
> his music, something of these works has become a mirror of what we
> ourselves experienced in our innermost hearts in feelings and struggles, in
> the uplifting of the mind and the sorrowing of the heart. And what at any
> rate we all understand is that in Sibelius we possess one of the richest
> spirits that were ever born in this country and the greatest creative power
> now living among us … [He] has taken his place as the representative of
> his people among the noblest in art.*

There were, inevitably, some dissenting views, most notably from
the critic known as 'Bis' in *Hufvudstadsbladet*, who vented his spleen
on the new symphony (and would again on its revision), and the
writer Elmer Diktonius, who in his essay 'Brahms, Tchaikovsky and
Sibelius' upbraided all three for their political conservatism. Nor did
Sibelius's celebrity provide any immunity to the harsher realities of
daily life. Barely had any household dust time to settle on a Steinway
piano presented to him on his birthday before an official from the
Justices' Debt Office claimed the instrument in order to offset it
against some of the composer's debts. A hastily arranged collection
and the proceeds from the celebratory concerts ultimately saved the
composer from the ignominy of repossession by the bailiff.

In January 1916 he began to prepare the symphony for publication.
As he did so, he became increasingly dissatisfied with its structure,
noting on 26 January, 'I am wrestling with God. I'd like to give my
new symphony another, more human form. Something closer to the
earth, something more alive. The problem is that during the course of
the work I have changed.' A full recomposition was a daunting task

and Sibelius's diary records no work on it from mid February until the beginning of October, when the necessity of finalizing the changes in time for a re-première on his fifty-first birthday was of increasing urgency. Work may have continued intermittently; in the meantime there remained the still-embryonic Sixth Symphony and the ever-constant need for small pieces to sell to publishers, and conducting engagements in Sweden and Norway. After the excellence of the American musicians in Connecticut, the standards of performance in the Nordic orchestras, the only ones he had access to with the war raging as intensely as ever, depressed him greatly. 'Am I no more to experience,' he asked himself, 'the delight that a first-class orchestra gives me when I conduct my works?' More congenial creative work came in the form of the composition of five songs for the soprano Ida Ekman, who had over the years proved one of the staunchest champions of his songs. (A sixth was added in 1917, the set eventually being published as Op. 86 by Wilhelm Hansen in 1923.)

On 22 July his second daughter Ruth, who had had some success of her own as an actress, appearing in plays by Minna Canth among others, was married to Samuel – commonly known as 'Jussi' – Snellman. Much of the summer was occupied fulfilling a commission for incidental music for a Finnish National Theatre production of Hugo von Hofmannsthal's *Jedermann* ('Everyman'; *Jokamies* in Finnish). Hofmannsthal's 1911 rewriting of the medieval mystery play provided the composer with an excuse to revisit a medieval sound world, which he had so enjoyed doing in *Scènes historiques*. But the morality's sacred tone required music of a very different cast, which Sibelius relished integrating with the text. So successful was he that some of the *Jedermann* numbers almost approach ballad opera in style. He also realized that, especially in wartime, a concert suite would not be viable, though he did arrange three short extracts for piano.

During 1916, with even the Scandinavian concert trips at an end, Sibelius began to miss his annual expeditions to Europe. These had been vital throughout his career for refreshing his creative faculties, even if the people and music that he did encounter in Berlin, Paris, Vienna or London proved to be not always so inspiring. Cooped up in Finland, in Ainola, Sibelius became increasingly restless. This, along with his uncertainty over the symphony, and resumption of drinking

The soprano Ida Ekman,
a lifelong champion of
Sibelius's songs, and for
whom Sibelius wrote
his final three sets, Opp. 86,
88 and 90. Her son, Karl,
published a biography of
Sibelius in 1935.

and smoking – which last had incurred Aino's unconcealed disgust (in later years Aino regarded the seven years of Sibelius's abstinence as the happiest years of her married life) – took its toll on the marriage. Tension within the household rose dramatically, and in September it was Aino, exhausted and depressed by their unrelenting hand-to-mouth existence, who escaped for a month to visit Eva and Arvi Paloheimo in Petrograd (as St Petersburg was now called). Sibelius was not unsympathetic to her condition, but seemed powerless to alleviate it in any way. Matters worsened on her return. Heated rows centring with some ferocity on the subject of alcohol ensued; weeks might go by without 'a smile or laugh' and 'always tears and tears. Her whole life thrown away.' In November Sibelius broached, if only to himself, thoughts of separation in his diary. But the conventions of Finland in 1916 did not easily brook such notions. In the last resort, however ill-treated she may have felt, Aino had an unwavering belief in her husband's genius and stayed with him.

The second version of the Fifth Symphony was completed in November 1916 and unveiled in Turku on 8 December, under the composer's direction, being repeated six days later in Helsinki. The most significant change from the original conception was the telescoping of the first two movements: the opening span's inconclusive close was removed as were the first sixty-four bars of the scherzo, and a connecting bridge passage inserted. Sibelius still thought of this new compound construction as two distinct but interrelated movements, not unlike the opening pair of the *Voces intimae* string quartet. The original's third movement, a slow-paced set of variations, was substantively rewritten, as was the finale which was increased in size to balance effectively the joined first two movements. Critical reaction was mixed, and this time there was no gala atmosphere to rein in adverse comment. With a performance proposed for Stockholm, Sibelius set to work to tidy the piece up once again, but by early January he realized that yet another recomposition was required. On the sixth of that month he wrote to his brother-in-law Armas Järnefelt, who was the conductor of the Stockholm Opera, ruling out the performance and, indeed, withdrawing the work:

I am deeply unhappy. When I composed the Fifth Symphony for my fiftieth birthday, time was very short. The result was that during this last

*year I've gone back to it and revised it, but I'm not satisfied. and I can
not, unequivocally can not, send it off.*

A diary entry from a week later is gloomier still:

*My soul is sick. And it looks like this is going to last a long time. How
did I end up here? For many reasons. The direction of my composing has
led me up a blind alley … I didn't make it round the cape.*

With that, he put the Fifth aside for well over a year to concentrate on
other works, sketches for the *Fantasia*-cum-Sixth-Symphony not least.

During the protracted hiatus between the interim and final
versions of the Fifth Symphony, external events at last began to
overtake Finland's isolation from World War I. The stalemate
slaughter of the trenches in north-west Europe continued unabated, as
at Vimy Ridge and Passchendaele, but in Russia two political
revolutions turned the vast Tsarist Empire upside down. Nicholas II
himself at first abdicated, but the decision by the new administration
to pursue the war led inexorably to the second, more catastrophic
revolution by the Bolshevik Communists under Lenin. Finland found
herself with a sudden and not-to-be missed opportunity to become a
fully independent nation, and seized the chance eagerly. In July the
Provisional Government in Petrograd at first accepted Finland's right
of self-determination in all matters except defence and foreign affairs,
but rescinded this agreement after Lenin fled to Finland in the wake
of his failed first coup. In the chaos following the Bolshevik's
successful seizure of power in November (the 'October' Revolution –
so called because the Russian calendar lags a fortnight behind that of
Western and Central Europe) the Eduskunta took matters into their
own hands, electing a Regency Council under the provisions of a still-
valid Swedish law of 1772 which assumed supreme authority. Their
position was immediately challenged by a Revolutionary Council of
largely left-wing sympathizers which tried – unsuccessfully – to stage
its own Bolshevik revolution, an unco-ordinated affair which rapidly
degenerated into widespread looting, pillage and killings by various
small disaffected groups. The Eduskunta, reinforced by the return of
many political exiles, such as Pehr Svinhufvud, passed a law reducing
working hours which placated the majority of the workers, and

decided to have their independence constitutionally ratified by the new Soviet government. Preoccupied in securing his own position, Lenin acceded to this demand in early January, formal independence taking effect retrospectively from 31 December. Simultaneously, 60,000 Russian troops were withdrawn, though the bulk of the garrisons remained in place. Freedom had been achieved without a shot being fired but, ironically, before the month was out, Finland was plunged into civil war.

The left-wing elements, which still possessed their own paramilitary force in the 'Red' Guard, still hankered after power. They aimed to set up a separate Soviet-style state aligned with Lenin's Union of Soviet Socialist Republics. The Regency Council, almost exclusively dominated by conservative, 'White' interests, formed a Civil Guard to oppose the Reds. However, the southern segment of the country was predominantly Red in orientation, so that the Parliament and White forces quickly evacuated the capital and set up their base in Vaasa on the west coast. From there, under the command of Lieutenant General Karl Gustav Emil Mannerheim, a Fenno-Swede, the Whites with assistance provided by German troops and the *Jäger* Division swept the Reds from their strongholds – including the second city of Viipuri also – in three months of extremely bitter fighting. Mannerheim had served with great distinction in the Russian Army but had returned home after being relieved of duty on account of the tension in Finland in the latter part of 1917. He made a triumphant entry into Helsinki on 16 May, but resigned at the end of the month in protest at the continuing German military presence. During the summer, at the instigation of Juho Paasikivi, now Prime Minister, the Senate formally declared Finland to be a constitutional monarchy (somewhat after the British model) and in October elected Kaiser Wilhelm's brother-in-law Prince Friedrich Karl of Hessen as King. Germany's collapse the following month made his enthronement a political impossibility, and he formally abdicated in December leaving Finland a republic.

Sibelius was far from indifferent in the conflict, taking the side of the White cause. Indeed, dismayed at what he felt to be prevarication by the Fennoman politicians, he had long hoped the Swedish Finns would make common cause with Germany to oust the Russians. Late in 1917 he composed his popular March for the Finnish *Jäger* Battalion

who sang it on campaign the next year. He had remained largely
isolated during the surge towards independence, composing various
small items and the six 'Flower Songs', Op. 88, and Six Songs on texts
by Johan Runeberg, Op. 90, his final two sets. They were written
expressly with Ida Ekman in mind and made some concessions to the
then limited range of her voice. He continued to sketch what would
become the Sixth Symphony, reaching the third movement by the
outbreak of the civil war, but the only large-scale orchestral piece was
a collection of Six Humoresques for violin and orchestra. These were
published in two groups, Nos. 1–2 as Op. 87 and Nos. 3–6 as Op. 89,
and while they can be performed individually the six pieces make a
very effective suite. They may have started life as sketches for the
second violin concerto he had had in mind since 1915 but, whether he
found the musical material too intractable to develop in that way, or

The end of the brief but
bitter civil war: Lieutenant
General Mannerheim
enters Helsinki in triumph in
May 1918.

his difficulties with the Fifth Symphony made him wary of pursuing such a design, they remained as miniatures despite his assertion to Carpelan that they were 'on a grand scale'. If the Violin Concerto represents a cohesive symphonic argument in sound, the delightful Humoresques, expressing in the composer's own words 'the anguish of existence ... fitfully lit up by the sun', are sound-bites by comparison, yet which might have been expanded and conjoined into a second concerto had the will been there.

The civil war did not leave the composer unaffected. His *Jäger March* had been hijacked by the pro-German White faction at a Helsinki concert, and was seen widely as a public demonstration of support, which made Sibelius feel distinctly uncomfortable. When the Reds occupied Järvenpää in early February, he was forbidden to leave the confines of Ainola, 'even to stroll' as he noted in his diary. He believed himself to be a natural target by virtue of his celebrity, not without cause. 'All educated people are in danger of their lives. Murder upon murder. Soon, no doubt, my hour will come, for I must be specially hateful to them as the composer of the *Jäger March*.' In fact, the Reds had not made that connection, despite being aware of his standing. On 12 February, and again a day later, Ainola was searched by some Red Guards (who did not know who he was), looking for hidden food and arms. Sibelius later described these to his biographer Karl Ekman, but anonymity seems rather to have been the threat:

The men presented a terrifying appearance with their pock-marked, deformed faces. They were not from the Järvenpää district, a circumstance that made my position all the more dangerous. They had no idea of who I was and behaved in a very threatening and rough manner. I actually had a revolver hidden in a room on the ground floor of the villa. The house-porter, who was present during the search, knew of this, and if he had betrayed me my life would not have been worth much.

On 15 February Sibelius considered changing his appearance by shaving his head, though he postponed a permanent alteration until the following year; it is unclear whether a wish to disguise himself or hair loss was the root cause. These experiences, and a Red delegation from Helsinki headed by Kajanus and Eero Järnefelt, finally persuaded Sibelius to take himself and his family away from his now defiled sanctuary of Ainola, despite the capital still being under Red control. They stayed variously and at times separately with Christian, who was a doctor at a hospital in Lappviken, Eero Järnefelt and Arvi Paloheimo's father. But even in Helsinki, with shells landing nearby, they were not wholly safe; and Christian was even arrested by the Reds at one point – though only for a day.

After the relief of Helsinki and the collapse of the Red forces, Sibelius felt able to return to Ainola, where he resumed as best he could the various compositional threads he had been weaving prior to his flight. The accumulation of civil war, displacement, Aino's depressive illness, marital strain and acute food shortages made this no easy task. Inflation had made his financial plight so critical that he seriously considered selling Ainola, and had electricity installed in response to the dearth of paraffin and as a potential selling-point. His feelings of neglect and conspiracies against him proved further distractions, near-disabling ones for a composer too readily assailed by self-doubt and paranoia in even the sunniest of times.

The most important of his projects were for yet another revision of the Fifth Symphony, actually begun in February, as well as its successors. On 20 May he wrote to Axel Carpelan:

… the Vth Symphony in its new form almost completely recomposed. The first movement is totally new. The second recalls the old one. The third is reminiscent of the ending of the old first movement. The fourth movement, the old motives, but developed in a leaner, firmer way. The whole, if I can call it that, is a vital rise to the end. Triumphal … The VIth Symphony is wild and impassioned in character. Sombre with pastoral contrasts, probably in four movements with the end rising to a sombre roaring in the orchestra, in which the main theme is drowned. The VIIth Symphony. Joy of life and vitality, with appassionato passages. In three movements – the last an 'Hellenic rondo'. All this with due reservation … it looks as if I was to come out with all these three symphonies at the same time … the plans may possibly be altered according to the development of the musical ideas. As usual, I am a slave to my themes and submit to their demands.

Carpelan, who was gravely ill, rather more than the preoccupied composer perhaps appreciated, was supportive but dismayed at what he perceived to be a reversion back to the original design of the Fifth. Sibelius himself was evidently unconvinced also, since he effectively abandoned work on it in June. The remainder of the summer was frittered away writing trifles to earn a little income more often than not drunk away in binges in the capital.

Finland's independent status led the composer to produce a number of choral works of a more or less patriotic nature, most notably two with orchestral accompaniment, *Our Native Land* (Oma maa) and *Song of the Earth* (Jordens sång; commissioned by Åbo Academy in Turku, there is no connection at all with Mahler's symphonic song cycle of the same name), and one without: *Outside the Storm Rages* (Ute hörs stormen). The best of these is *Our Native Land*, a minor masterpiece though it does not sound particularly Finnish in character, unlike some of his earlier efforts in this vein like *Sandels* or *The Origin of Fire*. But the Fifth kept calling to him, not least because Carpelan's illness had become terminal, and Carpelan had from the first responded so readily to the work's kernel – the 'swan-hymn beyond compare'. Between February and April 1919 Sibelius worked in earnest on the symphony. The 1918 plan was rejected *in toto*, as he reported to his friend in late February:

> *In these past few days something great has happened. I regained my sight. The [second] version of the first movement ... is among the best things that I have ever composed. I cannot understand my blindness. Amazing, that you always supported it.*

If Sibelius did compose a new first movement in 1918, it has not survived in recognizable form. (It may have been absorbed into one of the later symphonies.) The second movement, which Carpelan had thought unsuccessful, was overhauled completely and, like the finale, greatly simplified. In layout the final version of the Fifth Symphony resembles that of No. 3 in reverse, with a fusion of scherzo and in this case opening movement leading to a straightforward central set of variations and a dynamic finale. Like the Fourth Symphony, the first movement charts once more a landscape bleak in places, but its brighter second half is nothing short of invigorating. The other two movements both have dissonant outbursts, yet the entire symphony is expressed in warmer colours and fuller, less stark harmonies than in its predecessor. The prominent use of brass and timpani also lends the final version a more heroic aspect than its prototypes. Most crucially, it concludes with a series of six resounding hammer blows unequivocally in the home key; there could be no doubt as to when this symphony had finished.

Axel Carpelan never heard the final Fifth Symphony, dying on 24 March 1919. Bereft of his friend's counsel, which had been of immense value over the past nineteen years, Sibelius had a brief and acute loss of confidence about the finished work a week after completing it. A diary entry for 28 April notes how he proposed removing the second and third movements altogether to leave the first as a 'Symphonic Fantasia' – perhaps even the first of several such works. But by the first week of May, the battle between fantasia and symphony was finally resolved in favour of the latter. In the end, it was not possible to issue the work without its main defining moment – Carpelan's 'swan-hymn'. After working over the finale for the fourth time, he dispatched the score to the copyist. He later claimed that on laying down his pen 'twelve white swans settled down on the lake, and then circled the house three times before flying away.' The final version was unveiled in Helsinki on 24 November, along with the Humoresques and in company with *Song of the Earth*, to triumphant acclaim.

7

Sibelius on the podium with
the concertmaster of the
Viipuri orchestra; he
conducted the orchestra in
his Second Symphony on
28 April 1923.

*Each of my seven symphonies has its own style,
and their creation in every case took a lot of
time. But I never talk about my own work; for
the next morning I would regret having done so.*

Jean Sibelius to Santeri Levas

Pure, Cold Water 1919–27

Finland in 1919 was still in a state of national uncertainty. The birth of the new state had been accompanied by economic chaos, civil war and famine. Foreign governments had been slow to recognize her independence, due partly to the role the now prostrate Germany had played in that struggle, and partly to the unknown quantity that was Soviet Russia, itself riven by civil war on a vast scale, with whom Finland had territorial disputes in Karelia. The Finnish government got on with exercising the newly won freedom. The prohibition on alcohol, designed to combat the nationwide problem of drunkenness and which had been approved by the Eduskunta a decade earlier but not implemented, was formally instituted in March. Yet its enforcement was less than wholehearted; even at official state banquets, alcohol was served clandestinely for those that wanted it.

With the idea of a monarchy firmly buried, executive power was formally instituted in the office of President, with elections for its first incumbent by the members of the Eduskunta in July. But Finland was no more at peace with herself than she was with her Bolshevik neighbour. Red sympathizers were by no means extinct, as much in reaction to the scale of the Whites' reprisals against the Reds after hostilities had ceased. Even Sibelius was a target for criticism (in a 1921 article entitled 'Aphorisms' by Elmer Diktonius), since the *Jäger March* had come to be so closely associated with the Whites. Communist activity, fronted by the Socialist Labour Party (since the Communists were a proscribed organization), increased markedly within the trades unions. The pro-right, nationalist lobby countered with emotive appeals to the notion of a 'Greater Finland', to incorporate Russian East Karelia, whose population was ethnically Finnish (but which showed little enthusiasm for a new political union). An anti-White backlash was inevitable, and even the hero of the hour was not immune: in that first Presidential election, Mannerheim was defeated by Kaarlo Ståhlberg.

The war years had put a great strain on all areas of Sibelius's life. Compositionally, he had been stretched to breaking point by the Fifth Symphony, whose birth-pangs had been extraordinarily public for such a highly sensitive composer, and aside from the music to *Jedermann* and the Humoresques he had little else of real quality to show for the time. At home, matters were still on the brink. His financial situation had eased briefly with the successful first performances of the Fifth Symphony, but Sibelius's taste for the high-life remained undiminished. While he was fully aware of alcohol's debilitating effect on his marriage – Aino's health suffered constantly from the nervous strain – he seemed powerless to stop himself. Nor was his self-control perfect in public: while attending a Nordic Music Festival in Copenhagen in June 1919, he had become so enraged at being asked to pay for champagne he had ordered while giving a party (he felt the festival organizers should have underwritten his expenses) that he threw his money around the room, so that several of his compatriots had to scramble on all fours to retrieve it. Only Aino's iron will brought him back to his senses.

As with the Fifth Symphony, Sibelius worked on ideas for its successor without knitting them together into coherent movements – though at the end of the year he would still be wondering whether it should not take the freer form of a fantasia. The success of the Fifth's final version put into sharp relief the uncertain progress of the Sixth, and early in 1920 work on it petered out. To try and clear the impasse, the composer spent increasingly long visits to Helsinki to attend concerts, not least Kajanus's programming that season of all five symphonies in chronological sequence, and to frequent the local restaurants. The nation's social life, so badly disrupted during the war, renewed itself and as a national celebrity Sibelius was in demand both at functions hosted by such luminaries as the architect Eliel Saarinen, Siloti and Mannerheim, as well as conducting at gala concerts, as on 26 June, in the presence of President Ståhlberg.

With the symphony on hold, Sibelius continued to produce smaller works, both to commission and on his own volition to sell. One such was the cantata *Maan virsi* ('Hymn to the Earth'), to a text by Eino Leino, given its première under Heikki Klemetti's baton in Helsinki on 4 April. It was not received well, the kindest comment referring to it as a 'well-sounding novelty', the most embarrassing

Following page, composers and musicians gathered together for the Nordic Music Days Festival in Copenhagen, 1919. Sibelius is seated in the second row, fourth from right; second from right is his rival, the great Danish symphonist Carl Nielsen; Kajanus is second from Sibelius's left, with Stenhammar seated on the ground at Sibelius's feet.

being Bis's mistaking it for a Finnish-language version of the cantata
Song of the Earth that Sibelius had written for Åbo Academy the
previous year. The critic only realized his error three months later.
Commissions for larger works were turned down, including two ballet
projects, one of which came from Poul Knudsen, scenarist of
Scaramouche which was still awaiting its first staging. The
indefatigable Adolf Paul, now writing film scripts in Sweden, tried in
vain to interest the composer in writing music for the silver screen.
One approach that did meet with his wholehearted acceptance came
from Rosa Newmarch, acting on behalf of the impresario Robert
Newman, who wanted to engage Sibelius as conductor for a series of
concerts – the precise number to be settled later – in Britain in
February and March 1921.

As 1920 wore on, Sibelius's financial predicament worsened.
The effects of inflation and the cessation of trade with Russia had
devastated the Finnish economy, the mark having fallen in value to
under ten per cent of its value fifteen years before. With the German
currency collapsing, the royalty payments from Breitkopf und Härtel
were in consequence becoming worthless, though in truth Sibelius
was one among many in the same situation. His German publishers
tried to forestall any move to a rival firm, especially after he had sent
them a list of works written since the outbreak of the war. They were
dismayed at the number that had been published elsewhere, even if
only to local Finnish publishers, but were fearful of his connections
with Wilhelm Hansen. And with good reason, as the Danish firm that
summer easily outbid them for the Fifth Symphony. Sibelius was in
two minds about switching publisher again, but perhaps the deciding
factor was the sounder economic basis of the Danish crown over the
German mark.

In August a quite unexpected lifeline was offered to the composer
from the USA. He was invited to become the director for one year of
the Eastman School of Music in Rochester, New York State, at a salary
of $20,000. His duties were to include teaching and the conducting of
five concerts. The chief negotiator for Eastman, Alf Klingenberg,
visited Sibelius at Ainola in early September to discuss the proposal
further. The composer had mixed feelings about the prospect: he had
not relished his earlier academic roles, and was uneasy even in the
one-to-one of a tutorial. But the money was a temptation he could

not resist and he told Klingenberg he would accept on condition that he received an advance of $10,000 – in order for him to settle his affairs in Finland. The School authorities baulked at this, but finally compromised and agreed to pay it into an American bank when Sibelius was ready to travel.

The encouraging contacts from Britain and the USA spurred the composer back to his writing desk, but not initially to the Sixth Symphony, for which he may have been considering a descriptive title, *Runes historiques*. The idea for a tone-poem on the subject of *Kuutar* appealed to him, and he made several sketches for it – later taken up into the symphony. But his mind was looking to less ambitious horizons. His paltry return from the composition of *Valse triste*, one of the pieces he was most often asked to conduct, had long rankled and he desired to repeat its success while securing a better commercial deal with Hansen. In September and October he looked again at a deliberately lighter piece for two sopranos and orchestra written the previous year, the 'pastoral scene' *Autrefois*, using a text by Hjalmar Procopé. His diary entry for 4 October noted that *Autrefois* was 'no good … a reworking is necessary.' Hansen, however, thought it could be a new *Valse triste*. Its pallid Nordic lyricism did have sufficient appeal at early performances for it to be encored, but such optimism was not justified. *Autrefois* shows how deep the divide had become between Sibelius's 'quality' output, such as the symphonies, and note-spinning trifles of limited commercial success and less artistic value. Aino in particular was alarmed at this dichotomy in her husband's music, viewing works like *Autrefois* as a betrayal of his talent, for which she had endured and sacrificed so much over the years. But worse was to follow.

On 1 December his brother-in-law Armas conducted the first foreign performance of the Fifth Symphony in Stockholm. Sibelius had worked himself up into a state of severe nervous tension in the weeks prior to the performance, made worse by Katarina's contraction of pneumonia and fears for Heidi. Matters were not much improved by the mixed reviews the symphony received, although its publication was greeted far more positively in Germany a few months later. The best fillip he received came on his fifty-fifth birthday, when the singer Wäino Sola presented him with a cheque for 55,000 Finnish marks on behalf of a group of patriotic and music-loving businessmen. Sibelius promptly took himself off to Helsinki for a week to indulge in some serious socializing and drinking, leaving Aino at home. Even before this, on 2 December, he recorded in his diary his pangs of conscience concerning his wife, but the will power to give up the bottle was not there; rather, after avoiding spirits assiduously on resuming drinking in 1915, he now took to whisky.

> *Day in and day out I sit and stare disconsolately in front of me, and think depressing thoughts. Where will this get me? To inertia and loneliness. Poor Aino. What a dreadful fate. Alone, alone with her sick children. I cannot bear to think about it. And why? Just tell me. We have just slowly drifted into this despondency. If only I could find something to improve my nerves. My nerves are really very bad. I can't leave home – Aino would then be on her own. Though I can't see what we get out of each other's company. We are both down and she avoids my gaze and then there's that implied criticism of me in all her movements. But cheer up – death is round the corner!*

Only after the Stockholm performance did the nervous composer release the score of the Fifth Symphony to Sir Henry Wood, so that he could prepare it with his orchestra for Sibelius to conduct in the following February. His reticence extended even to providing details of the work to Rosa Newmarch, who was writing the programme notes for the concerts and in letters barely concealed her exasperation at the delays. At the turn of the new year, he finally telegraphed his formal acceptance of the professorship in Rochester, and the school placed an announcement in the *New York Times* later in the month.

Sibelius left for Britain at the end of January, after a brief diversion to Berlin first, arriving on 6 February. In contrast to previous visits, he was looked after by the Finnish diplomatic staff, Marcus Tollett and Ossian Donner in particular, which gave him the aura of a cultural ambassador. His concert schedule had expanded to include not only appearances (conducting only his own pieces in larger mixed programmes) in London's Queen's Hall and in Birmingham, but also in Bournemouth, Bradford and Manchester, as well as *En saga* with the student orchestra of the Royal College of Music. The works he presented included – inevitably – *The Swan of Tuonela*, *Valse triste* and *Finlandia*, all guaranteed to fill the house, but also the Third, Fourth

Opposite, 'Old Timber': Sir Henry Wood, co-founder of the Proms and the first to conduct a Sibelius score in Britain (King Christian II in 1921), who invited the composer on his last trip to London in 1921

and Fifth Symphonies, as well as *The Oceanides*. Symphony No. 5 was an undoubted success with the Queen's Hall audience on 12 February, and critical reaction was generally positive for so new a work. The polite reception accorded shortly afterwards to the still difficult Fourth was in marked contrast to the ovation given to Busoni's *Red Indian Fantasy*. Given the Finn's long-standing incomprehension of Busoni's music, his irritation at being overshadowed was entirely in character, but it did not interfere with the two old friends' long-delayed reunion. This, incidentally, caused Henry Wood a considerable headache, as he recalled years later:

> *I could generally manage Busoni when I had him to myself, but my heart was always in my mouth if he met Sibelius. I never knew where they would get to. They would forget the time of the concert at which they were to appear; they hardly knew the day of the week ... I ... had to commission a friend never to let these two out of his sight. He had quite an exciting time for two or three days following them about from restaurant to restaurant. He told me he never knew what time they went to bed or got up in the morning. They were like a couple of irresponsible schoolboys.*

Irresponsible or not in his behaviour, it was clear to almost everybody that the pale, gaunt Busoni was not a well man; years of overwork and straitened financial circumstances had taken a heavy toll on his physical health. Yet Sibelius seems not to have noticed, and recalling their meeting a decade later to his biographer Karl Ekman said of this 'assiduous champion of my music ... I could not imagine that it was to be the last time that I saw my faithful old friend. He seemed so full of vitality and buoyant.' (In fact, it proved to be the last time that Sibelius would see England, Wood, Bantock or Rosa Newmarch as well.) On 1 May, Busoni conducted the first Italian performance of the Second Symphony in Rome to great acclaim, which ironically his own Violin Concerto and *Two Studies from 'Doktor Faust'* failed to receive. The Italian was not ignorant of the nature of his relationship to 'Sibban', writing to Adolf Paul on 10 November:

> *In spite of our affectionate dealings he never seems quite at ease with me and there is at the same time a childish, ingratiating manner which*

'I never knew where they would get to': the 'irresponsible schoolboys' Busoni (left, looking gaunt) and Sibelius in London, 1921

makes me feel awkward. I met him last in London in February. All the same I am very fond of him.

Quite what Paul's motives were in passing these comments on verbatim to Sibelius can only be guessed at.

The moving force behind this successful tour had been Rosa Newmarch, who adopted a rather maternal attitude to the composer

(who was less than ten years younger than her). While unshakeable in her belief in his music, other aspects of his person gave her cause for concern. Perhaps the most disturbing was his association with the 25-year-old Harriet Cohen. She had made a great impression on the composer both by playing *En saga* at the piano for him from memory, and resembling his mother in looks. Cohen was known to be engaged in a long-running, if intermittent, affair with the English composer Arnold Bax (his world-famous tone-poem *Tintagel* being inspired by her), and Newmarch did not think it good for Sibelius to be seen with her. There is no concrete evidence of any impropriety between them, though they were undoubtedly on familiar terms. Harriet Cohen possessed an obvious magnetism which enthralled a whole host of composers over the years. Their familiarity and her charisma might account for a certain coolness to her on Aino's part when Cohen visited Ainola in 1932 in the company of Bax, and again on her own in 1956.

Rosa Newmarch also lost no opportunity throughout Sibelius's month in England to argue with him against taking the Eastman post. She also wrote to Aino in Finland explaining how important it was for him not to go to the USA, and kept up the pressure on Sibelius by letter after his departure on 10 March (from Newcastle, crossing to Bergen in Norway):

Opposite, the pianist Harriet Cohen, or Tania as she was usually called, 'that fantastic volatile and delightful creature' in the words of her long-time lover, the English composer Arnold Bax, in 1913; eight years later Sibelius's attraction to her caused Rosa Newmarch some anxiety.

> *… I beg you not to squander your energies in teaching young Americans harmony and orchestration … à la Sibelius. They can find all that by studying your works. You are a composer not a pedagogue; possibly the greatest creative musician of our times – and certainly one of the noblest and most individual. That is your mission. Au diable les dollars! Spend the summer in Järvenpää; don't smoke too many Corona cigars for the sake of your finances; don't drink too often … and compose your Sixth (on the Almighty's command). This will give your life real meaning. You do not have the right to freely dispose of those years that remain to you, which most certainly do not belong to young Americans.*

But the composer was already having second thoughts, due mainly to the enthusiasm of his reception in England. Perhaps the most encouraging aspect of this for his always fragile self-confidence was the fact that his artistic sensibility was given the benefit of the doubt in works such as the Fourth and Fifth Symphonies which were not wholly understood. This had never been the case in Germany or Sweden, and was rarely so even in his own country. It seemed to him that conducting and composing was what he should do now, not get bogged down in academia, and as early as 21 February he wrote to this effect to Aino. On his return to Finland after further successful concerts in Bergen and Oslo, he wrote (on 25 April) to Rochester withdrawing from the post on the grounds that he could not teach. Klingenberg telegraphed back on 3 May that the teaching could be excluded, replaced by criticism of the students' compositions. Sibelius wired his acceptance three days later and asked that the advance be deposited in the bank. But on 9 May he changed his mind yet again: 'Have realised cost of living in America. Arrival impossible. Sibelius.' Christian Sinding was appointed in his place, followed in 1923 by Selim Palmgren, the young Finnish composer-pianist of whose successes – especially that of his Second Concerto, 'The River' – Sibelius was often irrationally jealous.

After the excitement of the British tour, the rest of 1921 was spent in more mundane fashion composing small, light pieces to raise cash, encouraged by the moderate success of *Autrefois*. But the next year or so would prove difficult for his self-esteem. Works like the *Suites mignonne, champêtre* and *caractéristique* for strings, the *Cinq Morceaux* ('Five Pieces') for piano, and *Valse lyrique* and *Valse chevaleresque* suffered the ignominy of rejection from the various international publishers he submitted them to, such as Chappell in London (who were eventually quite blunt in their comments, though they did finally accept the *Suite mignonne*). Hansen ultimately took many of them, but as much to keep the composer sweet as for their worth (and even here there were one or two ill-natured exchanges). That his name alone would not sell such items clearly showed that his standing internationally was not as great as he had supposed, putting his withdrawal from the Eastman post in a very different light.

However much he tried to justify the composition of these smaller pieces by, for instance, reference back to the waltz music of Johann Strauss that he had loved since his student days in Vienna, there was no disguising their poor quality. In a 1947 essay, the English composer Ralph W. Wood dismissed them in a vitriolic outburst as 'absolute hackwork', 'worthless … cheap and irritating … quite meritless and, indeed, offensive.' The view seemed to be that they were not worthy of the man who could write *The Oceanides*, let alone the symphonies. 'Salon music of genius' was how one critic once evaluated *Valse triste*, whereas the newer pieces, created to try to replicate its success, were salon music without talent. However harsh this judgement was, it paled against that of Aino, who loathed especially the *Valse chevaleresque*. Sibelius had told her it would be a gold mine; Aino thought it the product of someone whose senses were sodden with champagne. When Chappell rejected it and Hansen paid less than half the composer's asking-price to publish, the atmosphere in Ainola could be cut with a meat cleaver.

If Sibelius appeared to be unable to compose anything on a large scale, or of unquestioned appeal, the most recent of his major works were steadily making headway in the wider world. Hermann Scherchen, already establishing himself as the firebrand of avant-garde composition, had attracted great acclaim in Leipzig with a performance of the Fourth Symphony, and Busoni likewise with its successor in Berlin the next month. Indeed, the Fifth was progressing from triumph to triumph in North America. Leopold Stokowski had given its American première in October 1921 in Philadelphia; the audience took to the work immediately although the critics were cool. Repeat performances in other major cities won these over as well. In May *Scaramouche* finally made it onto the stage. The production failed to please, unlike the music: 'a masterpiece from beginning to end,' one critic called it, and few dissenting voices were raised. These successes prompted Hansen to attempt to put Sibelius back on the track of larger works by commissioning a piano concerto. His response that he was 'a slave of my ideas so that I can no longer write what I want, but what I must' does not sit well with the churning-out of works such as the *Suite caractéristique*.

With Katarina in Stuttgart studying the piano, Sibelius felt more isolated than usual. But just as *Scaramouche* was proving such a musical triumph, tragedy struck. His brother Christian, who had been ailing for some time, was diagnosed as suffering from pernicious anaemia, for which there was then no cure. He died on 2 July, a few days after Sibelius had visited him and played on the piano the *Elegy* from *King Christian II*. After the deaths of Carpelan and his daughter, Kirsti, this was the most devastating loss of his adult life. But life had

The English-born conductor Leopold Stokowski at the time of his first marriage, in 1911, aged twenty-nine. In the 1920s he conducted the North American premières of several Sibelius works.

to go on; in August he was received into the Masons with the rank of 'master mason' and for the next decade or so was active in the organization (which had, of course, a most active social life), even composing – in 1926–7 – vocal pieces for masonic ritual. And in September 1922 he picked up the reins of the Sixth Symphony.

Sibelius's Symphony No. 6 is a quite extraordinary and unique masterpiece. The character of the music is unlike anything else in the modern repertoire. It captures in sound the rarified, limpid quality of the light of the Nordic countries, and is almost – though not quite – bereft of the 'wild and impassioned' character he had forecast to Carpelan in 1918. There is a luminosity in its textures that is in stark contrast to the heroism depicted in the Fifth Symphony, seeming to depict the streams and forests of his country in the full flood of spring – the same landscape, perhaps, as that conjured up in the Fourth, but in a more benevolent season. The composer himself stated that it was 'very tranquil in character and outline … and is built, like the Fifth, on linear rather than harmonic foundations.' In it he had given expression to the 'rare sense of rapture' he had experienced as a boy in Hämeenlinna, and there is a pronounced mystical atmosphere. This led him in time to comment how when so many other composers were concocting strange cocktails of outlandish colours, he offered 'pure, cold water' (the most refreshing drink of all). 'In any case,' he declared, 'I do not think of a symphony only as music in this or that number of bars, but rather as an expression of a spiritual creed, a phase in one's inner life.'

The period of sustained construction of this most beautiful of symphonies coincided with his grief over Christian's death (and with a time of stormy negotiations over his bank debts). So intense was his concentration on it that he passed on a commission for a second ballet collaboration with Poul Knudsen to Leevi Madetoja. The first three movements were complete by January, when he had to break off to conduct in Norway and Sweden, and the whole symphony finished in February 1923, barely in time for the first performance on the nineteenth of that month. That concert was a sell-out, despite a bizarre programme which also featured *La Chasse* from the second set of *Scènes historiques*, the *Suites champêtre* and *caractéristique*, *Autrefois* and *Valse chevaleresque* (Aino must have had to grit her teeth through that), and was repeated three days later.

On 24 February Sibelius and Aino left for Stockholm, where he was due to conduct several concerts of his works, to include the First, Second and Sixth Symphonies and the usual collection of popular numbers at the start of a tour taking in Uppsala, Gothenburg and Rome. This was, excursions to St Petersburg aside, the first time Aino had set foot outside Finland for twenty-two years, yet she spent much of her time looking back to Ainola, fretting over her two youngest children (Margareta was fourteen, Heidi eleven) and writing epistles to the servants about what to do in the garden. The Stockholm concerts proved to be a great success; of the second, even the usually vitriolic Peterson-Berger was bowled over: 'His tone-painting, *The Oceanides*, was totally and completely different from three years ago under Schnéevoigt … In this beautiful poem one really heard something of the sound of the Aegean sea and of Homer …' But an even greater surprise was in store: 'the Sixth Symphony sounded not only clear and comprehensible but was full of tasteful and individual, yet expressive and vital beauty. The last three symphonies were for me more or less a torment, thanks to the lack of concrete ideas and pure melody … were I to hear [them] under his own direction, I should have appreciated them more.'

After a brief stop-over in Berlin to meet up with Adolf Paul, Aino and Janne reached Rome on 11 March. Sibelius had a week to prepare for his concert at the Augusteo, at which the main work was the Second Symphony. In contrast to Busoni's success with the piece just two years earlier, the Finn was unable to make the same kind of impression, being regarded as primarily a local, Finnish phenomenon. The couple took time out to stay on the isle of Capri, then at the beginning of April headed north for Gothenburg. On the way they tried to call in on Busoni, who was too ill to receive them. Sibelius, still oblivious to the nature of Busoni's condition, took this as a slight and refused a later invitation to call round. When his friend died the following year Sibelius bitterly regretted not having swallowed his misplaced pride.

So far the tour had been successful, with husband and wife getting on tolerably well. But in Gothenburg, matters began to go awry. The two concerts, at which he presented the Fifth, Sixth and Second Symphonies, *The Oceanides*, *Pohjola's Daughter* and *Rakastava*, were received rapturously, but before the start of the second, on 11 April,

Following page, Aino and Sibelius at home: 'The sort of marriage centring solely on rearing children is anathema to me – there are other things to think about if you are an artist.'

Sibelius was found to be missing. After an increasingly anxious search, he was located sitting calmly in a local restaurant, oblivious of the time, eating oysters and drinking champagne. Whether he was shame-faced at being found out, or had just drunk too much, the start of the first piece broke down and had to be commenced over again. Despite the applause, Sibelius knew that he had disgraced himself – if only in his own and Aino's eyes; as they left the concert hall he took out a small bottle of whisky and smashed it on the steps.

On his return home, Sibelius began to work on his next orchestral work, the last of the three symphonies he had outlined to Carpelan in 1918, which was to conclude with a 'Hellenic Rondo'. Yet if the artistic successes of the tour encouraged the development of what became the Seventh Symphony, more mundane matters distracted him: the collapse of the German currency and the hyperinflation that followed rendered his royalties from Lienau and Breitkopf worthless, plunging his finances into another desperate state, and Aino was still seething over Gothenburg. The unexpected award of a prize of 100,000 Finnish marks from the Kordelin Foundation did much to alleviate the most immediate of his money worries, but it also encouraged him to do the rounds of his old haunts in Helsinki. Eero Järnefelt's sixtieth birthday in November provided just such an excuse, but it is clear from several of his diary entries that, however well or badly progress on the new piece was going from day to day, the tension at home caused by his drinking was driving him away from his desk. He persuaded himself that alcohol, whisky at this point in his life, was essential to inspiration, referring to it in his diary as his '… most faithful companion. And the most understanding. Everything and everyone else have largely failed me.' These were sentiments hardly calculated to endear him to his wife.

His working method was to stay up all night writing and drinking. Aino would appear in the morning to find him asleep or half-asleep at his desk, bottle to hand, which she would then remove. Neither would speak a word to the other. He was, as ever, not insensible to her state of mind, but equally as usual, lacked the will to do anything about it. On 6 January, he recorded in his diary:

Aino has been badly ill for some time. She is at the end of her tether. I won't get my pieces ready now. Hope at least that one of them will be finished. That is imperative. But I am on the wrong rails. Alcohol to calm my nerves and state of mind. How dreadful old age is for a composer! Things don't go as quickly as they used to, and self-criticism grows to impossible proportions.

One morning, she finally cracked; with the première of the new work, which Sibelius had decided was to be a 'Symphonic Fantasia', scheduled for Stockholm in March, one morning she handed him a note. In it she declared quite bluntly that she would not accompany him to Sweden, or indeed be seen at all in public with him, in the drunken state he had been in in Gothenburg. (This note was found by Erik Tawaststjerna long after Sibelius's death amongst papers held by the composer's eldest daughter Eva Paloheimo.)

Aino stuck by her decision and the composer went alone to Stockholm, where he conducted three concerts. These featured not only the première of the new *Fantasia sinfonica*, as it was billed, and the usual old standards, but also the Fifth Symphony. All three concerts were received well, the new work in particular. Constructed in a single, integrated span the *Fantasia* in its twenty or so minutes emulates the topography of a conventional four-movement symphony, with episodes redolent of opening and closing allegros, slow movement and scherzo. Just as each of the symphonies from the Third onwards had been of markedly different character to its predecessors, so the music of the *Fantasia* possessed a nobility of utterance quite at variance with the Sixth Symphony, or indeed with the extrovert heroism of the Fifth. One of the *Fantasia*'s most striking features is the role assigned to a solo trombone. Leaving aside that for obviously colouristic effect, Sibelius had been sparing in his use of solo instruments in key roles in his orchestral works, the clarinet at the start of the First Symphony, and the cello in the Fourth and *The Oceanides* being perhaps the most notable examples. In the *Fantasia*, the trombone is entrusted with the long, majestic theme in C major which serves as a distillation or encapsulation of the whole conception. The grandeur of both the theme and the work as a whole quickly persuaded him that it really was a symphony in a single movement; by August, when he was arranging concerts in Bergen and Copenhagen, he proposed including it as Symphony No. 7, and it was under this title that it was published.

August 1924 saw two other events of personal importance to him –
early in the month the melancholy news of Busoni's death (which had
occurred on 27 July) reached him, and at its end his favourite
daughter Katarina, by then returned from Stuttgart, married Eero
Ilves in Tuusula. The next month, he was off – again alone – to
Copenhagen and Malmö to conduct a total of six concerts. These
went well, but towards the end of the tour Sibelius reached a state
euphemistically described as nervous exhaustion, although alcohol
poisoning would be nearer the mark. He pleaded with Aino to join
him in the Danish capital, redoubling his efforts after a doctor had
advised him to refrain from conducting – for the sake of his heart, the
hypochondriac composer claimed later – and to take a rest cure in
Italy. After much hesitation, Aino agreed; Sibelius slowly drank away
his fee and a payment from Hansen waiting for her, but then she
changed her mind. Sibelius returned to Ainola.

Sibelius now entered a fallow period with no major project to
occupy his mind. Nor was there any major commission in prospect.
At the turn of the new year (1925), he was still kicking his heels,
besieged by self-doubt and bemoaning how his music was
misunderstood to his diary. 'How little the public and the critics
realize what I have given them … My time will come.' He occupied
himself with trifles, a *Morceau romantique* on a theme by one of
Mannerheim's relatives for a charity concert, some desultory
arrangements, the last of his six melodramas to accompany the
recitation of a poem, *A Lonely Ski-trail*, and a couple of liturgical
items with organ accompaniment. An offer to conduct the new
symphony at the Three Choirs Festival in September cheered him
until Rosa Newmarch confirmed that financial crises in London made
any concerts there out of the question. But on May Day, his luck
turned. Wilhelm Hansen wrote to ask if he had ever written music for
Shakespeare's *The Tempest*, since the Royal Theatre in Copenhagen
wanted to use his music in a production of extraordinary lavishness
planned for the end of the year. The producer was to be Adam
Poulsen, who had previously directed *Scaramouche*. Sibelius replied
that he had not, but the idea fired his imagination, especially when
the Theatre pressed him to undertake the commission. Poulsen
provided the composer with a translation of the play (it was to be
spoken in Danish) and a detailed scheme which involved thirty-four

pieces of music, ranging from the briefest snatches of music lasting a handful of seconds, to fuller-scale movements of four minutes' length or more. At the start, the entire first scene was to be replaced by a musical depiction of the tempest itself, for which Sibelius created perhaps the most vivid example of orchestral onomatopoeia ever penned. The score, his largest to have survived after *Kullervo* and *Scaramouche*, teemed with invention, reflecting the kaleidoscopic range of the play itself, from the terrific opening storm music, to the exquisite delicacy of that for Prospero's daughter Miranda, to the uncouth, dangerous rusticity of Caliban. The spirit Ariel was represented by various songs, short depictions where he flies on and off stage, and a fine miniature where he takes the shape of an oak tree playing a flute.

Sibelius completed the score during the summer but for a variety of reasons the first night was delayed until March 1926. The production itself prompted mixed reactions, but both the décor and the music were accorded the greatest praise. Indeed the reputation of the music's dramatic effectiveness quickly became known outside Denmark. In Germany, the young conductor of the Berlin Philharmonic Orchestra Wilhelm Furtwängler took the Prelude with him on tour to North America the following year. Sibelius later told Hansen that 'In the music for *The Tempest* there are a mass of motives which I would liked to have developed more exhaustively but which within the bounds of the play, I had to content myself with merely sketching'; it was largely the power of suggestion generated by the concision of the best of the pieces that created such an impact. He never attempted to forge anything larger, to 'develop more exhaustively' these motives, contenting himself with extracting for publication a slightly shortened version of the Prelude, and two concert suites, some of which telescoped otherwise distinct items.

Sibelius did not attend the première in Copenhagen, even though he had arranged to sail from Turku to Stettin (now Szczecîn) at almost the same time. The reason for this avoidance lay in another new commission, this time from Walter Damrosch and the New York Philharmonic, for a fifteen to twenty-minute symphonic poem for the 1926–7 concert season. This had arrived by telegram just after the New Year when he had recovered from the celebrations for his sixtieth birthday. Sibelius had wanted to go to Italy to avoid any fuss, but this

Following page, poster for the lavish Finnish production of Shakespeare's *The Tempest* using a slightly extended version of Sibelius's incidental music, in November 1927. The role of Ariel was taken by the composer's daughter, Ruth.

Myrsky

(The Tempest)

5-näytöksinen näytelmä, (9-kuvaelmaa.) Kirjoittanut *William Shakespeare*. Suomentanut *P. Cajander*. Säveltänyt *Jean Sibelius*. Ohjannut *Pekka Alpo*. Näyttämökoristeet ja puvut suunnitellut *Matti Warén*. Tanssit järjestänyt ja harjoittanut *Maggie Gripenberg*.

HENKILÖT:

Alonzo, Neapelin kuningas . . . . *Jussi Snellman*

Sebastian, hänen veljensä . . . . *Aku Korhonen*

Prospero, Milanon laillinen herttua . . . . . . *Urho Somersalmi*

Antonio, hänen veljensa, Milanon herttua-

vallan anastaja . . . . *Eero Kilpi*

Ferdinand, Neapelin kuninkaan poika . . . . *Urho Seppälä*

Gonzalo, vanha rehellinen valtaneuvos . . . *Hemmo Kallio*

Caliban, kuvaton metsäläis-orja . . . . *Aarne Leppänen*

Trinculo, ilvehtijä . . . . *Ilmari Unho*

Stephano, juopunut juomanlaskija . . . . . . *Yrjö Tuominen*

Laivamies . . . . *Uuno Montonen*

Miranda, Prosperon tytär . . . . *Aili Somersalmi*

Ariel, ilmahenki . . . . *Ruth Snellman*

Iris ⎫   ⎧ *Heidi Korhonen*

Ceres ⎬ henkiä . . . . ⎨ *Tyyne Juntto*

Juno ⎭   ⎩ *Glory Leppänen*

Henkiä, (Maggie Gripenbergin oppilaita) Prosperon palveluksessa olevia. Hoviherroja ja laivamiehiä.

Väliajat IV, VII ja VIII kuvaelman jälkeen.

SUOMEN KANSALLISTEATTERIN JA SUOMEN NÄYTTELIJÄLIITON ELÄKERAHASTOJA SOPII AINA AVUSTAA proved impractical. In the event, Kajanus arranged several concerts, the composer was awarded the Grand Cross of the Order of the White Rose, one of his country's highest honours, his annual pension was increased more than threefold from 30,000 to 100,000 marks and in addition he received over a quarter of a million marks from a public collection. Of this, 125,000 marks was invested to generate a regular income, the rest was given over to him. Italy now beckoned so that he could work on the new piece. Aino planned to accompany him (there were no conducting engagements and the public aspect of his alcoholism seems to have been in check for the time being), but this plan was scuppered by the insistent presence of his childhood friend, Walter von Konow, who wanted to gatecrash the expedition. Sibelius went by himself in the end in March, but von Konow managed to catch up with him in Rome at the end of the month, much to the composer's irritation. None the less, Sibelius managed to get to grips with the music, and alighted on the title *Tapiola*, the domain of the forest-god of Finnish legend.

He passed through Berlin on both the outbound and northbound legs of his journey. He met the desperately penurious Adolf Paul on the way south, who had pawned his best clothes to raise money. Sibelius managed to help a little by getting his clothes out of hock but there was little more that he could do. On his return he stayed for a fortnight in the former Imperial capital, working on the symphonic poem and meeting Hellmuth von Hase, head of Breitkopf und Härtel, who were anxious to restore the Finnish master to their fold (and wean him away from Hansen). With the stabilization of the German economy in 1925 they had expanded their activities and had increased the rate of his royalties. They discussed the new work and Sibelius promised the completed score to them. Breitkopf undertook to publish it quickly and produce the parts for the orchestra to play from, though in the event this caused some anxiety for both parties. Having sent the finished piece to Leipzig in August, Sibelius withdrew it in mid September to make cuts. Breitkopf were displeased, as their work was far advanced (perhaps they recalled his complete rewrite of *In memoriam* at proof stage in 1909–10), but sent it back, with two sets of proofs. Sibelius was unable to look at these until after he had conducted what proved to be his last public concert, in Copenhagen, but contented himself with minor changes of no great consequence.

His nervousness over what proved to be his final full orchestral score to have survived is not unlike that he suffered over his very first, thirty-five years before, when he had sent the Overture in E major and 'Ballet Scene' to Kajanus, then begged him not to perform them. It may be that with *Tapiola* the publication of the music before its first performance – which he would not be able to attend – would make it that much more difficult to amend the composition should he later feel the need to do so. As it turned out, his fears were groundless.

From the outset, Sibelius conceived of a representation of the immense Finnish forests for his New York symphonic poem. In this it is reminiscent of his other great American commission, *The Oceanides*, in 1914 and there are certain common points of reference between the two works. Both are vividly orchestrated and impressionistic, though far removed from the delicate sensibilities exhibited by Debussy's and Ravel's works; both contain a darkening of the musical imagery towards the close which ushers in the principal climax of each work. In the case of *Tapiola*, this is expressed in music of terrifying and elemental power; Sibelius had pushed orchestral resource into quite new regions and in this respect at least *Tapiola* was thirty or forty years ahead of its time. Damrosch appreciated its quality, writing to the composer at New Year 1927:

I consider Tapiola *to be one of the most original and fascinating works from your pen. The variety of expression that you give to the one theme in the various episodes, the closely-knit musical structure, the highly original orchestration, and, above all, the poetic imagery of the entire work, are truly marvellous. No one but a Norseman could have written this work. We were all enthralled by the dark pine forests and the shadowy gods and wood-nymphs who dwell therein. The coda with its icy winds sweeping through the forest made us shiver.*

Walter Damrosch, who conducted the first performance of *Tapiola* in New York in 1927

The critics, however, were not so impressed by the novelty. Olin Downes noted the 'powerful atmosphere [which] evokes with extraordinary mastery the deep mysteries of ... the primaeval forest' but thought it 'a work of style and manner rather than inspiration'. Lawrence Gilman in the *New York Herald Tribune* was disappointed that it was not a 'great masterpiece' like the Fourth Symphony. Others found 'signs which indicate that Sibelius's powerful imagination is beginning to run out'. Greater familiarity over the years raised its critical stock rather higher. 'Even if Sibelius had written nothing else,' wrote one of Sibelius's most ardent admirers, Cecil Gray, in the 1930s, 'this one work would be sufficient to entitle him to a place among the greatest masters of all time', a sentiment endorsed a decade further on still by Ralph Wood who declared of that remark: 'It is not an overstatement.'

8

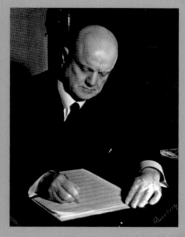

'At the height of his powers':
Sibelius at his work desk
apparently composing in the
1930s

*The thing that has pleased me most is that I
have been able to reject. The greatest labour I
have expended, perhaps, was on works that have
never been completed.*

Jean Sibelius to Karl Ekman

The Silence of Järvenpää 1927–57

With the completion of *Tapiola*, and an additional number for the Finnish National Theatre's production of *The Tempest* in November 1927, Sibelius's major period of productivity – as far as it was perceived by the outside world – came to a close. Although he would live for another thirty years, he released no work of comparable stature to *Tapiola*. This silence, more apparent than real since a stream of smaller items were produced over the next few years, attracted considerable speculation from the late 1920s onward, centred principally on the Eighth Symphony, speculation the composer himself encouraged at first by various pronouncements. He continued to compose into the 1930s but by the end of the decade had effectively ceased, bar one or two minor arrangements (such as of *A Lonely Ski-trail* in 1948).

But in January 1927 there was no question of Sibelius being written out. In fact, his pattern of working continued largely intact from that established at the start of World War I, with instrumental miniatures for violin (with piano or string orchestral accompaniment) and vocal items – such as a large collection for Masonic Ritual – orbiting around the larger potential mass of the Eighth Symphony. To stimulate composition, the composer and his wife went to sniff the cultural air in Paris, a city he found highly convivial – but its musical establishment paid him only scant attention, and rather less regard. A crushing example of the latter took place in June of this same year when, with the composer back in Finland, *Scaramouche* was roundly rubbished at its French première, sending composer and wife into black despondency. At first he was much taken by some of the new music he heard there, particularly an orchestral score by Albert Roussel (perhaps the Second Symphony, or just possibly the Suite in F) and some pieces for two pianos by Florent Schmitt, but after a few weeks grew tired of the over-ripeness and heavily rich textures prevalent in nearly all the works he heard. And while the symphony should have been demanding his attention, he preferred to work on

Sibelius, with his 'most faithful companion' in a caricature by John Minnion

two concert suites from *The Tempest*. In the event, these would not be ready to send to Hansen's until August.

On the way home, Janne and Aino stopped off in Berlin, where the composer renewed contact with both of his German publishers and also Adolf Paul. There, Sibelius was plagued by a racking cough which had developed by the time he returned home into full-blown influenza. This disease, an inconvenience in the world of antibiotics, was still a killer in the 1920s; indeed, a worldwide epidemic during the winter of 1918–19 had caused the deaths of 150,000 in Great Britain, but over 16 million in India.

On 25 April Kajanus finally gave the first performances in Finland of the Seventh Symphony, *Tapiola* and the Prelude from *The Tempest*.

For reasons that are obscure, Kajanus took none of these new pieces to the Nordic Music Festival in Stockholm, but the 'plain and monotonous' (to quote one critic) cantata *Song of the Earth*. The lack of a major score by Finland's acknowledged principal composer was much commented on and served to fuel the composer's intermittent mistrust of Kajanus. As always when things were not going his way, either in the concert hall or on his work desk, Sibelius turned to drink and poured out his feelings of self-pity in his diary.

> *Isolation and loneliness is driving me to despair. Not even my wife is talking to me. Life has been tremendously difficult … In order to survive, I have to have alcohol … And that's where all my troubles begin. Am abused, alone, and all my real friends are dead. My prestige here at present is rock bottom. Impossible to work. If only there were a way out. A sad but deep truth: When things go well, I have plenty of friends and am happy. When things go badly, everyone leaves me alone.*
>
> *Must make the best use of the time I have left … Tried to have an alcohol-free day despite the fact that there is so much annoying me and no one to talk to. Aino said I have only myself to blame for losing all my friends. I lost some when my reputation abroad began to soar and others faded away when I was no longer young and all the rage. In reality all they want is to bask in my reflected glory. Perhaps it is all my fault.*

His hand tremor had been troubling him more and more, though he noted ruefully less so when the 'atmosphere at home is better.' Work on *The Tempest* suites proved a continual torment. 'It's like having to do your homework all over again.'

Towards the end of May Sibelius received the first letter in what would prove to be a correspondence running for nearly three decades from the American critic Olin Downes. However much Sibelius may have felt neglected or kept out of the limelight at home, in Germany and in France, in the Anglo-Saxon countries (Great Britain and the USA, primarily) his music was still regarded very highly. Downes in particular championed his cause with conductors and public alike, and in the fullness of time came to be known as 'Sibelius's Apostle'. To Downes, the Finnish master was the epitome of all that was best in modern music and the rod with which to castigate Stravinsky, whose music he abhorred. Downes wanted Sibelius to conduct in North

America, but for all that this had been his great dream of a decade before, now the idea was out of the question. He had not conducted in public for several years, his tremor, alcoholism and lack of self-confidence were obstacles that could not be overcome. And there was the Eighth Symphony. But it took until the middle of August before Sibelius cabled that he could not consider such a tour 'at the present moment'. Downes was not to be so easily put off; if he could not get

'Sibelius's Apostle', the American critic Olin Downes. Downes's committed advocacy of Sibelius helped elevate the Finn to the position of 'most popular living composer' in a poll of New York Philharmonic concertgoers, but attracted equally partisan detractors, such as Virgil Thomson and Theodor Adorno.

his composer to the USA to present his works he continued to canvass the best conductors to do so instead. He achieved some spectacular successes: Leopold Stokowski had already programmed several Sibelius scores, including the Fifth Symphony, but now Downes went to work on the expatriate Russian Serge Koussevitzky in Boston. In the meantime, the budding apostle paid Sibelius a visit during a prolonged European tour. The latter received him cordially in a Helsinki hotel and proceeded to drink his visitor under the table.

In February 1928 Sibelius was back in Berlin – this time alone – for his annual foreign trip. His letters home reveal that he was again working on more than one piece, though their identity is unclear. Certainly one was the symphony, but alongside it he was probably sketching ideas for what would prove to be his last published sets of miniatures, the *Five Esquisses* for piano, Four Pieces and Three Pieces, both for violin with piano (Opp. 114–16), as well as a short Suite for violin and strings, eventually printed in 1995 as Op. 117. None of these pieces would see the light of day until the following year, however, and the suite was marked almost immediately as 'to be reworked'. The final known example of Sibelius's bland, note-spinning manner, in quality the suite's three movements lie somewhere between the anonymous doodling of the *Suites mignonne, champêtre* and *caractéristique* on the one hand and the inspired writing of the Humoresques. And with thoughts of solo violin pieces uppermost in his mind, it was singly appropriate that Wilhelm Furtwängler, chief conductor of the Berlin Philharmonic Orchestra, should conduct the Violin Concerto on 9 March, with Ferenc von Vecsay as soloist. The critical reception was not good: one typical review echoed Joseph Joachim's verdict at the 1905 première in finding it 'boring'.

During the summer, another distraction away from the symphony came from Sibelius's Masonic colleague, Wäino Sola, who on 25 September was to give the first public performance of the *Masonic Ritual Music* (Op. 113). Sola's idea was for a new orchestral work – perhaps a symphony – to inaugurate the completion of the Imatra Hydro-electric Station, built to harness the natural power of the Falls which fascinated the composer. (In 1911, when Sibelius took Rosa Newmarch to Imatra, she had thought that he seemed to be trying to capture in his head the fundamental sound made by the water's constant roaring, like a huge sustained 'pedal' note on the piano – or the orchestra. Sibelius used these 'pedals', a marked feature of his orchestration, as platforms on which he constructed his major compositions.) No official commission was ever made, although several letters were exchanged between Sibelius, Sola and Malmi, the chief engineer at Imatra. The composer was initially interested, but true to form quickly changed his mind even though Sola took him out to see the station for himself in the hope of making him change it back. On the way back, Sola and Sibelius stopped for a picnic. Having opened a bottle of wine, they realized they had not brought any glasses with them, so Sola made some cups from note paper. The first one given to Sibelius did not last long: his hand tremor was so severe he crushed the cup, showering wine everywhere. An 'Imatra Symphony' was never to be written.

By 1929 the fragile balance between the different cultural and political groupings in Finland was under severe strain, and finally began to break down, unleashing a period of civil disorder. The language problems of the nineteenth century between ethnic Finn and Fenno-Swede had been simmering with increasing heat since independence. The Finnish tongue had achieved constitutional parity with Swedish in all administrative and educational areas, but the numerically superior Finnish-speakers now demanded dominance. Sibelius heartily disapproved of the conflict, believing staunchly in a 'one nation, two cultures' policy, and was dismayed by the 'coarseness' of the Finnish lobby. But other, darker forces were coming to the surface that cut across ethno-cultural lines, echoing the political polarization that was rife in continental Europe. The old battle-lines of White and Red had never been properly solved and throughout the 1920s Communist agitators, led by Arvo Tuominen, stirred up the conservative elements into a rabid fury. The explosion occurred at Lapua, a market-town in Ostrobothnia where a rally of 400 red-shirted members of the Young Workers' Educational Association was violently disrupted and broken up by an impromptu popular rising of local people.

The 'Lapua movement', as it has become known, was dedicated to the eradication of Communism from Finland and appealed across a wide spectrum of Finnish society. At its root, Lapua was militantly pro-Finnish as were the majority in the language dispute, but anti-Soviet feeling had outstripped anti-Swedish sentiment. Farm workers, clerics, teachers, industrialists, military officers, intellectuals and academics were all swept along in the early stages, even such public figures like Mannerheim and Sibelius, the latter for once not avoiding to take a conscious political stance. In 1930 the Lapua movement's leader Kosola organized a 'Peasants' March' on Helsinki with the aim of coercing the government into anti-Communist legislation. This attracted huge support and the government duly presented proposals to the Eduskunta to legally curb the Communists' freedom of action. The Parliament, led by the Social Democrats who Lapua believed were merely fronting for the Red faction, rejected the proposals.

Lapua's response was to indulge in several high-profile stunts, such as abducting prominent socialists (including former President Ståhlberg and his wife), and driving them to the Soviet border where they were handed over to the bewildered Russian guards. However, lack of governmental action resulted in an escalation of illiberalism and violence, such as the assault on the Social Democrat Speaker of the Eduskunta, Väinö Hakkila. These acts lost the movement a great deal of its liberal support, and proved too much for the likes of Mannerheim and Sibelius. The final throw occurred in 1932 when the increasingly marginalized Lapua hardliners vainly attempted a coup and occupied Mäntsälä, a suburb of the capital. Astutely placed army detachments and a radio broadcast from President Svinhufvud persuaded the rebels to disarm and disband, but from the ashes of Lapua arose the Fascist 'Patriotic Peoples Front' (whose initials in Finnish were IKL).

Economic crises had contributed to the groundswell of Lapua's popularity. Despite large-scale government investment in projects such as the construction, completed in 1929, of the Arctic Highway between Rovaniemi, the capital of Finnish Lapland, and Liinahamari, the ice-free port on the Barents Sea (acquired with Petsamo by treaty from the Soviet Union in 1920), Finland had still been in the process of recovering from World War I when hit by the ensuing worldwide economic depression that followed in the wake of the Wall Street Crash. Unemployment, widespread insolvency triggering the sale of property – particularly in the agricultural sector – which in turn proved so extensive that some banks were forced to merge in order to survive, the fall of timber prices and the rise in the cost of living plunged the country into chaos. And the language problem still rumbled on fitfully, even provoking isolated riots between groups of students, and would only peter out in the 1950s. (Sickan Park, Cultural Attaché at the Finnish Embassy in London in the mid 1990s, was born into a Swedish-speaking family. She recalled how as a schoolgirl she and others would often be pelted with stones by Finnish children on her way to the local Swedish-language school.)

Against this backdrop of constant political turmoil and increased financial uncertainty, Sibelius continued his struggle with the new symphony. His personal circumstances continued much as before, although there was never enough money. With the marriages of his daughters Katarina and Heidi to the brothers Armas and Yrjö Blomstedt (the former changed his name to Jussi Jalas in 1945) in 1929 and 1932 respectively, his outgoings had reduced and so he was able to avoid the undignified churning out of insubstantial pieces to raise funds. The Swedish composer Wilhelm Stenhammar, who had done sterling service to Sibelius's cause in Gothenburg, had died in 1927; two years later, Aino's mother Elisabeth also passed away. As usual Sibelius did not attend the funerals, but in March 1931 he was forced to break his rule to act as pall-bearer for his erstwhile 'Symposium' confederate Axel Gallen-Kallela. Sibelius had agreed additionally to provide a short commemorative organ piece for the artist, but then tried unsuccessfully to withdraw from the promise. In the event, he produced the short *Surusoitto* ('Funeral Music', Op. 111, No. 2 – published with another short organ miniature from 1925), which it is believed was derived, according to the composer Joonas Kokkonen, from the slow movement of the Eighth Symphony (a contention supported by Aino in her final years). These were melancholy times for the composer as colleagues and friends steadily went to their graves: before the year was out, so had the other pre-eminent symphonist from the Nordic world, Carl Nielsen. The two composers had never struck up the kind of personal relationship that had existed between Sibelius and Stenhammar. Although each man greatly respected the other's work, the relationship for both was tempered by feelings of potential rivalry.

Further distractions were provided by visitors, not least the conductor Basil Cameron who persuaded Sibelius to conduct in Britain – Sibelius characteristically withdrew from this arrangement shortly afterwards – and Cecil Gray. The latter became the composer's

first biographer in English and proved as staunch a supporter in
Britain as Downes was in the USA. Gray wrote of his meetings – one
of which started at lunch and broke up at seven o'clock the next
morning – with Sibelius:

> *The intellectual feast he spreads before his guests is … magnificent; …*
> *of himself and his work he speaks diffidently and unwillingly. One quickly*
> *realizes that he prefers to discuss any and every other subject on earth, and*
> *does – literature, philosophy, psychology, painting, politics, science … To*

This concert saw only the
second British performance
of *Luonnotar*, written for and
given its first performance at
the Three Choirs Festival in
Gloucester twenty-one years
earlier.

QUEEN'S HALL
LONDON
Sole Lessees - - Messrs. Chappell & Co., Ltd.

THE
FINNISH NATIONAL ORCHESTRA

Conductor   -   GEORG SCHNÉEVOIGT

Soloist :
HELMI LIUKKONEN
(Soprano)

Monday,
June 4th, 1934

Programme

give any adequate idea of all the wisdom and wit – enigmatic, gnomic, aphoristic, paradoxical – which flows from Sibelius on such occasions would be impossible.

Between 1930 and 1933, the first recordings of the symphonies began to be issued in state-funded releases from The Sibelius Society in London, conducted mainly by Kajanus (though Georg Schnéevoigt and Koussevitzky also contributed). Successful as these were, still uppermost in the minds of all the commentators on Sibelius was the matter of the Eighth Symphony. Already by the close of 1928, Koussevitzky in Boston and Hansen in Denmark had written to enquire after the work's progress. Over the following four years this interest rose to a clamour. In mid April 1931 Sibelius made his last trip outside Finland to Berlin, to concentrate on the work, which he had promised to Koussevitzky. A letter to Aino on 22 May gives details about the symphony and other concerns.

Am worried about the political situation. How are things at home? … Here I am living in my music. Am engrossed in my work – but anxiety about everything gets me down … My plan is to stay on until the end of June … The symphony is making great strides and I must get it finished while I am still in full spiritual vigour. It's strange, this work's conception.

Work was interrupted in May when the composer was admitted into a clinic with a stomach complaint, although the doctor believed that Sibelius had also been suffering from pleurisy, and he was prescribed injections of an experimental drug, Eutonan. Back in Finland in the summer, the composer promised the European première to Cameron. On 20 August Sibelius wrote to Koussevitzky 'In the event of your wishing to perform my new symphony next spring [i.e. 1932], this will, I hope, be possible.' Yet one month later when Olin Downes asked to be sent a copy of the score at his expense, Sibelius's response was tart indeed: 'Regret very much having told of my eighth symphony [sic] not yet finished'.

A cat-and-mouse game ensued over the next eighteen months, with the composer alternately blowing hot and cold about releasing the new work, which was presumably in at the very least a near-complete state, and the conductor arranging, cancelling and re-arranging the

The conductor Serge
Koussevitzky, to whom
Sibelius on several occasions
promised the première of
the elusive Eighth Symphony

première. Matters came to a head in the early summer of 1932. Sibelius
wrote to Koussevitzky offering Symphony No. 8 for an October
première in Boston. He would send a hand-written score, probably in
order for him to keep a tighter control over the piece than had been
the case with *Tapiola*. The delighted Russian, who was planning to
programme all of the symphonies for the 1932–3 season, rapidly
arranged a second performance of the Eighth Symphony in New York
for November and started advertising both concerts. Downes wrote
for details so he could prepare programme notes. Suddenly, Sibelius
froze and in July told Koussevitzky not to advertise any performance;
though whether this arose from the thought of the publicity, Downes's

increasingly strident claims which would place a heavy burden of expectation on the new piece, or his own hyper-criticality about this 'strange conception', is not clear. After months of negotiation, the première was re-fixed to crown the Boston season – and Koussevitzky's Sibelius series – for April 1933. But in January of that year with repeated enquiries from the USA about the score's readiness, Sibelius backed out again: 'Regret impossible this season.'

Although later that year Sibelius did send part of, if not the whole, score to his copyist, this was the closest the Eighth Symphony came to a public hearing. Koussevitzky became resigned to the fact that the work would not appear (though he remained ready to play it at the drop of a hat). He continued to conduct Sibelius's other works regularly – including a recording in London of the Seventh Symphony in 1933 and in Helsinki at the opening concert of the 1935 Sibelius Festival, held in honour of the composer's seventieth birthday. Downes, however, who had invested a considerable amount of his personal reputation in promoting Sibelius (and through whose efforts the Finn's music was played so widely he was voted the most popular living composer in a 1935 New York Philharmonic Society poll), was less inclined to let the matter drop. On his fourth visit to Finland, in 1936, he pressed the composer insistently about the Eighth Symphony. As Downes himself reported later, Sibelius's evasive replies grew increasingly tense:

> *He muttered a few inconsequential words. His face assumed a most unhappy expression. Then he turned to me in frustration. 'Ich kann nicht!', burst out in German and he gave a deep sigh. He will not speak about his work before it is ready.*

But if no new score was available from his pen, several old and long-forgotten ones had emerged during 1935, his seventieth-birthday year and the centenary of the *Kalevala*. Robert Kajanus, the earliest and – despite Sibelius's recurrent fears that his old friend had been trying to do him down – longest-serving of his champions, had died two years before. Amongst his papers were found the two *Lemminkäinen* tone-poems, *Lemminkäinen and the Maidens of Saari* and *Lemminkäinen in Tuonela*, that had been suppressed at the turn of the century. Sibelius permitted performances of these, and the large third movement of the

Kullervo symphony, as part of the *Kalevala* celebrations. The *Lemminkäinen* pieces were eventually published by Breitkopf und Härtel in 1954, but *Kullervo* remained under interdict. In the festival devoted to Sibelius at the end of 1935, Hofmannstahl's play *Jedermann* was revived featuring the score written in 1916, as well as his daughter Ruth in the role of Paramour. And at the special gala event, Sibelius's official status as a 'national symbol' required the attendance of all the Presidents of Finland since independence – with the exception of the then current incumbent Svinhufvud who was ill. A good deal of attention was paid to the composer abroad, particularly in Scandinavia, Britain and the USA, where performances were constantly increasing, and also in Germany, where Hitler bestowed on him the Reich's foremost arts award, the Goethe medal.

As Europe slowly slid during the late 1930s towards World War II, so an inevitable reaction set in against Sibelius's music. The committed advocacy of critics like Gray and the composer Constant Lambert in Britain, and of Downes and others in the USA, began to become self-defeating. This was in part due to intellectual arguments within the critical establishment over the relative merits of the leading living composers, of whom Sibelius and Stravinsky led the way. But in the USA, in the wake of the Jewish mass emigration from Nazi Germany, a third figure emerged who drew even more fanatical attention from his admirers, and detestation from Downes: Arnold Schoenberg. The pro-Stravinsky and pro-Schoenberg camps were united in their castigation of Sibelius as a reactionary nationalist, refusing to admit that works such as the later symphonies and *Tapiola* were of any merit because of the outmoded forms – symphony, tone-poem – that they employed. Leading the way respectively for each lobby was the composer and critic of the *New York Herald Tribune* Virgil Thomson, and the emigré theorist and Schoenberg pupil Theodor Adorno. Thomson took great glee in besting Downes in print, while Adorno had been incensed by the elevated claims made in a book by Bengt de Törne for Sibelius's stature in world art, with comparisons to Beethoven, Dante and Velázquez. Sibelius became a cultural football kicked around between these unyielding aesthetic prejudices: on the one hand Downes's evangelism for mass culture, communicated primarily via the radio, of which Sibelius was a cornerstone, and on the other the espousal by Adorno, who hated

Opposite, the Finnish Pavilion, designed by Alvar Aalto, at the New York World Fair, 1939, for which Sibelius conducted his *Andante festivo* in a live relay from Helsinki, and Bax composed his Seventh Symphony

radio, of Schoenberg's dictum, 'If it is art, it is not for all, and if it is
for all, it is not art.' Downes's gimmick in coaxing the composer out
of retirement to conduct in Helsinki the *Andante festivo* for string
orchestra – composed in 1922 for string quartet and arranged eight
years later – for a live radio relay on New Year's Day 1939, was grist to
the mill for both sides. Yet through it all, Sibelius's music remained as
popular with audiences as it had been, and the dichotomy between
critical and popular evaluation, at least in the Anglo-Saxon world,
maintained largely unaltered for the next half-century. Finland's heroic
but short-lived defence against the Soviet Union in the Winter War of
1939–40 once more turned the spotlight on the composer as 'national
symbol'. Requests were made for the Eighth Symphony, including one
from the Royal Philharmonic Society to raise money for the Finnish
Red Cross.

But if the squabbling of critics failed to affect the audience's esteem
in the slightest, another event – just as irrelevant to the actual quality
of the music – did, if only for a brief period. His seventy-fifth
birthday that year was celebrated around the world with
unprecedented enthusiasm, so another falling-off of performances was
to be expected. But in June 1941 Nazi Germany launched Operation
Barbarossa and invaded Russia, while providing military support to
Finland, who now – in the Continuation War of 1941–4 – reclaimed
her lost territory and pressed on to conquer land to which she had no
legal right. Sibelius was induced in July to present his country's case in
newspaper articles in the Allied countries, but to little avail. Britain
bombed the Arctic port of Petsamo, held by German troops 'for
Finland' and declared war a few months later. In the USA, still
ostensibly neutral, there were calls for Sibelius's music to be barred
from performance. Consequently the composer's royalties evaporated,
and while performances of his works resumed after the end of the war,
it was not until 1954 that the non-payment of his American royalties
was satisfactorily resolved.

The early 1940s were a dark time for the composer. His son-in-law
Arvi Paloheimo, with whom he had broken his abstinence from
alcohol during the previous world war, died in March 1940.
Continuing press censorship and draconian government control
depressed him greatly. In 1942 even members of the Eduskunta,
antipathetic to the dependence on German arms, were imprisoned for

Finnish troops retaking Viipuri from the Soviets, 2 August 1941

treason. In late 1943 Sibelius took up his diary again, recording there his disgust at creeping anti-Semitism and of a burgeoning sense of tragedy. He wrote that 'a heaviness of spirit paralyses me. The reason? Alone, alone. I cannot let myself tell of my great sorrow. Aino must be protected … But am I to blame? No.' The cause of this despair seems to have been occasioned by the growing presence of the Nazis, though he was aware that in order to keep Communism at bay, such pacts with 'barbarism' were essential. He was also concerned that Nazi racial theorists might be interested in his ethnic origins, and cursed Karl Ekman's 1935 biography which had given details of his ancestry. He was, however, cheered by hearing a broadcast from Britain of Vaughan Williams's Fifth Symphony which, as with that by Bax ten years earlier, had been dedicated to him. The gloom which had been lifted by Vaughan Williams's 'civilized and humane' manner, 'like a caress from a summer world' descended again when he learned of the death of Adolf Paul. With every year he grew more alone, with only Aino still with him from his youth.

The years 1944 and 1945 were still more difficult: the Soviet Union, having repulsed the Nazi armies besieging Leningrad (formerly St Petersburg) the previous year, now turned on Finland which quickly sued for peace. The Finns were required to turn their guns on their erstwhile allies and run the Germans out of the north. The Germans retaliated with a scorched earth policy in Lapland of unimaginable ferocity before being defeated in early 1945. Finland lost her access to the Barents Sea, her second city of Viipuri and huge swathes of Karelia, so joyously occupied three years before by the advocates of a 'Greater Finland'. The loss of Karelia deprived Finland of one-third of her hydro-electric potential, over a tenth of her productive forests, a little less of her arable area and a quarter of her chemical production. The losses of land in the two wars alone resulted in the relocation of over 400,000 Karelians (ethnic Finns) within the reduced land area of Finland.

After the war, Sibelius's life began to settle into the quiet rhythm of retirement and seclusion. The Eighth Symphony still weighed on his mind, and enquiries about it would still arrive from time to time. In 1945 he told Basil Cameron, and his own secretary of seven years, Santeri Levas, that the Eighth had been 'finished many times', but was still not ready. The carrot of this last masterpiece was deliberately left dangling for the remainder of his life, but for himself the composer had come to a decision about this work, of which hardly any details

'The bald-headed titan of later years': Sibelius in 1935 sitting for the sculptor Vaino Aaltonen

survive. As Aino was to tell Erik Tawaststjerna, during the 1940s (between March and August 1945 if Levas's recollections are to be believed) Sibelius burned a laundry basket full of manuscripts 'on the open fire in the dining room. Parts of the *Karelia Suite* were destroyed – I later saw remains of the pages which had been torn out – and many other things. I did not have the strength to be present and left the room. I therefore do not know what he threw on to the fire. But after this my husband became calmer and gradually lighter in mood. It was a happy time.' Given that a large number of the principal works of his youth have survived, usually in the collections of museums or libraries beyond his reach, it would seem likely that what went into the fire were compositions of more recent provenance. (He once remarked to Levas that had he 'published everything that [he] had written, the catalogue of [his] works would have been a great deal longer – in the region of one hundred and eighty opus numbers.') It would seem that the Eighth Symphony, which for the best part of two decades had tormented its creator and tantalized the outside world, also perished in the flames. Yet even as the constant stream of enquiries about the work persisted into the 1950s, the composer still maintained the pretence that he was working on it in his head.

Why did the composer destroy this work, which had cost him such labour and heartache? A huge array of theories have been proposed over the years to explain this decision, which to many people has remained inexplicable. One of the commonest, especially amongst critics who were not supporters of his music, was that he had at last written himself out, that there never was an Eighth Symphony on paper. Others have claimed that his hand tremor, whether occasioned by years of alcoholism or an ailment such as Parkinson's disease, made it physically next-to-impossible to write. Sibelius's letters from this time would seem to support this view, usually being typed – either by Aino or one of his secretaries, since the composer himself had a tendency to mistreat typewriters to such an extent that they collapsed – and signed by him using something very like a child's crayon (whose thick point obscured the shakiness of his hand). Yet it is clear now that the symphony was, in fact, complete in all essentials in the early 1930s, so his suppression of the score was made on qualitative grounds, not quantitative.

Aino believed that her husband's 'rigorous self-criticism' was the work's undoing. At first glance, this sits uneasily with the production of the vacuous suites for small orchestra of the early 1920s. But in this respect Sibelius was somewhat schizophrenic creatively, and did not apply the same criteria to a work like the *Suite mignonne* as he did to a symphony. After the protracted gestations of the Fifth and Sixth, and by implication the Seventh which was only made possible when its predecessors had been finalized, the birth of the Eighth was always likely to be difficult. His doubts over *Tapiola* and desire to cut it were outflanked by the publisher's rapid issue of the printed score, otherwise it, too, might have joined the Eighth in the pyre in the front room of Ainola. Perhaps the very nature of the symphony, its 'strange conception', gave him more cause for concern than with any of his previous pieces. *Tapiola* had advanced orchestral tone painting to a point beyond which he dare not proceed, just as the Fourth Symphony had done with tonality in 1911; the Fifth's charting of a new type of classicism had given him five years of toil and engendered a good deal of misunderstanding in the critical fraternity. It may be that the Eighth, so eagerly anticipated by a worldwide admiring audience, would have taken another new tack about which the hypersensitive composer no longer possessed sufficient strength of will to outface his detractors.

Opposite, Sibelius in retirement in the grounds of Ainola

By 1950 even the redoubtable Olin Downes had given up hope of ever seeing Sibelius's final symphony appear, so he switched his tack to the Finn's very first – *Kullervo*. Downes had been shown the score on a pre-war visit by Arvi Paloheimo, with whom the American had struck up a solid friendship, and allowed to study it for 'a few hours late one night in his apartment'. Having then only recently discovered that its highly self-critical composer had relented a little in permitting part of it to be played, Downes had formulated elaborate plans to launch the work, perhaps as a surrogate eighth Sibelius symphony, in the USA. He proposed a full American performance during the tour that year of the Finnish Polytech Choir, with Arturo Toscanini enlisted to conduct the work in a concert to be broadcast live on radio. He was even considering arranging for an American publisher to print the score. In fact, the Polytech Choir had already broached the idea with the composer – and been rejected – months prior to Downes's request. The American could not yet let the matter quite lie, and was able to

extract a photographic copy of the score for his pains, but there was
no question of the work being released for public hearing. That only
became possible, against Sibelius's express wish (which he became
resigned to having contravened), after his death when his son-in-
law Jussi Jalas gave a new première of the entire symphony on 12
June 1958.

Although there is no longer any tangible evidence that Sibelius was
active as a composer in the final two dozen years of his life (assuming
1933 to be the last period of sustained work on the Eighth Symphony),
he was not completely silent either. No new original work of any scale
came from his pen, but a very small number of arrangements did,
including the use of alternative texts for the choral *Finlandia Hymn*
(itself an extract of the big tune from the tone-poem's central episode),
minor additions to the *Masonic Ritual Music* in 1946, and the
orchestration of a handful of songs plus the melodrama *A Lonely Ski-
trail*. Commissions still came his way from time to time, as in 1949
from the Royal Philharmonic Society for a work to be given its first
performance at the 1951 Festival of Britain. Sibelius declined all such
offers, for with the immolation of the Eighth Symphony he had
irrevocably turned his back on original creation.

One of the most bizarre aspects of the final few years of Sibelius's
life after World War II was his unique role as a cultural ambassador
for his country who barely ever set foot outside his door. The Finnish
governments from 1945 were anxious to cast off the stigma of
collaboration with the Nazis during the war and being the stool-
pigeons of the Soviets afterwards. Cultural activities assumed as
important a role as political ones in the reinvestment of national
respectability, as in 1952 with the hosting of the Olympic Games in
Helsinki, the completion of war reparation payments to the Soviet
Union and the coronation of Armi Kuusela as 'Miss Universe'. The
popularity of Sibelius's music in the concert hall and on record helped
to keep Finland in the public eye, and at home he became a regular
attraction for dignitaries visiting the country. Sometimes there would
be several in a single day; on one occasion in 1953 the conductor
Eugene Ormandy and most of the Philadelphia Orchestra turned up!

Sibelius accepted this unofficial role without demur – although
the visits of official delegations from the Soviet Composers' Union
required a special fortitude. The young composer Einojuhani

Rautavaara was a not infrequent visitor to Ainola in the composer's last two years, by virtue of being able to drive. (Sibelius had recommended him for a scholarship in the USA after having heard some of his earliest pieces.) An incidental task of Rautavaara's duties as an assistant librarian for the Helsinki Philharmonic was the ferrying – in his mother's car – of visitors to Sibelius's villa. Rautavaara recalls a particularly trying visit when the nonagenarian composer had to stand politely listening to an interminable speech by the Russian delegation leader, Yurii Shaporin:

> *The expression on his [Sibelius's] face reminded me of something that I could not place. He wasn't smiling, I wondered, 'Why doesn't he smile?' And then I remembered some pictures I saw during the war, when Mannerheim got a visit from Hitler, in 1943 … the war was going rather badly and Hitler wanted to keep Finland in line … And the face of Mannerheim – who never liked Germans and especially Hitler and the Nazis – had that same look as Sibelius's with the Russians.*

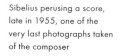

Sibelius perusing a score, late in 1955, one of the very last photographs taken of the composer

There was an even less welcome visitor two days before Christmas in 1952, when a burglar broke into Ainola and stole a small amount of cash. This incident was quite deliberately not reported widely since it was feared it would damage Finland's still fragile image in the world, but the composer himself was incensed by the invasion of his privacy. Levas reports that the 87-year-old composer took it as a personal insult and even briefly considered emigrating. He was prevailed on to stay without too much difficulty and security at Ainola was greatly improved.

Sibelius died of a stroke on 20 September 1957. At the time, Sir Malcolm Sargent – who had consulted the composer the evening before – was conducting the Fifth Symphony in a broadcast performance from Helsinki. Aino even considered turning on the radio to see if his own music might cause her husband to rally. His last reported words were 'Eva and Kaj', in acknowledgement of his daughters' arrival by his bedside. He was accorded a state funeral in the capital ten days later – Rautavaara was one of several young composers who acted as pall-bearers – at which, as he had foreseen in 1909, *In memoriam*, amongst other works, was performed. His body was borne back to Järvenpää and interred in the garden of Ainola. His widow survived him by almost twelve years, dying two months short of her ninety-eighth birthday on 8 June 1969. She too was buried at Ainola, alongside her husband, her name being inscribed unobtrusively along the edge of the massive stone memorial to the composer for whom she had endured so much.

Epilogue

Few composers have come to be seen, in the fullness of time, as the very embodiment of their country. In the older nation-states of Europe the cultural heritage is too diverse for any one figure, even of the stature of Beethoven, Mozart or Berlioz, to be cast in such a role. It could be argued that in a country such as England, Elgar and Vaughan Williams came close to fulfilling just such a position, though only fleetingly. A parallel case might be provided by the Norwegian Edvard Grieg – like Sibelius, unquestionably the greatest composer to have originated in his native country. But Grieg's music does not evince any particularly close connection to the land, and in the end this is perhaps the distinguishing feature of Sibelius's best music: an elemental power that seems to have sprung fully grown from the glacial boulders, lakes and forests of the Finnish landscape. And yet there is also in the later, less narrative tone-poems and the last three symphonies a more abstract quality that has rendered them intelligible in regions remote from the north of Europe.

For one of the most long-lived amongst major composers, Sibelius's mature career was, relatively, extremely short. All of the major utterances which entered the general repertoire and on which his reputation was founded were created within just over one-third of his life, starting with the original version of *En saga* in 1892 and concluding with *Tapiola* in 1926, a period of just thirty-four years. This is broadly commensurate with the compositional life-spans of, say, Beethoven, Brahms and Grieg, if one omits their apprentice efforts. In Sibelius's case, though, the true picture should include at least *Kullervo*, begun in 1891 and for so long suppressed, as well as the abortive Eighth Symphony (1926–33), which would extend his career by another eight years.

As became increasingly clear throughout his life, Sibelius – like Mahler – was first and foremost a symphonist. Whereas others who have specialized in this genre, like Beethoven and Shostakovich, put their most intimate and personal writing into the medium of the string quartet, reserving the symphony for public statements, Sibelius made the symphony the vehicle of his most profound thought. As far as can now be judged, he made eleven attempts at the genre. The first was the student effort composed whilst in Vienna and which broke down after only two movements (the Overture in E and 'Ballet Scene') were complete, the last, the eighth to be numbered, destroyed in 1945. His earliest conception of the symphony as a musical form was of a programmatic or narrative cast, in marked contrast to the mostly abstract designs expounded from Symphony No. 3 (1906–7) onwards. In this, he followed the line adopted by Richard Strauss (derived ultimately from Liszt) in writing symphonic poems. *Kullervo* was called quite rightly a symphony, albeit only in private between the composer and his fiancée, and the *Lemminkäinen* cycle (1893–5) is one in all but name. In his last years he even told Santeri Levas that he had in a way really written nine symphonies, although whether that was how he truly felt about these early attempts or was merely a way of diffusing the disappointment of the non-appearance of the Eighth is anyone's guess.

If it is on the later symphonies that his importance as a composer in the form rests, those of the 1890s – to which the Second (1901–2), still probably the most popular of all of them, belongs in spirit – were crucial to the evolution of that style. His reluctance to use wholeheartedly the term 'symphony' for *Kullervo* and the *Lemminkäinen* cycle suggests that even at such an early stage he was aware that his music might take a less programmatic direction. Neither work is too far removed from Classical models (Beethoven's Sixth, the 'Pastoral', is after all avowedly descriptive and in five movements, not the traditional four), and his contemporaries on the continent had few qualms about using the term 'symphony' in a much freer way than before. Yet what separates the early Sibelius symphonies from the later numbered ones is their lack of that 'severity' of which he would speak to Mahler in the wake of Symphony No. 3. And while the First and Second adhere to the Russian romantic-epic tradition, they mark definite moves away from the Lisztian–Straussian ethos of their unnumbered predecessors.

The Third Symphony marked a definite watershed in Sibelius's symphonies. He abandoned it in 1904, recognizing that he might be in danger of merely repeating the Second. On his return to it just two

years later, under contract to Lienau, he had become a different type
of composer. The increased contact with, and exposure of his music
in, Germany encouraged him to compete on terms with the Classical
orchestral tradition (as he had done so successfully in his first two
with that of the Russians). But the pared-down textures of this work
and especially its successor flew in the face of most radical composition in Europe, where larger and larger orchestras were being used in
more and more elaborate works. As often as not, these were not even
symphonies, since many regarded the form as outmoded if not dead,
the proof being in the inflated scale of Mahler's essays and Richard
Strauss's avoidance of the genre altogether.

German critics were largely cool about Sibelius's espousal and
brand of symphonism, their views coloured negatively by an arrogant
belief in the superiority of their own composers, and the undeniable
appeal of the Finnish upstart's smaller pieces, such as *King Christian II*
and *Finlandia*. Walter Niemann, who counted himself an advocate
of the composer and contributed the essay in Breitkopf und Härtel's
official book on Sibelius, argued that the Finn was primarily an
impressionist in a 'position of the first rank as a programmatic
composer and tone-poet and as a master of orchestral colour' but
the symphonies:

> *… when measured against Western yardsticks … are wanting to a
> significant extent the fundamental prerequisites of genuine symphonic
> writing, monumentality of form, the organic development and inner logic
> and sense of consummation. The loosely gathered mosaic-like musical
> ideas remain in the majority of cases harmonically undeveloped …
> Sibelius strives to write in the manner of Tchaikovsky … in a Finnish
> dialect and his music clearly follows a self-evident but unstated
> programme that contributes to a slightly incoherent overall impression.
> The symphonies from first to last all have the same concerns: the Finnish
> landscape and the Finnish people's soul.*

What few understood at the time was that Sibelius was reinventing
the symphony as a musical form for the new century, by reinterpreting
the heritage of the Classical past and filtering out the excesses of the
then late-Romantic present. He achieved this goal by a new concentration of expression, reflected in the relatively modest durations of

the symphonies, a reliance on the standard orchestra with few of the more exotic extras beloved of Mahler, Schoenberg and Strauss, and – with the exception of the Fourth (1910–11) – a strict adherence to tonality. The themes used within each symphony became more closely interrelated, often evolving from common intervals, such as the dissonant augmented fourth or 'tritone' in Symphony No. 4. The process of re-invention had already begun in the quietly revolutionary first movement of the Second Symphony and was writ large in the Third. Philosophically, Sibelius's music echoed the 'young classicality' that Busoni was propounding at much the same time, its watchwords being fusion and synthesis. The traditional divisions between movements within a symphony were being eroded and dovetailed by a number of composers contemporary with Sibelius, not least Nielsen in his Fourth (1914–16) and Fifth (1921–2), but it was the Finn in his Fifth and Seventh symphonies who took this further than anyone else. (By a curious twist of fate, when Sibelius was retitling his *Fantasia sinfonica* as the Seventh, his younger compatriot Aarre Merikanto was moving in the opposite direction with his Third Symphony of 1923, which he renamed *Fantasia*.) In parallel with these structural innovations, his musical language was synthesizing the severity of the Symphonies Nos. 3 and 4 with a very Nordic brand of impressionism. Starting with *The Oceanides*, this would be carried to its ultimate extreme in *Tapiola*, but it lies behind the 'pure, cold water' of Symphonies Nos. 6 and 7. Indeed, Sibelius used his tone-poems, however unconsciously, throughout his career as studies for his larger canvasses. And speaking once of his Sixth Symphony, which had attracted much analytical attention, Sibelius commented a trifle ruefully, 'most people forget it is, above all, a poem.'

The lessons of the symphonies were not lost on those composers prepared to listen with an open ear. Sibelius's persistence with the medium of the symphony may have attracted critical odium – as late as 1951 Nicholas Nabokov could write of 'so many rambling synthetic symphonies', which he also reviled as 'antediluvian monstrosities' – but it also greatly encouraged others to do likewise, such as Arnold Bax, Vaughan Williams and Walton in England, and a whole range of North American composers. When the New Zealander Douglas Lilburn, who had studied with Vaughan Williams, achieved prominence as a composer of vigorous and dynamic orchestral works in the

1950s, he was hailed as the 'Sibelius of the South'. It is no accident that when similarly exaggerated claims for the demise of the symphony as a form were being made in the 1960s and 1970s, it was composers with an audible debt to Sibelius, for example Robert Simpson and Vagn Holmboe, who kept the faith and showed what could be done. Thus it was that higher-profile creators such as Peter Maxwell Davies, Hans Werner Henze and Witold Lutosławski were able from the later 1970s onwards to resume acquaintance with a still living tradition.

Sibelius's other orchestral works divide into two very unequal categories. On the one hand, the tone-poems, although illustrative, follow symphonic principles in their design. The best of them, *En saga*, *Pohjola's Daughter*, *Night Ride and Sunrise*, *The Oceanides* and *Tapiola*, possess a cogency of musical argument that ranks them as scarcely less than the symphonies in quality, and fully the equal of the best examples by Liszt and Richard Strauss. Even less successful pieces like *The Wood Nymph* and *Spring Song* are still worthwhile. On the other hand, the various concert suites that he wrote throughout his life cover the entire gamut from excellence in the case of the extracts from *Pelléas and Mélisande*, *Belshazzar's Feast* and *Swanwhite* to the vacuity of the *Suites mignonne*, *champêtre* and *caractéristique*. A similar disparity is evident in his chamber and instrumental output after 1891, the string quartet *Voces intimae* and the Piano Sonatinas, Op. 67, representing the high points amongst a welter of mediocre sets for piano and/or violin. Yet prior to *Kullervo*, he had shown himself in works such as the B flat Quartet, Op. 4 to be an accomplished composer of chamber music. His few concertante pieces are much less uneven, although none has been established in the concert repertoire aside from the Violin Concerto – now an unquestioned standard.

Sibelius was a master of small forms when he was writing them from an artistic, rather than commercial, imperative, as the extraordinary success of the *Valse triste* showed. His output of songs may be variable in quality but the best of them can stand comparison with any produced in the twentieth century. The richest period of production ran from 1899, when *Black Roses* was composed, to 1910, with the completion of the Eight Songs, Op. 61. Thereafter, Sibelius returned to the medium only during World War I, concluding in 1918 with a group of six settings of Runeberg (Op. 90), the poet of his first set (Op. 13; 1890–2). His vocal works after World War I are almost exclusively choral.

Sibelius's failure to write a full-scale opera, bound up as it was with his flirtation with and rejection of Wagner's aesthetic, is deeply regrettable given his natural gifts as a melodist and writer for the voice. It is made all the more inexplicable by his obvious affinity with, and genius in writing music for, the stage. *The Maiden in the Tower* and *Scaramouche*, which proved to be his only large-scale stage enterprises outside the realm of incidental music, both enjoyed modest success. The pieces written for *Jedermann* and *The Tempest* also hint at operatic potential, but Sibelius had decided to abjure opera for the symphony (as Wagner had the symphony for opera), and much as he might toy with potential operatic subjects, music for them would not flow.

Sibelius's initial breakthrough had come in Helsinki in the field of chamber music, with the A minor String Trio and Quartet in B flat. With the triumphant success of *Kullervo*, he emerged on a national level, and continued to be closely associated with the nationalist cause, however uncomfortably, until well after independence. Yet Sibelius hankered after recognition as his own man, with no affiliations whether political or musical, a unique phenomenon uninfluenced by outside models, writing abstract works with a universal appeal. Part and parcel of this desire was his eagerness to succeed in the more cosmopolitan cultures of Germany and France rather than in the Russian Empire. His success in Germany ultimately proved limited, after a bright start in the early 1900s. Already before World War I broke out Sibelius had become marginalized, despite the championing of his works by Busoni and others. But without the committed and informed advocacy of a Downes or a Gray, Sibelius's music remained misunderstood in Germany. Even as distinguished a figure as Wilhelm Furtwängler once declared that Sibelius was not a symphonist at all, but an Impressionist. Otto Klemperer's judgement, however, was rather that his 'achievement was to create an altogether new music with completely classical means.' In France, his music never secured a foothold, much to his chagrin. Tone-poems such as *The Swan of Tuonela* did make an impression from time to time, but the French were historically resistant to Sibelius's principal medium of the abstract symphony. Not until the 1980s did a new generation of young

French composers wake up to the revolutionary methods of thematic growth and transformation that Sibelius had intuitively employed. He was held in greatest esteem in the Nordic countries and the Anglo-Saxon world, particularly Great Britain and the USA, where the popularity of his music has continued in concert and on record largely undimmed and unheedful of the attitudes of newspaper columnists.

Since his death, Sibelius has been associated increasingly in the public mind with the Danish composer Carl Nielsen. There were obvious parallels between them: almost exact contemporaries, both invested the symphony as a form with their most crucial inspiration, revitalizing the form as a consequence; both eschewed standard chamber music forms such as the string quartet in their maturity yet produced solitary masterpieces – *Voces intimae*, and Nielsen's Wind Quintet (probably the greatest example of that form ever set down on paper). Yet the differences between them were fundamental, not least in their approach to the common genre of the symphony itself. Nielsen's use as a basic structural principle of progressive tonality, where the course of the music is determined by the movement from an initial home key to a quite different one at the close, was quite alien to Sibelius. The Finn followed convention in opening and closing his works in the same key, developing instead to a greater degree the sophistication of internal thematic transformation within his scores. And no effort, even at a national level, would be mounted to record the Nielsen symphonies, as there had been for Sibelius before World War II, until well into the 1950s.

Sibelius's importance to Finland can scarcely be overstated, but his relationship with his countrymen is a deeply complex issue. Sibelius himself was equivocal about his role as a national figure, or at least the responsibilities such celebrity forced upon him. He assiduously and successfully avoided political involvements for most of his life, with one or two exceptions, most particularly with regard to the language issue between Finnish and Swedish. His eventual resignation to becoming a living national monument, an 'at home' ambassador of worldwide standing for the fledgling state, grew out of his self-imposed compositional silence. This contrasts with the role Nielsen assumed in Denmark, which was almost exclusively musical, with no avowedly political aspect. The Dane, however, died in 1931 before his time, with much yet to be achieved, unlike Sibelius who ultimately drew down the curtain on his life's work with effect from about the same time.

Musically, Sibelius like Beethoven cast a shadow that his successors have still not entirely come to terms with. All who came after him in Finland have been forced to choose whether to follow his lead or reject it entirely. Some, like Madetoja – who predeceased Sibelius in 1947 – took the former path but could not adequately fill the gap. The majority who opted to take a different path were forced to exchange their countryman's overpowering presence for equally dominant foreign ones, most usually French and Russian, often in combination. Composers such as Selim Palmgren, Uuno Klami and Einar Englund adopted musical styles remote from Sibelius but close to Ravel, Rachmaninov, Stravinsky or Shostakovich. In the late 1950s the music of the Austrian avant-garde composers Schoenberg and Webern became an equally potent force amongst Finnish composers, amongst whom Joonas Kokkonen and Paavo Heininen have been especially prominent. Some have gloried in the sheer diversity of different styles on offer, utilizing many of them at various points in their careers, such as Einojuhani Rautavaara (whose brilliant Third Symphony takes Bruckner as its starting point), Usko Meriläinen and Kalevi Aho. But in the end, the vast majority of post-Sibelian Finnish composers have felt compelled to face up to the ultimate challenge of the symphony. Only a few, such as Aulis Sallinen, Kokkonen in his Fourth Symphony or Tauno Marttinen in several of his nine, have sought and managed to achieve a convincing stylistic rapprochement with their great forebear.

Taken as a whole, the extreme variability in quality of Sibelius's music has caused many commentators, even avowedly well-disposed ones such as Robert Layton, to question his final standing amongst acknowledged 'greats' such as Beethoven, Brahms and Mozart. This is, in part, a reaction to the damage done historically to Sibelius's reputation – in critical circles at least – by the excessive zeal of Cecil Gray, Olin Downes, Ernest Newman and others, against which the equally prejudicial antagonism of Theodor Adorno and Virgil Thomson seem to count for little. And however sublime the very best of Sibelius's music is, the embarassing emptiness of a large section of his output is often held to have diluted the value of the whole of it. Yet while Sibelius must be counted as an uneven composer, as were Mahler and Shostakovich in very different ways, this was not due to the nature of his gifts but because of harsh financial imperatives and personal – but non-musical – weakness. He himself drew a distinct line between his bread-and-butter writing, over which his hyper-criticality was rarely exercised, and the symphonies and tone-poems that were his mission in life. And whether the critical fraternity likes it or not, it has very often been the smaller works, like *Finlandia, Valse triste* or the *Karelia Suite*, that have won Sibelius an immovable place in the affections of music-lovers at large.

Was Sibelius then a 'great' composer, or merely one who could at times achieve great things? This was a question he was all too conscious of, and the burden of his own – and what he perceived as others' – expectations of what constituted great music finally caused his creative instincts to seize up irreconcilably. What he produced in the meantime counts at its finest amongst the pinnacles of Western music of this or any other century. If his legacy has not until now been fully explored and developed, the blame can hardly be laid at his door. His music survived the vicissitudes of fashion across a century and has still been found to contain within it seeds for the future, especially with regard to the organic development of themes. These would seem the classic hallmarks of a great composer.

Classified List of Works

The following list takes as its starting point the published catalogue devised by Fabian Dahlström of 1987 which, by its author's own modest admission, was in some senses preliminary, so I have included subsequent refinements that have been made public by Dr Dahlström, Erik Tawaststjerna and Kari Kilpeläinen, the leading authorities on the manuscripts. Sibelius's arrangements of his own works are included here; those by other hands, however well known (e.g. of the *Canzonetta*, Op. 62a, by Stravinsky), are omitted. Some early student works and obvious fragments have been excluded. In general, the compositions are listed primarily under the most familiar title, whether Finnish, Swedish or English. Where it is appropriate, translations of a title, then any alternative titles and/or subtitles, are given in parenthesis. As to datings, many of the early chamber and instrumental pieces were only dated years, even decades, later and very approximately at that. Where compositions occur with a common date range (e.g. 'c. 1887–9'), they are listed alphabetically by title. Where first performances (fp) cannot be safely averred, a common feature of the instrumental miniatures and transcriptions for the home market, works are marked 'fp?'.

With regard to opus numbers, Sibelius generally did not assign these on his manuscripts, and in his worklists was very inconsistent in their application. These worklists were often compiled over several years rather than created at one time. The earliest (1896) bears no numbers at all; comparisons of those drawn up in 1905–9, 1911–2, 1914, 1915 (this last written out by his daughter Katarina), c. 1915–31, and others (not precisely dated) in the late 1930s and 1940s, show a wide divergence in the works assigned to particular numbers. Several compositions changed number between lists, such as the incidental music to *The Lizard*, Op. 8, variously listed as Op. 59, 40 and 29a, while others –

for instance Opp. 1 and 6 – were given to a wide variety of pieces over the years. Some, especially the early chamber works, vanish from, re-enter and exit the lists; some opus numbers, such as 4, 6, 8, 18, 21, 65 and 72, remained purposefully blank into the 1920s in order for the revisionist composer to modify his output. As the years went by, those works which had been published – with an opus number in view – needed to stay fixed, causing increasing congestion amongst the candidates for the remaining available numbers. (Even then some movement still occurred within groups of pieces collected under a single opus, such as in the cases of the collections of piano pieces, Opp. 76 and 94.) Some opus numbers covering several works were never completely filled; for instance, there is no piece assigned to Op. 21, No. 1 – No. 2 is *Natus in curas* – or Op. 53b (to accompany *Pan and Echo*, Op. 53a). Additionally, Sibelius from time to time gave late pieces early numbers deliberately to mislead prospective publishers and unwary biographers as to the actual date of composition. Examples of this practice include the song *Arioso*, Op. 3, written in 1911 (not in the 1890s as he claimed), the *Cassazione*, Op. 6 (variously Opp. 30 and 34 as well), actually composed in 1904, the Ten Bagatelles for piano, Op. 34, of 1913–16 rather than 1900, and the incidental music to *The Lizard*, Op. 8 (1909) which followed *Kullervo* not by a few months but by seventeen years. Even Op. 1 cannot be trusted – the Five Christmas Songs dating from between 1895 and 1909. For fuller exegeses of the problems of Sibelius's cataloguing of his works – often compounded by other writers who used these lists in good faith – see Dahlström's introduction to his published catalogue, Chapter 3 of the third English volume of Tawaststjerna's study and Kilpeläinen's papers to the International Jean Sibelius Conferences in August 1990 and November 1995.

The convention I have adopted here is to follow the final numbering, but to include within square parentheses known alternative numberings, as with *Malinconia* for cello and piano, Op. 20 [Op. 25] (1900); those works which at one time possessed but ultimately lost numbers can show only the parenthetical number, e.g. the Overture in E major [Op. 6] (1891).

Works are listed in the following categories: Stage Works, Incidental Music, Choral (unaccompanied), Choral with Instruments, Choral with Orchestra, Vocal with Piano, Vocal with Instruments, Vocal with Orchestra, Orchestral, Solo Instrument(s) with Orchestra, Chamber, Piano, Instrumental. Arrangements of the same work are listed separately in their respective categories, and cross-references have been added where helpful, particularly where forces are similar. In some instances, however, the inter-relationship between two or more works is explained fully within a single entry.

Except for the larger collections of miniatures, I have only shown separately works grouped under a single opus where it seemed appropriate to do so (as for instance in the Nine Part-Songs, Op. 18, later reduced to six, and the Four *Lemminkäinen* Symphonic Poems, Op. 22, where each individual component has its own performing history).

Stage Works

The Maiden in the Tower ('Jungfrun i tornet') [Op. 20], opera in one act, libretto by R. Herzberg (1896). fp Helsinki, 7 November 1896

Scaramouche, Op. 71, ballet-pantomime in one act, scenario by Poul Knudsen and M. T. Bloch (1913). fp Copenhagen, 12 May 1922

Incidental Music

(for orchestra unless otherwise stated)

Näcken ('The Watersprite'), for solo voice and piano trio, play by Gunnar Wennerberg (1888; in collaboration with Martin Wegelius). fp Helsinki, 9 April 1888

Scenic Music for a Festival and Lottery in Aid of Education in the Province of Viipuri [Opp. 10, 11], for solo voices and orchestra (1893). fp Helsinki, 13 November 1893

Music for the Press Pension Fund [Opp. 26, 25] (1899). fp Helsinki, 4 November 1899

King Christian II, Op. 27, for solo voice and orchestra, play by Adolf Paul (1898). fp Helsinki, 24 February 1898. Extended version (1898). fp Leipzig, 27 February 1899

Kuolema, Op. 44, for solo voice and orchestra, play by Arvid Järnefelt (1903). fp Helsinki, 2 December 1903. Extended version, Op. 62 (1911). fp Helsinki, 8 March 1911

Pelléas and Mélisande [Op. 46], for solo voice and orchestra, play by Maurice Maeterlinck (1905). fp Helsinki, 17 March 1905

Belshazzar's Feast [Op. 51], for solo voice and orchestra, play by Hjalmar Procopé (1906). fp Helsinki, 4 November 1906

The Lizard ('Ödlan'), Op. 8 [Opp. 59, 40, 29a], for solo violin and strings, play by Mikael Lybeck (1909). fp Helsinki, 6 April 1910

Swanwhite [Op. 54], play by August Strindberg (1908). fp Helsinki, 8 April 1908

Two Songs for William Shakespeare's *Twelfth Night*, Op. 60, for voice with guitar or piano (1909). fp Helsinki, 12 November 1909

Wedding March for Adolf Paul's *The Language of the Birds* [Opp. 64, 29b] (1911). fp Vienna, March 1911

Jedermann ('Everyman'), Op. 83, for solo voices, chorus and orchestra, play by Hugo von Hofmannstahl (1916). fp Helsinki, 5 November 1916

Elektra, arranged from *Pan and Echo* (Dance Intermezzo No. 3), for small orchestra, play by Hugo von Hofmannstahl (1921). fp Helsinki, 18 April 1921

The Tempest ('Stormen'), Op. 109, play by William
Shakespeare (1925). fp Copenhagen, 16 March 1926.
Extended version (1927). fp Helsinki, 4 November 1927

Choral (unaccompanied)

Heitä, koski, kuohuminen ('Cease Your Raging,
Waterfall'), for male chorus, text from the *Kalevala*
(1893; unfinished, completed by Erik Bergman, 1960–1).
fp Helsinki, 18 March 1961

Rakastava ('The Lover'), Op. 14 [Op. 18/1], suite for
baritone and male chorus, text from the *Kanteletar*
(1893). fp Helsinki, 28 April 1894. Revised version for
soprano, baritone and mixed chorus (c. 1898). fp?

Arrangement of Jazeps Wihtol's *Laulun mahti* ('The
Power of the Song'), for male chorus (c. 1895).
fp Helsinki, 7 December 1895

Juhlamarssi ('Festival March'), arranged from the
Cantata for the University Graduation Ceremonies of
1894, text by Kasimir Lönnbohm (Eino Leino)
(c. 1896). fp Mikkeli, 1897

Natus in curas (also *25. V. 1896*), Op. 21/2, hymn for
male chorus, text by Fridolf Gustafsson (1896).
fp Helsinki, 25 May 1896

Workers' March ('Työkansan marssi'), for mixed chorus,
text by J. H. Erkko (1896). fp?

Aamusumussa ('Morning Mist'), for children's voices,
text by J. H. Erkko (1896). fp? Revised version for
mixed chorus (c. 1898). fp? Revised version for male
chorus (c. 1920). fp?

Ten Songs from the Cantata for the University
Graduation Ceremonies of 1897, Op. 23, text by
A. V. Forsman (Koskiemies) (c. 1899). fp?

Carminalia [Op. 8], Latin songs from the eighteenth
century, for mixed chorus, texts anonymous (1898). fp?
(See also Choral with Instruments)

Soi kiitokseksi ('We Praise Thee, Our Creator'), song
from the Cantata for the University Graduation
Ceremonies of 1897 [Op. 23/6a], for female chorus,
text by A. V. Forsman (Koskiemies) (c. 1899). fp?

Nejden andas ('The Breath of the Countryside'), from
The Breaking of the Ice on the Oulu River [Op. 30],
improvisation for female chorus, text by Zachris
Topelius (1899). fp?

Nine Part-Songs [Op. 18], for mixed and male chorus,
texts by Paavo Cajander, Juhani Aho and Aleksis Kivi
and from the *Kanteletar* and *Kalevala* (1893–1904).
Revised as Six Songs, Op. 18, for male chorus
(1893–1902):
No. 1: *Isänmalle* ('To My Country') [Op. 18/1], for male
chorus, text by Cajander (1899). Never performed.
Revised version for mixed chorus (1900). fp Helsinki,
20 June 1900. Revised version for male chorus (not that
of 1902 usually performed, by Selim Palmgren) (1908).
fp (probably) Turku, 1908
No. 2: *Sortunut ääni* ('The Broken Voice'), Op. 18/1
[Op. 18/7], for male chorus, text from the *Kanteletar*
(1898). fp Helsinki, 21 April 1899. Revised version for
mixed chorus (1898). fp?
No. 3: *Veljeni vierailla mailla* ('My Brother's Abroad')
[Op. 18/2], for chorus of tenors, baritones and basses,
text by Aho (1904). fp Helsinki, 2 December 1904
No. 4: *Terve kuu* ('Hail, O Moon!'), Op. 18/2
[Op. 18/8], for male chorus, text from the *Kalevala*
(1901). fp Helsinki, 30 May 1901
No. 5: *Venematka* ('The Boat Journey'), Op. 18/3
[Op. 18/9], for male chorus, text from the *Kalevala*
(1893). fp Helsinki, 6 April 1893. Revised version for
mixed chorus (c. 1914). fp?
No. 6: *Saarella palaa* ('Fire on the Island'), for male
chorus, Op. 18/4 [Op. 18/3], text from the *Kanteletar*
(1895). fp Helsinki, 7 December 1895. Revised version
for mixed chorus (c. 1898). fp?
No. 7: *Min rastas raataa* ('The Thrush's Toiling')
[Op. 18/4], for mixed chorus, text from the *Kanteletar*
(c. 1897–8). fp?

No. 8: *Metsämiehen laulu* ('The Woodman's Song'),
Op. 18/5, for male chorus, text by Kivi (1899).
fp Helsinki, 4 April 1900
No. 9: *Sydämeni laulu* ('Song of My Heart'), Op. 18/6,
for male chorus, text by Kivi (1898). fp Helsinki,
1 December 1898. Revised version for mixed chorus
(c. 1908). fp?

Kotikaipaus ('Nostalgia'), for female chorus, text by
Walter von Konow (1902). fp Sääksmäki, summer 1902

25 October 1902, to Thérèse Hahl, for mixed chorus, text
by Nils Wasastjerna (two versions, both 1902). fp?

Ej med klagan ('With No Dirges'; 'in memoriam Albert
Edelfelt, 24. VIII. 1905'), for mixed chorus, text by
Johan Runeberg (1905). fp (at Edelfelt's funeral)
Helsinki, 24 August 1905

Primary School Children's March ('Kansakoululaisten
marssi'; *Una Cygnaeuksen muistolle*), for children's voices
(1910). fp (simultaneously in several schools) 10 October
1910

Cantata, for female chorus, text by Walter von Konow
(1911). fp Turku, 11 November 1911

Song for the People of Uusimaa, for male chorus, text by
Kaarlo Terhi (1912). fp Helsinki, 20 April 1912.
Alternative version for mixed chorus (1912). fp?

Män från slätten och havet ('People from Land and Sea'),
Op. 65a, for mixed chorus, text by Ernest V. Knape
(1911). fp Vaasa, 30 June 1912 (with string orchestral
parts by Hans Aufrichtig, for first performance only)

The Bells of Berghälls Church ('Kellosävel kallion
kirkossa'), Op. 65b, motet for mixed chorus, text by
Julius Engström (1912). fp Berghälls (Kallio) Church
inauguration, 1912

The Sun upon the Lake is Low (from Three Songs for
American Schools), for mixed chorus, text by Sir Walter
Scott (1913). fp?

Five Part-Songs, Op. 84, for male chorus, texts by
Gustaf Fröding, Bertel Gripenberg, Jonatan Reuter
(1914–17):
No. 1: *Herr Lager och Skön fager* ('Mr Lager and the Fair
One'), text by Fröding (1914). fp Helsinki, 27 April 1915
No. 2: *På berget* ('On the Mountain'), text by
Gripenberg (c. 1914–15). fp Helsinki, 27 April 1915
No. 3: *Ett drömackord* ('A Dream Chord'), text by
Fröding (1915). fp (probably) Helsinki,
10 December 1920
No. 4: *Evige Eros* ('Eternal Eros'), text by Gripenberg
(1915). fp Helsinki, 14 December 1915
No. 5: *Till havs* ('At Sea'), text by Reuter (1917).
fp Helsinki, 30 April 1917

Kuutamolla ('In the Moonlight'), for male chorus, text
by Aino Suonio (1916). fp Helsinki, 11 April 1916

Drömma ('Dreams'), for mixed chorus, text by Jonatan
Reuter (1917). fp?

Fridolins dårskap ('Fridolin's Folly'), for male chorus,
text by Erik Axel Karlfelt (1917). fp?

Jone havsfärd ('Jonah's Voyage'), for male chorus, text by
Erik Axel Karlfelt (1918). fp?

Outside the Storm Rages ('Ute hörs stormen'), for male
chorus, text by Gösta Schybergson (1918). fp Viipuri,
5 April 1919

Honour March of the Singing Brothers of Viipuri, for
male chorus, text by Eero Eerola (1920). fp Viipuri,
2 May 1921. Second, alternative setting (1929). fp?

Brusande rusar en våg ('Surging the Wave Rushes
Forward'), for male chorus, text by Gösta Schybergson
(1918). fp Turku, 19 March 1921

Likhet ('Alikeness'), for male chorus, text by Johan
Runeberg (1922). fp Turku, 13 March 1926

Koulutie ('The Way to School'), for mixed chorus, text
by V. A. Koskenniemi (1924). fp?

Two Part-Songs, Op. 108, for male chorus, texts by
Larin-Kyösti (1925). fp Helsinki, 23 March 1926
No. 1: Humoresque
No. 2: *Ne pitkän matkan kulkijat* ('Wanderers on the
Long Way')

Suur' olet Herra ('The Lofty Heaven'), from Ode: *Den
höga himlen och den vida jorden* [Op. 107], for mixed
chorus, text by Simo Korpela (1927). fp?

Siltavahti ('The Guard of the Bridge'), for male chorus,
text by Wäinö Sola (1928). fp (probably) New York,
1929

Julsång ('Christmas Song'), for mixed chorus, text by
A. V. Jaakkola, alternative text by V. I. Forsman
(c. 1929). fp?

Jouluvirsi ('Christmas Song'; *Julvisa, En etsi*) [Op. 1/1],
for solo voice and male chorus, text by Zachris Topelius
(c. 1935). fp Helsinki, 1935. Version for solo voice and
female chorus (1942). fp?

Finlandia Hymn, for male chorus, from orchestral
tone-poem *Finlandia*, text by V. A. Koskenniemi
(1940). fp Helsinki, 7 December 1940. Version for
mixed chorus (1940). fp?

There are, additionally, various unaccompanied songs
of unknown date:
Ack! hör du fröken Gyllenborg ('Oh Listen You Miss
Gyllenborg!'), for mixed chorus, text unknown
Eilaa, eilaa, for tenor and mixed chorus, text from the
Kanteletar
Ensam i dunkla skogarnas famn ('Alone in the Depths of
the Forest'), for mixed chorus, text unknown
Morgonens och aftonens portar ('The Gates of Morning
and Evening'), for mixed chorus, text unknown
När sig våren åter föder ('When Spring Once More
Comes to Life'), for mixed chorus, text unknown
Skolsång ('School Song'), for children's or mixed chorus,
text by Nino Runeberg
Tanke se hur fågeln svingar ('Imagine, See How the Bird
Swoops'), for mixed chorus, text unknown

Choral with Instruments

Carminalia, Latin songs from the eighteenth century
[Op. 8], for female chorus and harmonium or piano,
texts anonymous (1898). fp? (See also Choral
(unaccompanied))

Har du mod? ('Have You Courage?'), Op. 31/2, for
unison male voices and piano, text by Josef Wecksell
(1904). fp? Revised version (1911). fp? (See also Choral
with Orchestra)

A Cavalry Catch (from Three Songs for American
Schools), for unison male voices and piano, text by
Fiona Macleod (1913). fp?

March of the Finnish Jäger Battalion ('Jääkärimarssi')
[Op. 91a], for male chorus and piano (1917).
fp (unofficial, 'on the march') Libau and Helsinki,
November–December 1917 (See also Choral with
Orchestra)

Scout March ('Partiolaisten marssi'), Op. 91b, for chorus
and piano, text by Jalmari Finne (1921). fp? (See also
Choral with Orchestra)

Den höga himlen och den vida jorden – Suur' olet Herra
('The Lofty Heaven'), ode [Op. 107], for male voices
and organ, text by Jacob Tegengren and Simo Korpela
(1926). fp Sweden (on tour), autumn 1926

Karjalan osa? ('Karelia's Fate'; *Patriotic March*) [Op.
31/2], for unison male voices and piano, text by
A. Nurminen (1930). fp Sortavala, 7 September 1930

Finlandia Hymn, Op. 113/12, for male chorus and
harmonium, from orchestral tone-poem *Finlandia*, text
by Wäinö Sola (1938). fp Helsinki, 4 April 1938

Masonic Ritual Music, for voice(s), male chorus and
harmonium, texts (in Finnish) by Franz von Schober
(trans. Eino Leino), Pao Chao (trans. Eino Tikkanen),
Johann Wolfgang von Goethe (trans. Eino Leino),
Aukusti Simelius, Viktor Rydberg, Jacob Tegengren,
Simo Korpela, Samuli Sario, Wäino Sola. Extended
version of 1926–7 work (1946). fp Helsinki, 24 October
1946. (See also Vocal with Instruments)

The World Song of The World Association of Girl Guides and Girl Scouts (*Our Way Is Clear*) [Op. 91b], for female voices and piano, text by Ewart (1950–2, based on 1921 *Scout March*). fp?

There are, additionally, three songs of unknown date:
Skyddskårssång ('Song of the Skyddskår'; *Skyddskårsmarsch*), for male chorus and piano *ad lib*, text by Nino Runeberg. fp?
Upp genom luften, bort över haven ('Up through the Air and over the Seas'), for mixed chorus and piano, text by Per David Atterbom. fp?
Vi kysser du fader min fästmö här? ('Oh Father Will You Kiss My Fiancée Now?'), for female chorus and piano, text unknown. fp?

Choral with Orchestra
(for mixed chorus and orchestra unless otherwise stated)

Kullervo, symphony/symphonic poem, Op. 7 [Op. 8], for mezzo-soprano, baritone, male chorus and orchestra, text from the *Kalevala* (1891–2). fp Helsinki, 28 April 1892

Cantata for the University Graduation Ceremonies of 1894 [Opp. 15, 14], for soprano, baritone, chorus and orchestra, text by Kasimir Lönnbohm (Eino Leino) (1894). fp Helsinki, 31 May 1894

Cantata for the Coronation of Tsar Nicholas II [Op. 19], text by Paavo Cajander (1896). fp Helsinki, 2 November 1896

A Song for Lemminkäinen, Op. 31/1, for male chorus and orchestra, text by Yrjö Weijola (1896). fp Helsinki, 12 December 1896

Cantata for the University Graduation Ceremonies of 1897, for soprano, baritone, chorus and orchestra, text by A. V. Forsman (Koskiemies) (1897). fp Helsinki, 30 May 1897

Sandels, Op. 28 [Op. 28a], improvisation for male chorus and orchestra, text by Johan Runeberg (1898). fp Helsinki, 16 March 1900. Revised version (1915). fp Helsinki, 14 December 1915

Song of the Athenians ('Atenarnes sång'), Op. 31/3, for unison boys' and men's voices, brass septet and percussion, text by Viktor Rydberg (1899). fp Helsinki, 26 April 1899. Revised versions (1911, 1912). fp?

The Breaking of the Ice on the Oulu River, Op. 30 [Op. 28c], improvisation for reciter, male chorus and orchestra, text by Zachris Topelius (1899). fp Helsinki, 21 October 1899

Snöfrid, Op. 29 [Op. 28b], improvisation for reciter, chorus and orchestra, text by Viktor Rydberg (1900). fp Helsinki, 20 October 1900. Version with alternative text of final chorus by Volter Kilpi (1902). fp Helsinki, 9 April 1902

The Origin of Fire ('Tulen synty'; *Ukko the Firemaker*), Op. 32, cantata for baritone, male chorus and orchestra, text from the *Kalevala* (1902). fp Helsinki, 9 April 1902. Revised version (1910). fp?

Impromptu (*Livslust*), Op. 19, for female chorus and orchestra, text by Viktor Rydberg (1902). fp Helsinki, 8 March 1902. Revised version (1910). fp Helsinki, 29 March 1910

Har du mod? ('Have You Courage?'), Op. 31/2, for unison male voices and orchestra, text by Josef Wecksell (1904). fp Helsinki, 8 February 1904. Revised versions (1911, 1912). fp? (See also Choral with Instruments)

The Captive Queen (cantata for the centenary of the birth of J. V. Snellman), Op. 48, ballade for mixed or male chorus and orchestra, text by Paavo Cajander (1906). fp Helsinki, 12 May 1906

March of the Finnish Jäger Battalion ('Jääkärimarssi'), Op. 91a, for male chorus, brass septet and percussion (1918). fp Helsinki, 19 January 1918 (See also Choral with Instruments)

Our Native Land ('Oma maa'), Op. 92, cantata for chorus and orchestra, text by Kallio (1918). fp Helsinki, 24 October 1918

Song of the Earth ('Jordens sång'), Op. 93, cantata for chorus and orchestra, text by Jari Hemmer (1919). fp Turku, 11 October 1919

Maan virsi ('Hymn to the Earth'), Op. 95, cantata for chorus and orchestra, text by Eino Leino (1920). fp Helsinki, 4 April 1920

Scout March ('Partiolaisten marssi'), Op. 91b, for chorus and orchestra, text by Jalmari Finne (1921). fp? (See also Choral with Instruments)

Väinön virsi ('Väinö's Song'), Op. 110, cantata for chorus and orchestra, text from the *Kalevala* (1926). fp Sortavala, 28 June 1926

The Rapids-Rider's Brides ('Koskenlaskijan morsiamet') [Op. 33], arrangement for male chorus and orchestra of 1897 work for baritone/mezzo-soprano and orchestra, text by A. Oksanen (c. 1943). fp (probably) Helsinki, 22 April 1945

Vocal with Piano

Serenad ('Serenade') [Op. 6/1], text by Johan Runeberg (1888). fp?

En visa ('A Song'), text by Baeckman (1888). fp (probably) Loviisa, 1888

O, om du sett ('Oh, If You Had Seen'), melodrama for reciter and piano, text by Johan Runeberg (c. 1889). fp?

The Wood Nymph ('Skogsrået'), text by Erik Stagnelius (c. 1889). fp?

Likhet ('Alikeness'), text by Johan Runeberg (1890). fp?

Seven Songs, Op. 13, texts by Johan Runeberg (1890–2):
No. 1: *Under strandens granar* ('Beneath the Fir Trees') (1892). fp Helsinki, 16 December 1892
No. 2: *Kyssens hopp* ('Kiss's Hope') (1892). fp?
No. 3: *Hjärtats morgon* ('Heart's Morning') (1890). fp Helsinki, 19 October 1891

No. 4: *Våren flyktar hastigt* ('Spring Is Flying Swiftly') (1890). fp?
No. 5: *Drömmen* ('The Dream') (1891). fp Helsinki, 19 October 1891
No. 6: *Till Frigga* ('To Frigga') (1892). fp Helsinki, 16 December 1892
No. 7: *Jägargossen* ('The Young Sportsman') (1891). fp?

Kullervo's Battle-Cry, for baritone and piano, from *Kullervo*, text from the *Kalevala* (1892). fp?

Kullervo's Lament, for baritone and piano, from *Kullervo*, text from the *Kalevala* (1892). fp?

Seven Songs, Op. 17, texts by Johan Runeberg, Karl August Tavaststjerna, Oscar Levertin, A. V. Forsman (Koskimies), Ilmati Calamnius (1891–c. 1904):
No. 1: *Sen har jag ej frågat mera* ('And I Questioned Them No Further'), text by Runeberg (1894). fp Vienna, 1895
No. 2: *Sov in!* ('Slumber!'), text by Tavaststjerna (1894). fp?
No. 3: *Fågellek* ('Enticement'), text by Tavaststjerna (1891). fp Helsinki, 19 October 1891
No. 4: *Vilse* ('Astray'), text by Tavaststjerna (1902). fp?
No. 5: *En slända* ('A Dragonfly'), text by Levertin (c. 1904). fp Helsinki, 10 November 1904
No. 6: *Illalle* ('To Evening'), text by Forsman (1898). fp?
No. 7: *Lastu lainehilla* ('Driftwood'), text by Calamnius (1902). fp?

Five Christmas Songs, Op. 1, texts by Zachris Topelius, Wilkku Joukahainen (Nos. 1–3: 1895; No. 4: 1909; No. 5: 1901). fp? Revised version of No. 5, *On hanget korkeat* ('The Shining Snows Are Driven High'), for two female voices and piano (1942). fp?

Segelfahrt ('Sailing') [Op. 6/3], text by Johannes Öhnqvist (1899). fp?

Souda, souda, sinisorsa ('Row, Row, Duck'), text by A. V. Forsman (Koskimies) (1899). fp?

Seven Songs, Op. 36, texts by Ernst Josephson, Johan Runeberg, Gustav Fröding, Josef Wecksell (1899–1900):
No. 1: *Svarta rosor* ('Black Roses'), text by Josephson (1899). fp Helsinki, 21 September 1899
No. 2: *Men min fågel märks dock icke* ('But My Bird Is Long in Homing'), text by Runeberg (1899).
fp Helsinki, 21 September 1899
No. 3: *Bollspelet vid Trianon* ('Tennis at Trianon'), text by Fröding (1899). fp Helsinki, 24 October 1900
No. 4: *Säv, säv, susa* ('Sigh, Sedges, Sigh'), text by Fröding (1900). fp Finland (on tour), 1900
No. 5: *Marssnön* ('March Snow'), text by Wecksell (1900). fp?
No. 6: *Demanten på marssnön* ('The Diamond on the March Snow'), text by Wecksell (1900). fp Helsinki, 8 February 1901

Andantino, song without words (c. 1900). fp?

Five Songs, Op. 37, texts by Johan Runeberg, Zachris Topelius, Tor Hedberg, Josef Wecksell (1900–2):
No. 1: *Den första kyssen* ('The First Kiss'), text by Runeberg (1900). fp (probably) Helsinki, 1900. (There also exists a second, completely different and undated setting of this poem. fp?)
No. 2: *Lasse liten* ('Little Lasse'), text by Topelius (1902). fp Helsinki, 8 October 1902
No. 3: *Soluppgång* ('Sunrise'), text by Hedberg (1902). fp Helsinki, 10 October 1902
No. 4: *Var det en dröm?* ('Was It a Dream?'), text by Wecksell (1902). fp Helsinki, 10 October 1902
No. 5: *Flickan kom ifrån sin älsklings möte* ('The Tryst'), text by Runeberg (1900–1). fp Berlin, January 1901

Five Songs, Op. 38, texts by Viktor Rydberg, Gustav Fröding (1903–4):
No. 1: *Höstkväll* ('Autumn Night'), text by Rydberg (1903). fp Helsinki, 12 September 1903
No. 2: *På veranden vid havet* ('On a Balcony by the Sea'), text by Rydberg (1903). fp Helsinki, 16 October 1903
No. 3: *I natten* ('In the Night'), text by Rydberg (1903). fp Helsinki, 16 October 1903

No. 4: *Harpolekaren och hans son* ('The Harper and His Son'), text by Rydberg (1904). fp Helsinki, 9 September 1904
No. 5: *Jag ville jag vore i Indialand* ('I Would I Were Dwelling in India'), text by Fröding (1904). fp Helsinki, 12 October 1904

The Three Blind Sisters, from *Pelléas and Mélisande*, text by Maurice Maeterlinck (1905). fp?

Six Songs on German texts, Op. 50 (1906):
No. 1: *Lenzgesang* ('Spring Song'), text by A. Fitger. fp?
No. 2: *Sehnsucht* ('Longing'), text by Emil Weiss. fp (probably) Helsinki, 26 October 1906
No. 3: *Im felden ein Mädchen singt* ('A Maiden Yonder Sings'), text by Margarete Susman. fp (probably) Helsinki, 26 October 1906
No. 4: *Aus banger Brust* ('O, Wert Thou Here'), text by Richard Dehmel. fp Helsinki, 11 October 1906
No. 5: *Die stille Stadt* ('The Silent Town'), text by Richard Dehmel. fp Helsinki, 11 October 1906
No. 6: *Rosenlied* ('Song of the Roses'), text by Anna Ritter. fp Helsinki, 26 October 1906

Solitude (*The Jewish Girl's Song*), from *Belshazzar's Feast*, for female voice and piano, text by Hjalmar Procopé (1906). fp?

Erloschen ('The Fire Has Died Out'), text by Georg Busse-Palmo (1906). fp (probably) Berlin, 1906

Jubal, Op. 35/1 [Op. 45/1], text by Ernst Josephson (1907–8). fp Helsinki, 24 September 1908

Teodora, Op. 35/2 [Op. 45/2], text by Bertel Gripenberg (1908). fp?

Eight Songs, Op. 57, texts by Ernst Josephson (1909):
No. 1: *Älven och snigeln* ('The Snail'). fp?
No. 2: *En blomma stod vid vägen* ('The Wild Flower'). fp?
No. 3: *Kvarnhjulet* ('The Millwheel'). fp?
No. 4: *Maj* ('May'). fp Helsinki, 1915

No. 5: *Jag är ett träd* ('The Tree', *Det kala trädet*).
fp Turku, 8 October 1910
No. 6: *Hertig Magnus* ('Baron Magnus'). fp Helsinki,
26 October 1906
No. 7: *Vänskapens blomma* ('The Flower of
Friendship'). fp Helsinki, 9 November 1910. (There also
exists a second, completely different and undated
setting of this poem. fp?)
No. 8: *Näcken* ('The Elfling'). fp Helsinki,
9 November 1910

Hymn to Thaïs, the Unforgettable, text (in English) by
Arthur H. Borgström (1909). fp?

Eight Songs, Op. 61, texts by Karl August Tavaststjerna,
Viktor Rydberg, Johan Runeberg, Bertel Gripenberg
(1910):
No. 1: *Längsamt som kvällskyn* ('Shall I Forget Thee?'),
text by Tavaststjerna. fp?
No. 2: *Vattenplask* ('Lapping Waters'), text by Rydberg.
fp?
No. 3: *När jag drömmer* ('When I Dream'), text by
Tavaststjerna. fp?
No. 4: *Romeo*, text by Tavaststjerna. fp Helsinki, 1915
No. 5: *Romans* ('Romance'), text by Tavaststjerna. fp?
No. 6: *Dolce far niente* ('I Live All My Hours in
Dreaming'), text by Tavaststjerna. fp?
No. 7: *Fåfäng önskan* ('Idle Wishes'), text by Runeberg.
fp Helsinki, 28 April 1910
No. 8: *Vårtagen* ('The Spell of Springtide'), text by
Gripenberg. fp Helsinki, 23 September 1912

Autumn Song (from Three Songs for American
Schools), for duet and piano, text by Dixon (1913). fp?

Tanke ('The Thought'), for two female voices and
piano, text by Johan Runeberg (1915). fp?

Six Songs, Op. 72, texts by Viktor Rydberg, Zachris
Topelius, Johan Runeberg, Larin-Kyösti, Martin Greif
(1907–16):
No. 1: *Vi ses igen* ('Farewell'), text by Rydberg (c. 1915;
lost). fp?
No. 2: *Orions bälte* ('Orion's Battle'), text by Topelius
(c. 1916; lost). fp?

No. 3: *Kyssen* ('The Kiss'), text by Runeberg (1915).
fp Helsinki, 9 May 1918
No. 4: *Kaiutar* ('The Echo Nymph'), text by Larin-
Kyösti (1915). fp?
No. 5: *Der Wanderer und der Bach* ('The Wanderer and
the Brook'), text by Greif (1915). fp?
No. 6: *Hundra vägar* ('A Hundred Ways') [Op. 6/2],
text by Runeberg (c. 1907). fp?

Six Songs, Op. 86, texts by Karl August Tavaststjerna,
Erik Karlfeldt, Carl Snoilsky, Mikael Lybeck (1916–17):
No. 1: *Vårförnimmelser* ('The Coming of Spring'), text
by Tavaststjerna (1916). fp Helsinki, 16 October 1916
No. 2: *Längtan heter min arvedel* ('Longing Vain Are
My Heritage'), text by Karlfeldt (1916). fp Helsinki,
16 October 1916
No. 3: *Dold förening* ('Hidden Union'), text by Snoilsky
(1916). fp Helsinki, 16 October 1916
No. 4: *Och finns det en tanke* ('And Is There a
Thought?'), text by Tavaststjerna (1916). fp Helsinki,
16 October 1916
No. 5: *Sångarlön* ('The Singer's Reward'), text by
Snoilsky (1916). fp Helsinki, 16 October 1916
No. 6: *I systrar, I bröder, I älskande par!* ('Ye Sisters, Ye
Brothers'), text by Lybeck (c. 1917). fp?

Six Songs, Op. 88, texts by Frans Michael Franzén,
Johan Runeberg (1917). fp Helsinki, 26 October 1917
No. 1: *Blåsippan* ('The Anemone'), text by Franzén
No. 2: *De bägge rosorna* ('The Two Roses'), text by
Franzén
No. 3: *Vitsippan* ('The Wood Anemone'), text by
Franzén
No. 4: *Sippan* ('The Primrose'), text by Runeberg
No. 5: *Törnet* ('The Thorn'), text by Runeberg
No. 6: *Blommans öde* ('The Flower's Destiny'),
text by Runeberg

Six Songs on texts by Johan Runeberg, Op. 90
(1917–18):
No. 1: *Norden* ('The North'; *Pohjola*) (1917). fp?
No. 2: *Hennes budskap* ('Her Message') (1917). fp?
Revised version, 1918. fp?
No. 3: *Morgonen* ('The Morning') (1917). fp?

No. 4: *Fågelfångaren* ('The Bird-Catcher') (1917). fp?
No. 5: *Sommarnatten* ('Summer Night') (1917).
fp Helsinki, 4 October 1919
No. 6: *Ven styrde hit din väg?* ('Who Has Brought You Here?') (1917–18). fp?

Små flickorna ('Small Girls'), text by Hjalmar Procopé (1920). fp?

Pastoral, arrangement for two voices and piano of part of *Autrefois: Scène pastorale* [Op. 96b] (1920). fp?

A Lonely Ski-trail ('Ett ensamt skidspår'), melodrama for reciter and piano, text by Bertel Gripenberg (1925). fp?

Narciss ('Narcissus'), text by Bertel Gripenberg (1925). fp?

Siltavahti ('The Guard of the Bridge'), text by Wäinö Sola (1928). fp?

There are, additionally, two undated songs, *The American Miller's Song*, text unknown, and *Orgier* ('Orgies'), text by L. Stenbäck, and another without title or text, in G major, c. 1900. Details of first performance are not known. There is also the 1895 edition, in collaboration with A. A. Borenius, of Finnish Runic fragments.

Vocal with Instruments

Svartsjukans nätter ('Nights of Jealousy'), melodrama for reciter and piano trio, text by Johan Runeberg (1888). fp?

Snöfrid, melodrama for reciter and ensemble, text by Viktor Rydberg (1893; lost). fp?

The Wood Nymph ('Skogsrået'), melodrama for reciter, piano, two horns and strings, text by Viktor Rydberg (1894). fp Helsinki, 10 March 1895 (See also Orchestral)

Herran siunaus ('God's Blessing'), for liturgist and organ (1925). fp?

Johdantovuorolauluja ('Introductory Antiphons' – for Palm Sunday, All Saints' Day and General Prayers), for liturgist, congregation/choir and organ (1925). fp?

Masonic Ritual Music, Op. 113, for voice(s) and harmonium, texts (in Finnish) by Franz von Schober (trans. Eino Leino), Pao Chao (trans. Eino Tikkanen), Johann Wolfgang von Goethe (trans. Eino Leino), Aukusti Simelius, Viktor Rydberg, Jacob Tegengren, Simo Korpela, Samuli Sario, Wäinö Sola (1926–7). fp Helsinki, 12 January 1927. Extended version with chorus (1946). fp Helsinki, 24 October 1946. Revised version (1948). fp?

Vocal with Orchestra

Suite for orchestra with baritone [Opp. 10, 11], from *Scenic Music for a Festival and Lottery in Aid of Education in the Province of Viipuri* (1893). fp Helsinki, 19 November 1893

Serenad ('Serenade'), for baritone and orchestra, text by Erik Stagnelius (1895). fp Helsinki, 17 April 1895

The Rapids-Rider's Brides ('Koskenlaskijan morsiamet'), Op. 33, for baritone or mezzo-soprano and orchestra, text by A. Oksanen (1897). fp Helsinki, 1 November 1897. Voice and piano reduction (1899). fp?

Sen har jag ej frågat mera ('And I Questioned Them No Further'), Op. 17/1, arrangement for soprano and small orchestra of 1894 voice and piano work, text by Johan Runeberg (1903). fp Helsinki, 10 November 1903

Demanten på marssnön ('The Diamond on the March Snow'), Op. 36/6, arrangement for mezzo-soprano and small orchestra of 1900 voice and piano work, text by Josef Wecksell (date unknown). fp?

Höstkvall ('Autumn Night'), Op. 38/1, arrangement for voice and full orchestra, or string orchestra, of 1903 voice and piano work, text by Viktor Rydberg (1903–4). fp?

På veranden vid havet ('On a Balcony by the Sea'), Op. 38/2, arrangement for voice and full orchestra, or string orchestra, of 1903 voice and piano work, text by Viktor Rydberg (1903). fp Helsinki, 10 November 1903

I natten ('In the Night'), Op. 38/3, arrangement for voice and orchestra of 1903 voice and piano work, text by Viktor Rydberg (1903). fp Helsinki, 10 November 1903

Grevinnans conterfej ('The Countess's Portrait'; *Porträtterna*), melodrama for reciter and strings, text by Zachris Topelius (1906). fp Vaasa, 6 January 1907

Arioso, Op. 3, for soprano and string orchestra, text by Johan Runeberg (1911). fp? Voice and piano reduction (1913). fp Helsinki, 18 September 1913

Luonnotar, Op. 70 [Op. 70a], tone-poem for soprano and orchestra, text from the *Kalevala* (1913). fp Gloucester, 10 September 1913. Voice and piano reduction (1914). fp?

Våren flyktar hastigt ('Spring Is Flying Swiftly'), Op. 13/4, arrangement for soprano and small orchestra of 1890 voice and piano work, text by Johan Runeberg (1914). fp Turku, 30 March 1914

Soluppgång ('Sunrise'), Op. 37/3, arrangement for soprano and small orchestra of 1902 voice and piano work, text by Tor Hedberg (1914). fp Turku, 30 March 1914

Autrefois, Scène pastorale, Op. 96b, for two sopranos and orchestra, text by Hjalmar Procopé (1919). fp Helsinki, 1919 (See also Solo Instrument(s) with Orchestra)

'Come Away, Death' [Op. 60/1], for baritone, harp and strings, text by William Shakespeare (trans. Kyllikki Solanterä) (1909, orchestrated 1957). fp Helsinki, 14 June 1957

Orchestral

Overture in E major [Opp. 6, 6a] (1891). fp Helsinki, 23 April 1891

'Ballet Scene' ('Scène de ballet') [Opp. 6, 7] (1891). fp Helsinki, 28 April 1891

Porilaisten March (*Björneborgarnas March*), for small orchestra, after a painting by Albert Edelfelt (1892; lost). fp Helsinki, 5 February 1892. Version for full orchestra (1900). fp Stockholm, 4 July 1900

En saga ('A Tale'), tone-poem, Op. 9 (1892). fp Helsinki, 16 February 1893. Revised version (1902). fp Helsinki, 2 November 1902

Impromptu [Opp. 5/5 and 5/6], transcription for string orchestra of Impromptu for piano, Op. 5, No. 5 (c. 1893). fp Turku, 15 February 1894

Karelia Overture, Op. 10, from *Scenic Music for a Festival and Lottery in Aid of Education in the Province of Viipuri* (1893). fp Helsinki, 24 April 1894 (may be performed with *Karelia Suite*, Op. 11, in concert as one item)

Karelia Suite, Op. 11, from *Scenic Music for a Festival and Lottery in Aid of Education in the Province of Viipuri* (1893). fp Helsinki, 24 April 1894 (may be performed with *Karelia Overture*, Op. 10, in concert as one item)

Spring Song ('Vårsång'; *La triste du printemps, Improvisation*), tone-poem, Op. 16 (1894). fp Vaasa, 21 June 1894. Revised version (1895). fp Helsinki, 13 April 1895

Presto (Scherzo), transcription for string orchestra of 1889–90 String Quartet in B flat, third movement [Op. 3] (1894). fp?

Menuetto (Menuett-Impromptu, Tempo di Menuetto; 1894). fp?

The Wood Nymph ('Skogsrået'), tone-poem (also ballade), Op. 15 (1894–5). fp Helsinki, 17 April 1895 (See also Vocal with Instruments)

Symphonic Poems on Motifs from the Lemminkäinen Myth (also *Four Legends, Lemminkäinen Legends, Lemminkäinen Suite*), Op. 22 (1893–5). fp Helsinki, 13 April 1896. Revised version (1897). fp Helsinki, 1 November 1897.
In 1947 the composer gave the following preferred order when performed complete:
Lemminkäinen and the Maidens of the Islands, Op. 22/1 (revised for publication, 1939)
The Swan of Tuonela, Op. 22/3 (revised for publication, 1900)
Lemminkäinen in Tuonela, Op. 22/2 (revised for publication, 1939)
Lemminkäinen's Return, Op. 22/4 (revised for publication, 1900)

Coronation March, arranged from Cantata for the Coronation of Tsar Nicholas II [Op. 19] (1896). fp?

Overture from opera *The Maiden in the Tower* (1896). fp (probably) Turku, 7 April 1900

Suite from *King Christian II*, Op. 27 (1898). fp?

Suite from *Music for the Press Pension Fund* [Opp. 26, 25] (1899). fp Helsinki, 14 December 1899. Revised for publication, 1911, as *Scènes historiques*: Suite No. 1 (without final movement *Finlandia*)

Symphony No. 1 in E minor, Op. 39 (1898–9). fp Helsinki, 26 April 1899. Revised version (1900). fp Helsinki, 1 July 1900

Finlandia ('Suomi'; Impromptu), Op. 26 [Op. 26/7], tone-poem from suite from *Music for the Press Pension Fund* (1900). fp Helsinki, 2 July 1900

Cortège (1901). fp?

Symphony No. 2 in D major, Op. 43 (1901–2). fp Helsinki, 8 March 1902

Overture in A minor [Opp. 6, 6b, 21] (1902). fp Helsinki, 8 March 1902

Cassazione, Op. 6 [Opp. 40, 34, 30] (1904). fp Helsinki, 8 February 1904. Revised version (1905). fp?

Valse triste, Op. 44/1, for small orchestra, from *Kuolema* (1904). fp Helsinki, 25 April 1904

Musik zu einer Szene ('Music to a Scene'; alternative title: *A Fir Tree … Dreams of a Palm*, also known, originally, as Dance Intermezzo No. 1), Op. 45/2 (1904). fp Helsinki, 5 March 1904. Revised version as Dance Intermezzo No. 1 (1907). fp?

Romance (originally Andante) in C major, Op. 42, for string orchestra (1904). fp Turku, 26 March 1904

Suite from *Pelléas and Mélisande*, Op. 46 (1905). fp?

Scene with Cranes, Op. 44/2, tone-poem, for small orchestra, from *Kuolema* (1906). fp?

Pan and Echo (Dance Intermezzo No. 3), Op. 53a (1906). fp Helsinki, 24 March 1906

Pohjola's Daughter, symphonic fantasia, Op. 49 (1906). fp St Petersburg, 29 December 1906

Suite from *Belshazzar's Feast*, Op. 51 (1907). fp Helsinki, 25 September 1907

Symphony No. 3 in C major, Op. 52 (1906–7). fp Helsinki, 25 September 1907

Night Ride and Sunrise, tone-poem, Op. 55 (1908).
fp St Petersburg, 23 January 1909

Suite from *Swanwhite*, Op. 54 (1908–9). fp?

In memoriam, funeral march, Op. 59 (1909). Never
performed. Revised version (1910). fp Oslo,
8 October 1910

The Dryad, tone-poem, Op. 45/1 (1910). fp Oslo,
8 October 1910

Symphony No. 4 in A minor, Op. 63 (1910–11).
fp Helsinki, 3 April 1911

Two Pieces from *Kuolema*, Op. 62 (1911). fp Helsinki,
8 March 1911
No. 1: *Canzonetta*, for string orchestra, Op. 62a
No. 2: *Valse romantique*, Op. 62b (1911)

Scènes historiques: Suite No. 1, revised version of suite
from *Music for the Press Pension Fund*, Op. 25 [Opp.
26/2, 26/5, 26/4] (1911). fp?

Rakastava ('The Lover'), Op. 14, suite for string
orchestra and percussion (1911–12, based on 1893 work
for male chorus). fp Helsinki, 16 March 1912

The Bard, tone-poem, Op. 64 [Op. 70b] (1913).
fp Helsinki, 27 March 1913. Revised version (1914).
fp Helsinki, 9 January 1916

Scènes historiques: Suite No. 2, three tone-poems,
Op. 66 (1912). fp Helsinki, 29 March 1913

The Oceanides ('Aallottaret'), tone-poem, Op. 73 (1914).
fp Norfolk, USA, 4 June 1914

Symphony No. 5 in E flat major, Op. 82 (1914–15).
fp Helsinki, 8 December 1915. Revised version (1916).
fp Turku, 8 December 1916. Final version (1918–19).
fp Helsinki, 24 November 1919

March of the Finnish Jäger Battalion ('Jääkärimarssi')
[Op. 91a], orchestral arrangement of 1917 choral work
(1918). fp Helsinki, 21 April 1918

Academic March ('Promootiomarssi') [Op. 91b] (1919).
fp Helsinki, 31 May 1919

Valse lyrique, Op. 96, orchestral arrangement of 1914
piano work *Syringa* (1921). fp Helsinki, 6 April 1922

Valse chevaleresque, Op. 96c, orchestral arrangement of
1920 piano work (c. 1921). fp Helsinki, 19 February 1923

Suite mignonne, Op. 98a, for two flutes and string
orchestra (1921). fp?

Suite champêtre, Op. 98b, for string orchestra (1921).
fp Helsinki, 19 February 1923

Suite caractéristique, Op. 100, for string orchestra and
harp (1922). fp Helsinki, 19 February 1923

Symphony No. 6 in D minor, Op. 104 (1918–23).
fp Helsinki, 19 February 1923

Symphony No. 7 in C major (originally *Fantasia
sinfonica*), Op. 105 (1922–4). fp Stockholm,
24 March 1924

Andante lirico [Op. 5/4], transcription for string
orchestra of Impromptu for piano, Op. 5, No. 6 (1924).
fp?

Morceau romantique sur un motif de M. Jacob de Julin,
for small orchestra (1925). fp Helsinki, 9 March 1925

Tapiola, symphonic poem, Op. 112 (1926). fp New York,
USA, 26 December 1926

Concert extracts from *The Tempest* [Op. 109] (1928). fp?
Prelude, Op. 109/1
Suite No. 1, Op. 109/2
Suite No. 2, Op. 109/3

Andante festivo, arrangement for strings and timpani of 1922 string quartet (c. 1930). fp?

A Lonely Ski-trail ('Ett ensamt skidspår'), arrangement for harp and string orchestra of 1925 melodrama for reciter and piano (1948). fp?

Solo Instrument(s) with Orchestra

Violin Concerto in D minor, Op. 47 (1903–4). fp Helsinki, 8 February 1904. Revised version (1905). fp Berlin, 19 October 1905

Two Serenades, Op. 69, for violin and orchestra (1912–13). fp Helsinki, 8 December 1915
No. 1 in D major, Op. 69a (1912)
No. 2 in G minor, Op. 69b (1913)

Two Pieces (*Serious Melodies*), Op. 77, for violin or cello and orchestra (1914–15). fp (cello version) Helsinki, 30 March 1916; fp? (violin version)
No. 1: *Laetare anima mea* (*Cantique*), Op. 77/1 (1914)
No. 2: *Devotion* (*Ab imo pectore*), Op. 77/2 (1915)

Six Humoresques (Impromptus), Opp. 87, 89, for violin and orchestra (1917). fp Helsinki, 8 December 1915
No. 1 in D minor, Op. 87/1. Revised version (c. 1939). fp Helsinki, 15 December 1940
No. 2 in D major, Op. 87/2
No. 3 in G minor, for violin and strings, Op. 89/1
No. 4 in G minor, for violin and strings, Op. 89/2
No. 5 in E flat major, Op. 89/3
No. 6 in G minor, Op. 89/4

Autrefois, *Scène pastorale*, Op. 96b, for two clarinets and orchestra (1920). fp? (See also Vocal with Orchestra)

Suite in D minor, Op. 117, for violin and string orchestra (c. 1928–9). fp Lahti, 8 December 1990

Chamber

Piano Trio (c. 1881). fp?

Menuetto in F major, for two violins and piano (c. 1883). fp?

Trio, for two violins and piano (c. 1883). fp?

Piano Trio in A minor (c. 1884). fp Loviisa, summer 1888

Quartet in D minor, for piano, two violins and cello (1884). fp?

Molto moderato - Scherzo: Allegretto, for string quartet (c. 1885). fp?

String Quartet in E flat major (1885). fp?

Movement in G minor, for string trio (1885). fp?

Piano Trio in A minor ('Korpo Trio') (1886). fp?

Allegro in D major, for piano trio (c. 1886). fp (probably) Loviisa, summer 1887

Andante-Allegro in A major, for piano and string quartet (c. 1886). fp (probably) Loviisa, summer 1887

Andante-Allegro molto in D major, for string quartet (c. 1886). fp?

Andantino in G minor, for piano trio (c. 1887). fp (probably) Loviisa, summer 1887

Allegro and Menuetto, for two violins and cello (1887). fp (probably) Loviisa, summer 1887

Quartet in G minor, 'Sucksdorff', for violin, harmonium, cello and piano (1887). fp Loviisa, summer 1887

Piano Trio in D major (1887). fp Loviisa, summer 1888

Theme and Variations in C sharp minor [Op. 1], for string quartet (1888). fp Helsinki, 31 May 1888

Piano Trio in C major ('Loviisa Trio') (1888). fp Loviisa, summer 1888

Fugue in A minor, 'For Martin Wegelius', for string quartet (1888). fp?

Allegro in E minor, for string quartet (c. 1887–9). fp?

Moderato-Allegro appassionato in C sharp minor, for string quartet (c. 1887–9). fp?

Più Lento in F major, for string quartet (c. 1887–9). fp?

Adagio in F minor, for string quartet (c. 1888–9). fp?

Alla marcia in E minor, for string quartet (c. 1888–9). fp?

Allegretto in D major, for string quartet (c. 1888–9). fp?

Allegretto in G minor, for string quartet (c. 1888–9). fp?

Allegretto in A major, for string quartet (c. 1888–9). fp?

Presto in F major, for string quartet (c. 1888–9). fp?

Serenata in D minor, for string trio (c. 1888–9). fp?

Andante molto sostenuto in B minor, for string quartet (c. 1889). fp?

String Trio (or Suite) in A major [Op. 4] (1889). fp Helsinki, 13 April 1889

Andantino in A major, for string trio (1889). fp?

String Quartet in A minor [Op. 2] (1889). fp Helsinki, 29 May 1889

Andantino in C major, for string quartet (c. 1889). fp?

Allegro, for brass septet (1889). fp?

String Quartet in B flat major, Op. 4 [Op. 3] (1889–90). fp Helsinki, 13 October 1890

Overture, for brass septet (1889–90). fp?

Piano Quintet in G minor [Opp. 10, 6] (1890). fp (first and third movements) Helsinki, 5 May 1890; fp (first four movements of five) Turku, 11 October 1890

Adagio in D minor, for string quartet (1890). fp?

Andantino-Menuetto, for brass septet (1890–1). fp Loviisa, 5 February 1891

Quartet in C minor, for piano, two violins and cello (1891). fp?

Praeludium, for brass septet (1891). fp Loviisa, summer 1891

Tiera, tone-poem, for brass septet and percussion (1894, possibly 1898). fp (possibly) Helsinki, 20 June 1900

Preludio, for wind and brass instruments (c. 1899). fp (possibly) Helsinki, 20 June 1900

String Quartet in D minor, *Voces intimae*, Op. 56 (1908–9). fp Berlin, 6 January 1910

Andante festivo, for string quartet (1922). fp Helsinki, 28 December 1922

Piano

Con moto, sempre una corda (1885). fp?

Au crépuscule (1887). fp?

Trånaden ('Longing'), suite (1887). fp?

Allegretto in B flat minor (c. 1887–8). fp?

Andante in E flat major (c. 1887–8). fp?

Andantino in B major (c. 1887–8). fp?

Andantino in C major (c. 1887–8). fp?

Moderato-Presto (c. 1887–8). fp?

Adagio in D major (c. 1888). fp?

Allegretto in G minor (c. 1888). fp?

Menuetto in F sharp minor (c. 1888). fp?

Scherzo (c. 1888). fp?

Vivace in E flat major (c. 1888). fp?

Andantino in E major (1888). fp?

Largo in A major (1888). fp?

Vivace in D minor (1888). fp?

Allegretto in E major (1889). fp?

For Betsy Lerché, waltz (1889). fp Helsinki, 1889

Florestan, suite (1889). fp?

Allegretto in F major (1890). fp?

Lento in E major (c. 1890). fp?

Six Impromptus, Op. 5 (1890–3). fp (various selections) Helsinki, 5, 19, 22 November 1893

Sonata in F major, Op. 12 (1893–5). fp Helsinki, 17 April 1895

Ten Pieces, Op. 24 (Nos. 1–5: c. 1894–6; Nos. 6–9: c. 1898–1901; No. 10 Barcarola [Op. 38, No. 10]: 1903). fp?

Excerpts from *The Wood Nymph* ('Skogsrået'), transcription from orchestral tone-poem (1895). fp?

Caprizzio (1895). fp?

Intermezzo and Ballade, transcriptions from *Karelia Suite* (c. 1897). fp?

Allegretto in G minor ('19. xii. 1897'; 1897). fp?

King Christian II, transcription of orchestral suite (1898). fp?

Finlandia, transcription of orchestral tone-poem (1900). fp?

The Cavalier (1900). fp?

Marche triste in E minor (c. 1901–3). fp?

Six Finnish Folk Songs, arranged for piano (1903). fp?

Har du mod? ('Have You Courage?'), transcription of choral song (1904). fp?

Song of the Athenians, transcription of choral song (1904). fp?

Dance Intermezzo No. 1, transcription of orchestral work (1904). fp?

Valse triste, transcription from *Kuolema* (1904). fp?

Kyllikki, three lyric pieces, Op. 41 [No. 1: Op. 31] (1904). fp?

Pelléas and Mélisande, transcription from orchestral suite (1905). fp?

Livets dans, Dödens dans ('Dance of Life; Dance of Death'), transcription from *Belshazzar's Feast* (1906). fp?

Belshazzar's Feast, transcription from orchestral suite (1907). fp?

Ten Pieces, Op. 58 (1909). fp (Nos. 1–5) Helsinki, 10 October 1911; fp? (Nos. 6–10)

The Dryad, transcription of orchestral tone-poem (1910). fp?

The Bells of Berghälls Church ('Kallion kirkon kellosävel'), transcription of choral motet (1912). fp?

Two Rondinos, Op. 68 (1911). fp Helsinki, 10 October 1911
No. 1 in G sharp minor
No. 2 in C sharp minor

Three Sonatinas, Op. 67 (1912). fp?
No. 1 in F sharp minor
No. 2 in E major
No. 3 in B flat minor

Pensées lyriques, Op. 40 [No. 2, *Chanson sans paroles*: Op. 36/2] (1912–16). fp?

Spagnuolo (1913). fp?

To Longing ('Till trånaden') (1913). fp?

Syringa (*Valse lyrique*) [Op. 75/6] (1914). fp?

Four Lyric Pieces, Op. 74 (1914). fp?

Five Pieces ('Morceaux'; *Trees*), Op. 75 (1914). fp?
Revised version of No. 5, *Granen* ('The Spruce') (c. 1919). fp?

Thirteen Pieces ('Morceaux'), Op. 76 (Nos. 1–3: 1911; Nos. 6, 11–12: 1913–14; Nos. 4, 7–10, 13: 1916). fp?

Ten Bagatelles, Op. 34 (1914–16). fp?

Five Pieces (*Flowers*), Op. 85 (1916–17). fp?

Episodio, *Canzone* and *Scèna*, transcriptions from *Jedermann* ('Everyman') (c. 1917). fp?

Mandolinato (1917). fp?

Six Pieces, Op. 94 (1914–19). fp?

To O. Parviainen by his Old, Faithful and Grateful Friend Jean Sibelius (c. 1918–20). fp?

Three Pieces, Op. 96 (1920). fp?
No. 1: *Valse lyrique*, Op. 96a (1920)
No. 2: *Autrefois*, Op. 96b, transcription of *Autrefois: Scène pastorale* (1920)
No. 3: *Valse chevaleresque*, Op. 96c (1920)

Six Bagatelles, Op. 97 (1920). fp?

Danse élégiaque and *Scène d'amour*, transcriptions from *Scaramouche* (1920). fp?

De danske Spejderes March ('Danish Scout March'; *Partiolaisten marssi*), transcription for chorus and orchestra of *Scout March* (1921). fp?

Suite mignonne, transcription of suite for string orchestra (1921). fp?

Suite champêtre, transcription of suite for string orchestra (1921). fp?

Eight Short Pieces ('Petits Morceaux'), Op. 99 (1922). fp?

Suite caractéristique, transcription of suite for string orchestra (1922). fp?

Five Romantic Pieces ('Morceaux romantiques'), Op. 101 (1923). fp?

Five Characteristic Impressions, Op. 103 (1924). fp?

Morceau romantique sur un motif de M. Jacob de Julin, transcription of orchestral work (c. 1925). fp?

Three Pieces, transcriptions from *The Tempest* (1927). fp?
Episode (*Miranda*)
Scene
Dance of the Nymphs

Five Esquisses, Op. 114 (1929). fp?

There are, additionally, nine pieces which bear neither title nor tempo marking, dating from c. 1884–9, and two others with titles but without dates: Molto andante in F sharp minor and Più Lento – Tempo di valse.

Instrumental

Water Drops, for violin and cello pizzicato (c. 1875–80). fp?

Adagio-Allegro, for two violins (c. 1880). fp?

Andantino in C major, for cello and piano (c. 1884). fp?

Violin Sonata in A minor (1884). fp?

Andante grazioso in D major, for violin and piano (c. 1884–5). fp?

Duo, for violin and viola (1886 or 1887). fp?

Allegretto in E flat major, for violin and piano (c. 1887). fp (probably) Loviisa, summer 1887

Theme (Adagio) and Variations in D minor, for unaccompanied cello (c. 1887). fp?

Andante cantabile in G major, for violin and piano (1887). fp (probably) Loviisa, summer 1887

Duo in E minor, for violin and cello (c. 1887–9). fp (probably) Loviisa, summer 1887

Violin Sonata (also Suite) in D minor (c. 1887–8). fp?

Romance in B minor and *Perpetuum mobile* (Epilogue), for violin and piano [Opp. 1, 2] (1888; 1891). fp? Revised version (1911). fp?

Allegretto in C major, for violin and piano (c. 1888). fp?

Suite in E major, for violin and piano (c. 1888). fp?

Tempo di valse in G minor, for cello and piano (c. 1888–9; piano part lost). fp?

Violin Sonata in F major (c. 1888–9). fp Loviisa, 1889

Andante molto in F minor, for cello and piano (c. 1889). fp?

Allegretto in A minor, for violin and piano (c. 1889). fp?

Fantasia for cello and piano [Op. 1] (c. 1889; piano part lost). fp?

Moderato-Maestoso in E flat major, for cello and piano (c. 1889). fp?

Canon (Tempo di menuetto) in G minor, for violin and cello (1889). fp?

Tempo di valse ('Lulu' waltz) in F sharp minor, for cello and piano (1889). fp Loviisa, 19 August 1889

Duo in C major, for violin and viola (c. 1891–2). fp?

Rondo [Op. 2], for viola and piano (1893). fp (probably) Helsinki, 10 March 1894

Valssi ('Waltz'), for violin and kantele (c. 1899). fp?

Malinconia, Op. 20 [Op. 25], fantasia for cello and piano (1900). fp Helsinki, 12 March 1900

Melody for the Bells of Berghälls Church (1912). fp Berghälls (Kallio) Church inauguration, 1912

Two Pieces (*Serious Melodies*), Op. 77, for violin or cello
and piano (1914–15). fp?
No. 1: *Laetare anima mea* (*Cantique*), Op. 77/1 (1914)
No. 2: *Devotion* (*Ab imo pectore*), Op. 77/2 (1915)

Four Pieces, Op. 78 [No. 4: Op. 77/3], for violin or
cello and piano (1915–17). fp?

Six Pieces, Op. 79, for violin and piano (1915–17). fp?

Violin Sonatina (originally Sonata) in E major, Op. 80
[Op. 78] (1915). fp Helsinki, 6 December 1915

Five Pieces, Op. 81, for violin and piano (1915–18). fp?

Novellette, Op. 102, for violin and piano (1922). fp?

En glad musikant, for unaccompanied violin (c. 1925).
fp?

Five *Danses champêtres*, for violin and piano, Op. 106
(1925). fp?

Scène d'amour, transcription for violin and piano from
Scaramouche (1925). fp?

Intrada, Op. 111/1, for organ (1925). fp Helsinki,
25 August 1925

Four Pieces, Op. 115, for violin and piano (1929). fp?

Three Pieces, Op. 116, for violin and piano (1929). fp?

Surusoitto, funeral music, in memoriam Axel Gallen-
Kallela, Op. 111/2, for organ (1931). fp Helsinki,
19 March 1931

There are, additionally, twelve pieces for violin with and
without piano accompaniment which bear neither title
nor tempo marking, dating from c. 1885–8, an Andante
cantabile for harmonium and piano, and two undated
works for organ, *Praeludium* and *Postludium*, probably
written as a pair.

Further Reading

This list contains the official sources of published material for *Jean Sibelius*. Unless stated otherwise, these are all in English, even those published in Finland which are available in translation. I have concentrated on book-length studies, including for the sake of manageability only those shorter articles of particular relevance to the narrative. Many of the books listed have extensive bibliographies which can also be used as guides for further reading. For ease of reference I have divided the list into categories dealing respectively with Finnish History and Art, Sibelius himself as principal subject, and finally a miscellany including those books where Sibelius is featured as an incidental figure.

Finnish History and Art

The volume of literature in English published in Finland is unusual, but English is to a certain degree the third language of the modern state (as can be readily observed on the Finnish rail service). Accessibility to this material is less easy within Great Britain, but the books should be available by import or by recourse to the Finnish Embassy. Histories published in Britain or the USA tend to concentrate on modern affairs, as in the case of the books by Hamäläinen, Juttikala and Pirinen, and Tillotson. Matti Klinge's and Fred Singleton's readable accounts are probably the best introduction for the general reader wishing to obtain an overview of Finnish history. The reminiscences by the former prime minister Oskari Tokoi have a particular relevance for students of the political background.

Hall, W. *Green, Gold and Granite* (London, Max Parrish, 1953)
Hamäläinen, P. K. *In Time of Storm: Revolution, Civil War and the Ethnolinguistic Issue in Finland* (Albany, New York, New York State University, 1979)
Juttikala, E. and K. Pirinen *A History of Finland* (London, Heinemann, revised edition, 1979)
Kallio, V. *Finland – Cultural Perspectives*, trans. P. Henning (Porvoo, WSOY, 1989)
Klinge, M. *A Brief History of Finland* (Helsinki, Otava, 1981)
— *The Baltic World* (Helsinki, Otava, 1994)
Singleton, F. *A Short History of Finland* (Cambridge, Cambridge University Press, 1989)
Smith, J. B. *The Golden Age of Finnish Art* (Helsinki, Otava, 2nd edition, 1985)
Tillotson, H. M. *Finland at Peace and War* (Norwich, Martin Russell, 1993)
Tokoi, O. *Sisu, 'Even through a stone wall'* (New York, Speller, 1957)
Wuorinen, J. H. *A History of Finland* (New York, Columbia University Press, 1965)
Zetterberg, S. *Finland after 1917* (Helsinki, Otava, 1991)

Jean Sibelius

The definitive biography of Sibelius is, of course, Erik Tawaststjerna's multi-volume survey, the fruit of a lifetime of study, available in English through Robert Layton's excellent translation. Layton himself is the author of a fine single-volume survey for the Dent 'Master Musicians' series, which concentrates on discussing the music. Earlier biographies are generally marred by lack of access to the source documents or the whole of Tawaststjerna's study, as in the case of that by the late David Burnett-James, or too close a reliance on the composer himself, who was not above misinformation. The first studies, by Furuhjelm, Gray and Ekman, are all now severely out of date and misleading, except in providing historical insights into perceptions of the composer. Furuhjelm's study has, as far as I know, never been available in English; Gray's, and Birse's translation of Ekman's biography, while currently out of print, can regularly be found in decent second-hand bookshops. So can Gerald Abraham's thoroughgoing symposium, which is excellent as far as it goes, although none of the then hidden early works was available to be covered. Of more modern studies, Glenda Goss's *Jean Sibelius and Olin Downes* is a fascinating study of how a composer's reputation can be moulded to advantage, and provides many incidental details not included even by Tawaststjerna. For those seeking more technical discussion of Sibelius's music, the studies by Hepokoski, Pike and Murtomäki are self-recommending.

Abraham, G. (ed.) *Sibelius: A Symposium* (London, Lindsay Drummond, 1947)

Adorno, T. W. 'Glosse über Sibelius', in *Zeitschrift für Sozialforschung* (Frankfurt, 1938) [in German]

Burnett-James, D. *Sibelius* (London, Omnibus Press, 1989)

Dahlström, F. *The Works of Jean Sibelius* (Helsinki, Sibelius Society, 1987)

Downes, O. 'Sibelius', chapter in *Symphonic Masterpieces* (New York, The Dial Press, 1935)

Ekman, K. *Jean Sibelius: His Life and Personality*, trans. E. Birse (London, Wilmer, 1936)

Furuhjelm, E. *Jean Sibelius* (Porvoo, Werner Söderström, 1916) [in Swedish]

Goss, G. D. *Jean Sibelius and Olin Downes: Music, Friendship, Criticism* (Boston, Northeastern University Press, 1995)

— *The Sibelius Companion* (Westport, Greenwood Press, 1997)

Gould, G. 'The Piano Music of Sibelius', in T. Page (ed.) *The Glenn Gould Reader* (London, Faber and Faber, 1984)

Gray, C. *Sibelius* (Oxford, Oxford University Press, 1934)

— *Sibelius: The Symphonies* (London, Oxford University Press, 1935)

Grier, C. 'Sibelius', in A. L. Bacharach (ed.) *The Music Masters*, Vol. 4: 'The Twentieth Century' (Harmondsworth, Pelican, 1957)

Hannikainen, I. *Sibelius and the Development of Finnish Music*, trans. A. Nopsanen (London, Hinrichsen Edition, 1948)

Hepokoski, J. *Sibelius: Symphony No. 5* (Cambridge, Cambridge University Press, 'Cambridge Music Handbooks', 1993)

Herbage, J. 'Jean Sibelius', in R. Hill (ed.) *The Symphony* (Harmondsworth, Pelican, 1949)

Johnson, H. E. *Jean Sibelius* (New York, Knopf, 1959)

Karttunen, A. 'True and False *Andante Festivo*', *Finnish Music Quarterly*, No. 4, 1996

Kilpeläinen, K. *The Jean Sibelius Musical Manuscripts at Helsinki University Library: A Complete Catalogue* (Wiesbaden, Breitkopf und Härtel, 1991)

Koskimies, Y. *Sibelius and Hämeenlinna* (Hämeenlinna, Sibelius Society, 1990) [in Finnish, Swedish and English]

Layton, R. *Sibelius* (London, Dent, 1965, revised edition, 1978)

— 'Sibelius, Germany and Karajan', *Finnish Music Quarterly*, No. 4, 1994

Leibowitz, R. *Jean Sibelius: Le plus mauvais compositeur du monde* ('Jean Sibelius, the World's Worst Composer') (Liège, Dynamo, 1955) [in French]

Levas, S. *Sibelius: A Personal Portrait*, trans. P. M. Young (London, Dent, 1972)

Murtomäki, V. *Symphonic Unity: The Development of Formal Thinking in the Symphonies of Sibelius*, trans. H. Bacon and the author (Helsinki, Helsinki University, 1993)

Newmarch, R. *Jean Sibelius: A Finnish Composer* (Leipzig, Breitkopf und Härtel, 1906)

— *A Short Story of a Long Friendship* (Boston, C. C. Birchard, 1939)

Niemann, W. *Jean Sibelius: A Finnish Composer* (Leipzig, Breitkopf und Härtel, 1917)

Nupen, C. *Jean Sibelius* (documentary film in two parts, 'The Early Years' and 'Maturity and Silence', London, Allegro Films, 1984; issued on video, Teldec Classics 9031–76373–3, 1994)

Otonkoski, L. (ed.) *Finnish Music Quarterly*, 125th anniversary issue, Nos. 3–4, 1990

Parmet, S. *The Symphonies of Sibelius*, trans. K. A. Hart (London, Cassell, 1959)

Pike, L. *Beethoven, Sibelius and 'the Profound Logic': Studies in Symphonic Analysis* (London, Athlone Press, 1978)

Ringbom, N. -E. *Jean Sibelius: A Master and His Work*, first published in Swedish (Helsinki, Schildt's, 1948); trans. G. I. C. de Courcy (Oklahoma, Oklahoma University Press, 1954)

Salmenhaara, E. 'Jean Sibelius and *The Tempest*', *Finnish Music Quarterly*, No. 4, 1993

Shore, B. 'Sibelius' and 'Sibelius's Second Symphony', chapters in *Sixteen Symphonies* (London, Longman, 1949)

Tawaststjerna, E. T. *Jean Sibelius*, originally in Swedish, first published in Finnish (5 Vols., Helsinki, Otava: Vols. 1–2 trans. T. Anhava, 1965, 1967; Vols. 3–5 trans. E. Salmenhaara, 1972, 1977, 1988); translated into English by R. Layton (3 Vols., London, Faber and Faber, 1976, 1986, 1997)

— 'Sibelius's Eighth Symphony: an Insoluble Mystery', *Finnish Music Quarterly*, Nos. 1–2, 3–4, 1985

Tarasti, E. (ed.) *Proceedings from the First International Jean Sibelius Conference, Helsinki, August 1990* (Helsinki, Sibelius Academy, 1995)

Törne, B. de *Sibelius: A Close-Up* (Boston, Houghton Mifflin, 1937)

Truscott, H. 'Jean Sibelius', in R. Simpson (ed.) *The Symphony – Volume 2: Mahler to the Present Day* (Harmondsworth, Pelican, 1967)

Miscellaneous

As a figure who occupied a dominant position in Western music during a large portion of his lifetime, Sibelius not surprisingly features in a considerable number of memoirs by others. However, few of those who knew him well and consistently over a long period, such as Armas Järnefelt, Busoni or Kajanus, left detailed reminiscences. Others, such as Rosa Newmarch and Harriet Cohen, filtered their accounts, leaving them not infrequently impersonal in tone, while those who gave more unbuttoned accounts (such as Bax) did not have the opportunity to know the man well. Adolf Paul's fictional account therefore assumes a greater value, despite its inadmissibility as historical evidence. George Dyson's book is included by virtue of its complete omission of Sibelius from the ranks of composers of new music in the 1920s (a host of long-forgotten British figures do appear, also Busoni and Schoenberg), though whether Dyson excluded the Finn's music because he did not hold it in high regard, or because he did not consider it particularly new (for the time) is unclear.

Bax, A. *Farewell, My Youth: An Autobiography* (London, Longman, 1943)

Boult, A. *Boult on Music* (London, Toccata Press, 1982)

Brook, D. *Composers' Gallery* (London, Rockliff, 1946)

Busoni, F. *Sketch of a New Aesthetic of Music*, trans. T. Baker (New York, Schirmer, c. 1911; reprinted by Dover Publications, 1962)

Cohen, H. *A Bundle of Time* (London, Faber and Faber, 1969)

Dyson, G. *The New Music* (London, Oxford University Press, 2nd edition, 1926)

Elkin, R. *Queen's Hall 1893–1941* (London, Rider and Co., 1944)

Foreman, L. *Bax: A Composer and His Times* (Aldershot, Scolar Press, 2nd edition, 1988)

Lambert, C. *Music, Ho! A Study of Music in Decline* (London, Faber and Faber, 2nd edition, 1948)

Mellers, W. *Romanticism and the Twentieth Century* (London, Barrie & Jenkins, revised edition, 1988)

Nabokov, N. *Old Friends and New Music* (London, Hamish Hamilton, 1951)

Paul, A. *En bok om en människa* ('A Book about a Man') (Stockholm, Albert Bonniers, 1891) [in Swedish]

Rickards, G. 'The Symphony in Finland since 1945: a British Perspective', *Finnish Music Quarterly*, No. 2, 1995

Russell, T. *Philharmonic* (London, Pelican, 1942)

Schoenberg, A. 'New Music, Old Music, Style and Idea', in L. Stein (ed.) *Style and Idea*, trans. L. Black (London, Faber and Faber, 1975)

Tovey, D. F. *Essays in Musical Analysis* (7 Vols., London, Oxford University Press, 1935–44)

Wallin, N. 'Järnefelt', in A. L. Bacharach (ed.) *The Music Masters*, Vol. 4: 'The Twentieth Century' (Harmondsworth, Pelican, 1957)

Wood, H. J. *My Life of Music* (London, Gollancz, 1938)

Selective Discography

Pride of place in any discography of the music of
Sibelius must go to the independent Swedish label BIS,
who are at the time of writing about two-thirds of the
way through recording all the known works – including
early, unpublished versions – which will take up some
sixty-five compact discs when complete. Of particular
value has been the uncovering of preliminary versions
of very well-known works, such as the Violin Concerto,
the Fifth Symphony and *En saga*. In a selective
discography such as this, one cannot include
everything, but the BIS edition forms the backbone of
my preferences and the benchmark in terms of
programming, performance and sound quality against
which to measure rival issues.

Sibelius has been, of course, a much-recorded
composer, although it might be more accurate to say
that certain areas of his output have been served
extremely well by the recording industry. At any given
time nowadays, there are probably around sixty
recordings of the Violin Concerto (excluding Leonidas
Kavakos's astounding interpretation of the 1904 first
version) and *Finlandia* – the latter in various guises for
orchestra, chorus and orchestra or keyboard
transcriptions. There are thirty to forty recordings of
The Swan of Tuonela (as a distinct tone-poem in its own
right, not as part of the *Lemminkäinen Suite*), *Karelia
Suite* and *Valse triste*. The Gramophone Classical
Catalogue lists some fifteen complete sets of the seven
numbered symphonies (only Berglund for EMI, Järvi
for BIS and Segerstam on Chandos included *Kullervo*),
and others are being added constantly – for instance by
Sir Colin Davis, currently engaged on his second for
RCA. Berglund's very fine 1980s cycle is only partially
resident in the catalogue, so I have chosen his
stablemate Sir Simon Rattle's revelatory cycle and
Davis's unfinished second (RCA). And this

superabundance reflects only what is currently available
on compact disc, without regard for what may have
existed before on LP and earlier formats.

A further restriction – self-imposed – has been to
concentrate almost exclusively on all-Sibelius issues,
avoiding 'Scandinavian' – misnamed, as Finland is not
part of Scandinavia – or 'Nordic' collections, or
arbitrary commercial pairings with other Nordic
composers, such as Nielsen and Grieg. By this rule
some very fine accounts have been excluded, such as
that of the Violin Concerto by Viktoria Mullova (in its
most popular coupling with the Tchaikovsky, Philips
416 821–2PH) or any of Jascha Heifetz's. Avoiding
duplications is a practical impossibility, so where they
occur it is usually because the coupling includes
another work of importance. By this token, Sir
Alexander Gibson's two-disc set of the then complete
tone-poems for Chandos (rendered incomplete by the
exclusion of the *Lemminkäinen Suite* – issued separately
– and the recent rediscovery of *The Wood Nymph*)
might have been passed over also, but at mid-price it is
exceptional value, and the second disc, comprising
*Pohjola's Daughter, Night Ride and Sunrise, The
Oceanides* and *Tapiola*, is one of the best programmes of
Sibelius's orchestral music on the market.

Many historic recordings have been re-released on
CD, the most valuable (in terms of the insight they give
of how orchestras sounded when Sibelius was writing
his music) being those made by the Sibelius Society
during the 1930s, particularly those by Robert Kajanus,
Georg Schnéevoigt and others. However, the recording
purporting to be of Sibelius conducting his *Andante
Festivo* in 1939 – the only recording that exists of him
interpreting his own music – has in most of its
incarnations on disc been spurious (actually a tape by
an unknown conductor). A special mention must be
made of Erik Tawaststjerna's recordings (for BIS) of all
of Sibelius's piano music known at the time, including
the transcriptions the composer made of his own works.

Works referred to are in their final versions unless
otherwise stated.

Historical/Collections

Symphony No. 1
Concert Suite, from Belshazzar's Feast
Pohjola's Daughter
Symphony No. 3
Symphony No. 5
Karelia Suite (extracts)
Tapiola
Symphony No. 2
London Symphony Orchestra conducted by Robert
Kajanus (1930–2 recordings)
FINLANDIA 4509–95882–2 (3 CDs)

Violin Concerto
Symphony No. 6
Anja Ignatius (violin), Städtisches Orchestra Berlin
conducted by Armas Järnefelt (1943 recording);
Helsinki Philharmonic Orchestra conducted by Georg
Schnéevoigt (1934 recording)
FINLANDIA 1576–58810–2

En saga
Luonnotar
Finlandia
Spring Song
The Bard
The Dryad
Pohjola's Daughter
Night Ride and Sunrise
The Oceanides
Tapiola
Phyllis Bryn-Julson (soprano), Scottish National
Orchestra conducted by Sir Alexander Gibson
CHANDOS CHAN 8395–6 (2 CDs)

Symphony No. 1
Symphony No. 2
Symphony No. 3
Symphony No. 4
Symphony No. 5
Symphony No. 6
Symphony No. 7
Scene with Cranes
Night Ride and Sunrise
The Oceanides
City of Birmingham Symphony and Philharmonia
Orchestras conducted by Sir Simon Rattle
EMI CDM7 64118–2 (4 CDs)

Opera and Ballet

The Maiden in the Tower
Karelia Suite
Mari-Ann Häggender, Erland Hagegård, Jorma
Hynninen, Tone Kruse; Gothenburg Concert Hall
Choir, Gothenburg Symphony Orchestra conducted by
Neeme Järvi
BIS CD–250

Scaramouche
The Language of the Birds: Wedding March
Gothenburg Symphony Orchestra conducted by
Neeme Järvi
BIS CD–502

Incidental Music

(excluding concert extracts)

Belshazzar's Feast
Jedermann
Melodrama: The Countess's Portrait
Various soloists; Lahti Chamber Choir and Symphony
Orchestra conducted by Osmo Vänskä
BIS CD–735

The Tempest (1926 version, sung in the original Danish)
Monica Groop, Raili Viljakainen, Jorma Hynninen,
Jorma Silvasti, Sauli Tiilikainen; Opera Festival Chorus,
Finnish Radio Symphony Orchestra conducted by
Jukka-Pekka Saraste
Ondine Ode 813–2

The Tempest (1927 version, sung in Finnish)
Lilli Paasikivi, Kirsi Tiihonen, Anssi Hirvonen, Heikki
Keinonen, Paavo Kerola; Lahti Opera Chorus and
Symphony Orchestra conducted by Osmo Vänskä
BIS CD–581

Orchestral

Tone-poem: The Wood Nymph
Melodrama: The Wood Nymph
Incidental music: Swanwhite
Melodrama: A Lonely Ski-trail
Lasse Pyösti (speaker), Lahti Symphony Orchestra
conducted by Osmo Vänskä
BIS CD–815

*Symphonic Poems on Motifs from the Lemminkäinen
Myth* (in original 1895 sequence, Nos. 1–4)
Tapiola
Helsinki Philharmonic Orchestra conducted by Leif
Segerstam
Ondine ODE 852–2

*Symphonic Poems on Motifs from the Lemminkäinen
Myth* (in revised 1947 sequence, Nos. 1, 3, 2, 4)
Tapiola
Philadelphia Orchestra conducted by Eugene Ormandy
EMI CDM5 65176–2

King Christian II (extracts from incidental music)
Concert Suite, from Pelléas and Mélisande
Swanwhite (extracts from Concert Suite)
Iceland Symphony Orchestra conducted by Petri Sakari
Chandos Chan 9158

Symphony No. 1
Symphony No. 3
Helsinki Radio Symphony Orchestra conducted by
Okko Kamu
Deutsche Grammophon 429 526–2GR

Symphony No. 1
Symphony No. 4
London Symphony Orchestra conducted by
Sir Colin Davis
RCA Red Seal 09026 68183–2

Symphony No. 2
Symphony No. 6
London Symphony Orchestra conducted by
Sir Colin Davis
RCA Red Seal 09026 68218–2

Symphony No. 3
Symphony No. 5
London Symphony Orchestra conducted by
Sir Colin Davis
RCA Red Seal 09026 61963–2

Violin Concerto (original version, 1903–4)
Violin Concerto (1905 version)
Leonidas Kavakos (violin), Lahti Symphony Orchestra
conducted by Osmo Vänskä
BIS CD–500

Violin Concerto
Overture in A minor
Menuetto
In memoriam
Silvia Marcovici (violin), Gothenburg Symphony
Orchestra conducted by Neeme Järvi
BIS CD–372

Concert Suite, from Swanwhite
Concert Suite, from Belshazzar's Feast
The Dryad
Dance Intermezzo No. 1
Pan and Echo
Gothenburg Symphony Orchestra conducted by
Neeme Järvi
BIS CD–359

Symphony No. 4
Symphony No. 7
Valse triste
Berlin Philharmonic Orchestra conducted by
Herbert von Karajan
Deutsche Grammophon 439 527–2GGA

Scènes historiques: Suite No. 1
Scènes historiques: Suite No. 2
Suite: Rakastava (for string orchestra and percussion)
Valse lyrique
Scottish National Orchestra conducted by Sir
Alexander Gibson
Chandos Chan6591

Two Serenades (for violin and orchestra)
Two Pieces (Serious Melodies) (for violin and orchestra)
Six Humoresques
Overture in E major
Ballet Scene
Dong-Suk Kang (violin), Gothenburg Symphony
Orchestra conducted by Neeme Järvi
BIS CD–472

Symphony No. 5 (original version, 1914–15)
En saga (original version, 1892)
Lahti Symphony Orchestra conducted by
Osmo Vänskä
BIS CD–800

Cassazione
Prelude and Concert Suites Nos. 1–2, from The Tempest
Preludio
Tiera
Gothenburg Symphony Orchestra conducted by
Neeme Järvi
BIS CD–448

Melodrama: A Lonely Ski-trail
Melodrama: The Countess's Portrait
Incidental music: The Lizard
Presto
Andante festivo (for string orchestra and timpani)
Suite: Rakastava (for string orchestra and percussion)

Romance in C major
Suite champêtre
Impromptu (for string orchestra)
Suite in D minor
Various soloists; Ostrobothnian Chamber Orchestra
conducted by Juha Kangas
Finlandia 4509–98995–2

Vocal/Choral

Song: Arioso
Six Songs, Op. 17
Song: Souda, souda, sinisorsa
Six Songs, Op. 36
Five Songs, Op. 37
The Three Blind Sisters, from Pelléas and Mélisande
Six Songs, Op. 88
Song: Narciss
Anne-Sophie von Otter (soprano), Bengt Forsberg
(piano)
BIS CD–457

Song of the Cross-spider, from King Christian II
Five Christmas Songs
Eight Songs on texts by Ernest Josephson
Hymn to Thaïs
Songs, Op. 72, Nos. 3–6
Six Songs, Op. 86
Små flickorna
Monica Groop (mezzo-soprano), Love Derwinger
(piano)
BIS CD–657

Song: Resemblance
Song: Serenade
Song: En visa
Seven Songs on texts by Johan Runeberg, Op. 13
Six Songs on German texts, Op. 50
Six Songs on texts by Johan Runeberg, Op. 90
Song: The Thought
Song: The Wood Nymph
Anne-Sophie von Otter (soprano), Bengt Forsberg
(piano)
BIS CD–757

Selected Songs for voice and piano, from Opp. 13, 17, 27, 35, 36–8, 57, 61, 86, 90
Tom Krause (baritone), Gustav Djupsjöbacka (piano)
FINLANDIA 4509–96871–2

The Rapids-Rider's Brides (for baritone and orchestra)
Luonnotar
Selected Orchestral Songs
Jorma Hynninen (baritone), Mari-Ann Häggander (soprano); Gothenburg Symphony Orchestra conducted by Jorma Panula
BIS CD–270

Kullervo Symphony
Karita Mattila (soprano), Jorma Hynninen (baritone); Laulun Ystävät Male Choir, Gothenburg Symphony Orchestra conducted by Neeme Järvi
BIS CD–313

Complete Works for Male Chorus
Helsinki University Male Chorus conducted by Matti Hyökki
FINLANDIA 4509–95849–2

Cantata: The Origin of Fire
Cantata: Sandels
Finnish Jäger March (for chorus and orchestra)
Song: Här du mod?
Song of the Athenians
Academic March, for orchestra
Finlandia (for chorus and orchestra)
Sauli Tiilikainen (baritone); Laulun Ystävät Male Choir, Gothenburg Symphony Orchestra conducted by Neeme Järvi
BIS CD–313

Cantata: Our Native Land
Improvisation: Snöfrid
Impromptu, Op. 19
Cantata: Väinön virsi
Cantata: A Song for Lemminkäinen
Cantata: Maan virsi
Finlandia (for chorus and orchestra)
Stina Rautelin (speaker), Finnish National Opera Chorus and Orchestra conducted by Eri Klas
ONDINE ODE 754–2

Chamber/Instrumental

String Quartet in E flat major
String Quartet in A minor
String Quartet in B flat major
String Quartet in D minor, Voces intimae
Sibelius Academy Quartet
FINLANDIA 4509–95851–2

Piano Trio in C major
String Quartet in E flat major
Piano Quintet in G minor
Tapiola Piano Trio, Erik T. Tawaststjerna, Sibelius Academy Quartet
FINLANDIA 4509–95851–2

Piano Quintet in G minor
String Quartet in D minor, Voces intimae
Anthony Goldstone (piano), Gabrieli String Quartet
CHANDOS CHAN 8742

Suite in E major (for violin and piano)
Adagio in D minor (for string quartet)
Fugue (for Martin Wegelius)
Duo in C major (for violin and viola)
Piano Trio in C major
Water Drops
Various soloists; Jean Sibelius Quartet
ONDINE ODE 850–2

Kyllikki
Three Sonatinas
Two Rondinos
Piano Sonata in F major
Finlandia (arranged for piano by the composer)
Marita Viitasalo (piano)
FINLANDIA 4509–98984–2

Complete Original Piano Music
Erik T. Tawaststjerna (piano)
BIS CD–153, 169, 195, 196, 230, 278 (6 Vols.)

Complete Piano Transcriptions
Erik T. Tawaststjerna (piano)
BIS CD–366, 367 (2 Vols.)

Quartet in C minor (for piano, two violins and cello)
Sonata in F major (for violin and piano)
Suite in A major (for string trio)
String Trio in G minor
Various soloists; Jean Sibelius Quartet
ONDINE ODE 826–2

Two Pieces, Op. 2 (original and final versions)
Scène d'amour, from Scaramouche (composer's
arrangement)
Two Pieces (Serious Melodies) (for violin and piano)
Four Pieces, Op. 78 (for violin and piano)
Six Pieces, Op. 79
Sonatina in E major (for violin and piano)
Nils-Erik Sparf (violin), Bengt Forsberg (piano)
BIS CD–525

Five Pieces, Op. 81
Novellette
Five Danses Champêtres
Four Pieces, Op. 115
Three Pieces, Op. 116
Nils-Erik Sparf (violin), Bengt Forsberg (piano)
BIS CD–625

Andante molto in F minor
Tempo di valse ('Lulu' waltz)
Andantino in C major
Theme and Variations
Two Pieces (Serious Melodies) (for cello and piano)
Four Pieces, Op. 78 (for cello and piano)
Malinconia
Torleif Thedéen (cello), Folke Gräsbeck (piano)
BIS CD–817

Index

Photographic Acknowledgements

Åbo Akademis Bildsamlingar, Åbo,
    Finland: 35, 65
The Lucien Aigner Museum,
    Great Barrington,
    Massachussetts: 177
AKG London: 51, 69, 82 (courtesy
    of the Legal Successors of Jean
    Sibelius), 190
Bundesarchiv, Koblenz: 189
Corbis-Bettmann, London: 2, 18,
    61, 173, 184
The Finnish National Gallery
    Ateneum, Helsinki: 49, 54
    (private collection), 59, 121
    (courtesy of Mrs Tirsi
    Savolainen)
Helsinki University Library: 126
    (courtesy of the Legal Successors
    of Jean Sibelius)
Imatra Tourist Service, Finland: 111
Imperial War Museum, London:
    140
The Lebrecht Collection, London:
    17, 27, 34r, 37, 42, 44, 53, 63, 67,
    71, 81, 84, 87, 95, 100–1, 108, 109,
    119r, 124, 128–9, 136, 153, 155, 156,
    159, 171, 175, 182
National Board of Antiquites,
    Helsinki: 72, 119l, 187
Österreichischen National-
    bibliothek, Vienna: 45, foto
    Krziwanek-Wien u. Ischl
Sibelius Museum, Åbo, Finland:
    23, 24, 29, 32–3, 34l, 39, 47, 75,
    77, 93, 132–3, 145, 148–9,
    162–3
The Sibelius Birthplace Museum,
    Hämeenlinna, Finland: 15, 20,
    90, 104–5, 192
Courtesy of Erik T. Tawastsjerna:
    86, 117, 168–9
Santeri Levas, *Sibelius: A Personal
    Portrait*, Dent: 1972, 195